Universal Craftsmen

J. L. Montgomery

Cadmus Publishing
www.cadmuspublishing.com

Copyright © 2022 J. L. Montgomery

Illustrations by Minh Duy Du

Published by Cadmus Publishing
www.cadmuspublishing.com
Haledon, NJ

ISBN: 978-1-63751-474-0
Library of Congress Control Number: 2022917465

All rights reserved. Copyright under Berne Copyright Convention, Universal Copyright Convention, and Pan-American Copyright Convention. No part of this book may be reproduced, stored in a retrieval system, or transmitted in any form, or by any means, electronic, mechanical, photocopying, recording or otherwise, without prior permission of the author.

ACKNOWLEDGEMENTS

With great Thanks and Admiration, I would like to recognize all of those whose personal influences and contributions aided in this work's development and completion, especially: Samuel Dworkins, Ellen Shultz, Matthew Engle, Meghan Shapiro; for all of the various contributions of literature that served in further cultivating my skills as a writer. For being long and avid supporters, and more importantly, a great team of friends. You are my NoVa. William Kracht; for the spiritual insight and countless instructions in the Divine Law. For the mentorship in my meditative practices and works of transmutation. Bro. Edward; for all of the jewels that were deliberately not given to me, but instead, the provisional tools afforded that you knew I would have to use in order to retrieve them. For raising out of the rubbish what some discarded as worthless. Your work was not in vain. Ever Eastward My Brother, Ever Eastward! Brothers of the U.O.C., for all the dedication and ceaseless labors of the Order, especially Bro. Tisdale and Bro. Du, whose lamps have been a most Strong and Beautiful source of Light and guidance in my life. James Ford; for being a living testament to what perseverence looks like in action, and the reward that results from such. And last, but certainly not least, to my son Jakeim; for all of the rays of joy that constantly reminds me of both the splendor and beauty of God's Love and Mercy. Remember Son, "Do Good And Be Strong...Because When You're Doing Good, You're Automatically Being Strong"

ILLUSTRATIONS

All illustrations herein are the contributive works of Minh D. Du. What one orates or perhaps scribes in a 1000 words, this most talented and artistic man, beautifully expresses in the strokes of his pen. His ability to bring ink to life is a gift that is remarkably astounding and can only be said to be masterful. I would truly be amiss if I did not express my deepest gratitude for all of his charitable contributions to this work. "Thank You" for all of your support and personal labors in the ideals for which the U.O.C. stands. Although, each illustration is attributed to its subject matter, they have been deliberately placed at the end of each essay so as to incite contemplation of some of the abstract ideas that lay within the artist's mind. It is his hopes that you come to appreciate and enjoy his work as much as he did crafting it. If you or perhaps someone you know may be interested in having some artwork done, Mr Du can be reached at the following point of contact: Shequilla L. Crawley (434) 710-7956

Front Cover---The Stone Builder
Inside Cover---The Stone Builder
Pg. 7: The Microcosmic Man With Clinched Lips
Pg. 15: The Microcosmic Man In Lotus Position
Pg. 22: The Mountain Range
Pg. 30: The Microcosmic Man Viewing Himself In The Waters
Pg. 38: The Microcosmic Infant Suspended In The Womb
Pg. 45: The Microcosmic Man Washing Another's Feet
Pg. 51: The Microcosmic Man's Submersion and Resurfacing
Pg. 57: The Microcosmic Man Transporting Stones
Pg. 65: The Microcosmic Man Physically Impaired
Pg. 74: The Microcosmic Man's Portal Entry
Pg. 82: The Right Hands Of Fellowship

Pg. 90: The Microcosmic Infant In Cradle
Pg. 96: The Microcosmic Man Giving And Receiving Alms
Pg. 105: The Microcosmic Man Standing In Corner
Pg. 112: The Microcosmic Man Creatively Drawing
Pg. 120: The Microcosmic Man Suspended Within Squares
Pg. 127: The Celestial Belt, Galaxy
Pg. 134: The Anatomical Brain
Pg. 141: The Anatomical Heart
Pg. 149: The Microcosmic Man Suspended In The 47th Problem Of Euclid
Pg. 159: The Microcosmic Man Walking The Straight Road
Pg. 166: The Microcosmic Man Climbing A Mountain
Pg. 173: The Microcosmic Man Working While Contemplating
Pg. 183: The Microcosmic Man Climbing Stairs
Pg. 191: Only When Truly Leveled Will The G Become Revealed
Pg. 200: The Microcosmic Men Crossing Over
Pg. 208: The Microcosmic Man Suspended As A Compass
Pg. 213: The Microcosmic Man Ascending Out of Grave
Pg. 221: The Microcosmic Man Sitting On A Level
Pg. 227 The Microcosmic Man Sculpting

ABOUT THE U.O.C.

The Universal Order of Craftsmen is a relatively small group of incarcerated men, who by adopting the various principles of Freemasonry and Rosicrucian exercises, have committed themselves to the works of personal redevelopment and self accountability. "To Educate And Instill The Virtues Of Manhood Essential For Moral Redevelopment" is the grand aim we have in mind. Although we realize discipline, change and healing are all under the governing scopes of time, we have come to also realize that true remorse and penitence doesn't lie in mere words alone, nor does justice lie in exorbitant sentencing times wherein one dies waiting for release to prove their reformation to society, but rather it is what one commits to doing here and now. Repentance is a work of the present that begins with a contrite heart which in return actuates purposeful restoration and willing atonement. It is in this aspect that we seek not to evade accountability, nor remain content in waiting for tomorrow's release in order to show what our hearts feel today. Therefore, the few men dedicated to the principles for which the U.O.C. stands, have sought to create a publication platform in which the reflection of our works in moral reformation can be viewed. This platform is composed of various literary and artistic works of its men in showing not only their advancements in moral redevelopment, but also the applicative means by which they continually achieve such. Its basis focuses on the education and understanding of the Divine Law that regulates both the spiritual and material states of our existences which further have their correlations to the inner and outer natures of man. The law's effectiveness to establish justice (that which is considered right, true, equitable and just), is only as effective as man's ability to uphold it. Therefore, if man is internally unjust so will the execution and performances of his laws be also. Let's face it, immorality wasn't birthed in prison and neither will it be eradicated by them. So who were these men before incarceration...? Exactly... free citizens. Therefore, this attests to the crux of the problem not being a prison issue, but rather a humanity issue, an issue of immorality whose roots are deeply buried in the way that we think, feel and subsequently act. The U.O.C. believes that by recalibrating the scales of justice first within ourselves (the foundational works that supports all subsequent labors), that true and lasting change will then come to be seen, a belief anciently expressed as "As Above So Below, As Inner So Outer," or perhaps more familiarly understood in the Lord's prayer as "...on earth as it is in heaven... ." This is why our curriculum and mentoring program focuses strongly on reconstructing the mind and directing one's energies so as to harmonize with the principles of these laws. One of these laws in particular is the Law of Reaping and Sowing. Recognizing under this law that the fruits of today's adversities stems from the ill seeds we formerly sowed, we now seek to sow seeds of life in hopes that the fruits of healing will come to be reaped tomorrow. Therefore, in keeping with this law, a monthly percentage of the royalties of this work will be further deducted as restitution for the victims and families of our crime related offenses. The remaining will go towards the existing and projected works of the U.O.C.'s efforts for further expansion. We hope and pray that this work, and many others to come, serve as mortar in rebuilding that which has been broken.

Fraternally Yours,

J. L. Montgomery

PREFACE

The following is a compilation of brief essays pertaining to the symbols and rites of Freemasonry in which the U.O.C. have adopted in their works of moral redevelopment. In reading these, you'll find several ideas and key points being repeatedly expressed throughout their entirety (as these were individually written over the course of a 3-year span as subject matters for student discussions). As many of these interpretations can be generally found in many publications pertaining to Freemasonry and its symbolisms, the U.O.C.'s overall understanding of these however, are more in line with the Hermetic principles of soul development, and so for those who may find some of the terminology herein somewhat foreign, a brief glossary has been afforded to partly explain some of their meanings. In presenting this work, we do not speak for any Masonic body or any other particular school of arcane study, nor do we advocate for any craftsman to exchange their monitorial explanations provided to them by their Grand Jurisdictions in favor for those offered herein (especially if unable to see the spiritual congruency between the two). Although you will find various endnotes expressing some of the U.O.C.'s standing beliefs found congruent with the general census of most Grand Lodge Jurisdictions, you will also find those that differ. In reading these, you'll find references often made to the Ancient Mystery Schools and Religions; however, in these given opinions, the U.O.C. is not suggesting that Freemasonry's origin is derivative of these institutions, but that many of their rites and symbols are. With little research you'll discover many of these symbolisms being employed in both institutions, despite the fact they can be found in two different time periods (a case in point being the Equilateral Triangle and Rite of Circumambulation). Therefore, by bringing to light their spiritual congruencies and not so much their material differences of mediums (their respective theological faiths and deities), it is the U.O.C.'s hope that the commonality of their regenerative work can then be had. It is in this aspect that the reader will be better afforded the benefits of the U.O.C.'s interpretative viewpoints intended to raise one's consciousness of Self. This spiritual understanding along with its material application are the works in which the students of the U.O.C. considers to be Universally One, despite creed, religion, race, politics, jurisdictional differences and civil statuses, all which have long proven to only corrode the spiritual integrity of its true purpose. This is why builders without such distinctions can be rightfully termed Universal Craftsmen. The nature of this work begins in the mind by means of introspection, speculative thought and meditative exercise, which in return, brings about the awakening need for moral betterment and personal change. It continues thenceforth with progressive application, whose works of accountability and support are had to self and also to the student body. Although the meditative exercises are not discussed herein (that being another literary work altogether), the spiritual and moral aspects of these are. Even though it is believed that the true wisdom of these symbols have been reserved only for the initiates, anyone; however, who has undergone a true initiation in the heart, and thereby earnestly seeks to live in Harmony with the Divine Law, will still no less procure for themselves the same Universal bequeathing of man's Divine Inheritance. Whether such becomes vividly seen or remains darkly veiled to some, it has no less been afforded to every man for their personal discovery. Therefore, when seeking to do so, one should bear in mind that material signs serve only to point to spiritual truths intended to aid in our soul's development, and that they should be scrupulously unveiled when attempting to ascend to its spiritual principles of understanding and application. This should be the manner of every Mason's approach regarding their monitorial studies (this being the intent of its early crafters), and is one that I attempt to incorporate in practice. Therefore, it is with sincere hopes that I have not mistakenly drank from some of the same wells of ignorances as some have before me. If such reveals to be the case, then may the corrective light of Truth be casted upon me, that I may in return properly represent that which I hold sacred in practice. Therefore, whatever errors that may still exist within these pages, as I have diligently sought to sift through its contents for such, please charge it to the fallacies of the mind's understanding and not the heart's purity of intent.

In the end, those Truths in which the reader comes to extract, are his and his alone to appraise according to the benefit they serve to render to his being. In short... Eat the fish and discard the bones... but seek to know which is which.

Table of Contents

ESSAY I SECRECY 1
ESSAY II WHY FREEMASONRY? 9
ESSAY III 133rd PSALM. 16
ESSAY IV HOODWINK 24
ESSAY V CABLE-TOW 32
ESSAY VI DISCALCEATION 40
ESSAY VII LUSTRATION 47
ESSAY VIII STONE QUARRY 52
ESSAY IX WHOLE STONES (PERFECT YOUTH) 58
ESSAY X PERAMBULATION 67
ESSAY XI THE RIGHT HAND 76
ESSAY XII THE RITE OF INVESTITURE 84
ESSAY XIII THE RITE OF DESTITUTION 91
ESSAY XIV THE CORNERSTONE 98
ESSAY XV WHAT IS A LODGE 107
ESSAY XVI FORM OF A LODGE 115
ESSAY XVII EXTENT/DIMENSIONS OF A LODGE 122
ESSAY XVIII PILLAR OF WISDOM 129
ESSAY XIX PILLAR OF STRENGTH 136
ESSAY XX PILLAR OF BEAUTY 142
ESSAY XXI THE SQUARE 151
ESSAY XXII JEWELS 161
ESSAY XXIII OPERATIVE AND SPECULATIVE. 168
ESSAY XXIV WINDING STAIRCASE 175
ESSAY XXV THE LETTER G 184
ESSAY XXVI PASS/PASSOVER 193
ESSAY XXVII COMPASSES 202
ESSAY XXVIII HIRAM ABIF 209
TRANSFORMATION OF THE MIND by Traer Tisdale 215
LIFE IS AN ART, LIVING LIFE IS AN ARTIST by Minh D. Du . . 222
GLOSSARY   231
REFERENCES AND BIBLIOGRAPHY   241
UPCOMING: AND THE MORAL OF THE STORY IS...   243

ESSAY 1

SECRECY

There are many things said about the characteristics of Freemasonry, one in particular being its secretive nature. Much of the ignorances surrounding this has led to many false accusations and erroneous assumptions regarding its purpose. I can't count the number of conspiracy theories, plots, and devil worshipping practices the Freemasons have been said to be a part of, not to mention those secret signs and handshakes that supposedly makes them immune to justice. I have heard some even contend that Freemasonry is anti-Christian and downright arbitrary to the ideals of God and government, and that if it was so much of a benevolent organization, then why the need for such secrecy? When I think of these opinions, I'm reminded of my father's own comments when I had informed him of my intent to petition, "...if it's so much about promoting light, then why so much mystery and darkness... why not let their light shine before the world?" At that time I had no answer. I now look back, with a more enlightened sense of perspective, and know I could provide him with not only an adequate response, but one I'm sure to be quite thought provoking. Unsurprisingly, there are many religious practitioners like my father who hold this same view in mind mainly because it wasn't explained to them in an understandable way, or their source of information wasn't the most creditable, or, as in my father's case, their was no information source at all. Therefore, in the short essay to follow, it is only befitting that this particular point be among the first to be discussed in hopes that some light can be shed on what is often a misunderstood virtue.

Freemasonry has often been referred to as a secret society, but the truth is that it isn't a secret society at all, but as often said, a society with secrets (all of society seeming to know well of its existence). Granted, there was a time when secrecy, as far as its membership, was a dire requisite, when the principles of Liberty and Equality was frowned upon, and any freethinker who dared to challenge the laws of their ruling authorities were met with death. These were under the despotic ages of certain monarchies and religious fanatics, when the cries of freedom were being strangled silent by the noose of oppression and the flames of justice were being quenched by the blood of the innocents. In such times, the cloak of invisibility was indeed worn for self preservation in planting the seeds of what would later give birth to democracy. Thankfully we no longer live in those times, and we can now openly express our opinions and differences without fear of the guillotine or the torture rack. The need for this type of secrecy has long died along with their tyrant leaders. The type of secrecy Freemasonry now stresses is an open and most commendable virtue and has always, in my opinion, been a divine right made exercisable the moment man was given the power of choice, a choice intended to set into motion the development of his Soul. This development is effected by both sides of what can be seen and what cannot be seen. When it can't be seen, it automatically becomes to be associated with obscurity, mystery, and the idea of secrecy (all conditions of darkness). It is in these same conditions that we find the operations of the law at work that fosters the development of life. Without these, maturation cannot be had. Take, for example, a rose, whose fragrance and beautiful appearances render such pleasing delights of aroma to our senses. We view its compositional designs with splendor and awe. It incites the warmest sentiments of affection in the hearts of all its would be recipients without the communication of one single word. But how common have we all enjoyed this revelatory wonder of life's natural beauty having never given thought to the invisible workings that transpired beneath the earth concerning its development? It is here, in this hidden recess of darkness, that we find not only a work that's amazingly beautiful, but more so vitally important for its proper growth and maturation. It is the nature of this concealed work that constitutes a secret to those uninstructed (those who haven't familiarized themselves with the law which governs such operations, which in this case would be the laws of botany and agricultural science). Without some prerequisite understanding of these studies, the workings beneath the earth would certainly remain a mystery. However, it should not be viewed in some sense that someone has arbitrarily withheld this knowledge from a person, but rather it should be seen that it is the prerequisites of the natural law requiring to be learned and understood that determines the imparting of its concealed truths. When these stipulations have been met then will the veil come to be lifted and the revelation of Truth be had. It's like possessing a key to a locked door. Giving a person a key doesn't automatically grants him access, but learning how to use that key is the requisites of the law having been met that does. These terms and conditions of life are Truth's natural safeguards against the foolish and ignorant(1). When one attempts to obtain unlawful entry by circumventing the law, it in return imposes detrimental harm to the natural order and development of a thing, a case in point being a rose. For if one was to ignorantly unearth and expose the roots of this rose to the rays of the sun, not understanding the purpose that darkness serves, it would retard the course of its development and ultimately destroy it all altogether(2). This shows that that which is concealed has its equal purposes as much as Light. In light of this understanding, it can easily be seen how the entire world's design is under the conditions (or principles) of Light and Darkness, that which is regarded as the seen and unseen, the revealed and concealed, the known and the unknown. Our great Creator beautifully displays this witnessing truth of dualities in all of the revelatory sciences of creation, but nothing more remarkably existing than within the nature of our own selves. In this aspect, Freemasonry's veil is not arbitrary to the ignorant, but is in harmony with the operations of the law, the law set into place to preserve both the natural harmony and development of a work and the beauty it affords to the world. When the requisites of the law have been met, then the same results are achieved as those who have also underwent such same natural process, and that, which was formerly shrouded in ignorance, darkness and secrecy, can now end up coming to light.

The second supporting claim for secrecy is founded more upon a moral basis of reasoning. There is a famous euphemism which reads, "... let not your left hand know what your right hand doeth. That thy alms may be in secret and thy Father which seeth in secret himself shall reward thee openly." This, with its moralistic interpretation found in the book of Saint Matthew 6: 1-6, figuratively stresses the necessity of secrecy in the performance of one's labors of love. The true spirit of benevolence, unfeigned charity, self sacrifice, pure devotion, all the outcroppings of love that emanates from the Father of Light, can never be had in self aggrandizement and self seeking recognition. The Angel Tree Corporation responsible for donating gifts to under privileged children during Christmas doesn't publicize the recipients of their charity, nor do the deacons of 1st Baptist Church publicize that Annie Mae was given money to have her electricity turned back on due to delinquent payments. Neither do one discusses the personal matters of their family affairs in the presence of visiting guests or strangers. In all these like examples Freemasonry also follows. Therefore, let not your good be spoken evil of. For what purposes has one truly achieved, if the charitable acts of love intended for the edification and betterment of the recipient ends up demoralizing them into shame and humiliation? Therefore, by sowing the seeds of Freemasonry's deeds in the womb of darkness and secrecy, it fosters that undisturbed state necessary for developmental growth whereby maturation can render forth its fruit's of love. This is very important because when considering the conditions in which secrecy cultivates, we inadvertantly come to discover its handmaiden--Silence, which allows in such same manner discussed above, the means for one's inner maturation to be had. It is only in the still and quiet chambers of the heart that we can come to hear the voice of reasoning, the admonishments of Truth, and the lessons of wisdom. When the clangings of mental and emotional disturbances are present, distorted judgements are soon to follow.

A third, and in my opinion, an under stressed reason for the requisite of secrecy, esoterically involves imparting light out of season. In considering this, it should be understood that Freemasonry imitates the governing order set forth in the designs of the Divine Law whereby we, as her employees, have been commissioned to build a spiritual temple made not with hands. The architectural blueprint which display these laws are in the very designs of all creation and have been made discernable to us by means of our cultivated consciousness. Without these laws existence would no longer continue to evolve, immediate chaos would ensue, and world annihilation would soon follow. Among some of these laws are the Law of Dualities, the Law of Cause and Effect, or what some would term as Reaping and Sowing, or Action and Reaction. A law particularly relevant to this topic is the Law of Accountability. This teaches that with the increase of knowledge comes also the responsibility of its use and abuse. This law was depicted in the biblical parable concerning the talents (St. Matthew 25: 14-30). In a precise understanding of this lesson, it teaches that Truth, once imparted, automatically become the inherent responsibility of the possessor by default. The power of Truth is not merely gauged by its possession, but more so by its proper use. It's like Uncle Ben told Peter Parker in the movie Spider-Man, "...with great power comes great responsibility." I offer this jewel. The possession of a hammer can build and uplift humanity in the hands of a wisely developed man, while on the other hand, this same hammer can be used to tear down humanity in the hands of an impulsive and mentally underdeveloped one. Therefore, he who possess the knowledge and power of a thing doesn't becomes the master of what he possess until he first becomes the Master of himself. I repeat, he who possess the knowledge and power of a thing doesn't becomes the master of what he possess until he first becomes the Master of himself. It is then that he not only comes to know the when's, where's why's, as well as for what means and purposes to employ it uses, but even more importantly, he comes to understand the full ramifications and parameters of its effects upon all things in relationship to himself and others. Such Mastership comes only by way of achieved wisdom having been properly developed during the diurnal seasons of his life, or in Masonic terms, "... ones several stations in life." Therefore, attempting to cause or impart knowledge prematurely is an attempt to induce wisdom out of season, which in return, enacts upon both the possessor and recipient the effects of the law. Once received, a possessor becomes held accountable for how he wields the power of Truth that's been invested to him (whether he wants to accept it or not). To render a practical example, I submit the following for your consideration. Would you, as a licensed and well experienced driver, give your keys over to a five year old kid to drive? I would think sound reasoning would prevent such. But let's just say if you were to hear of somone who did, which in return resulted in a fatal car crash killing several motorists. Who would you then hold accountable, the ignorant five year old, or the irresponsible adult? As a result of the contractual violation between the licence holder and DMV, the resulting effects would come to not only impact both the adult and the kid, but also the innocent victims, their families and also their friends. This would all have been set into motion from the negligence of the parent not being responsible with the knowledge that he had been entrusted with. Therefore, it would be better to allow one to remain in ignorance, concealing from them that which would destroy them and possibly others until such time is proper, rather than enlighten them out of season to their demise or the demise of others. For if we as parents having such care and protection for our own earthly children, withhold from them those things which seem prudent to our judgement, how much more is this spiritually true in respects to the hidden laws of Science and the Grand Architect of The Universe(3). Therefore, in like imitation (expressed in the dictates of its Obligations and Charges), Freemasonry not only symbolically instructs its students of the protective care and responsibility that becomes self imposed upon them as a result of being brought to Light (receiving Truth), but also the penalties that the Divine Law imposes upon them if found in such violations. These are not the horrendous penalties of bodily dismemberment as presumed by the ignorant, these having their moral and esoteric implications, but rather these are the stings felt upon one's consciousness as reminders of their responsibilities and duties to properly wield and exercise the Truth as sacredly sworn. It is upon this same understanding that signs are employed in Freemasonry, so that the greater virtues of morality that are to be cultivated within and among every member, serve as reminders of the lessons underwent pertaining to this work. It is a true fact that ignorance and improper use of knowledge can be fatal, as knowledge out of season can certainly get you killed. Therefore, be not anxious to expose the roots of one's rose. For what none other is this rose, but a symbolization of man's Soul.

Universal Craftsmen

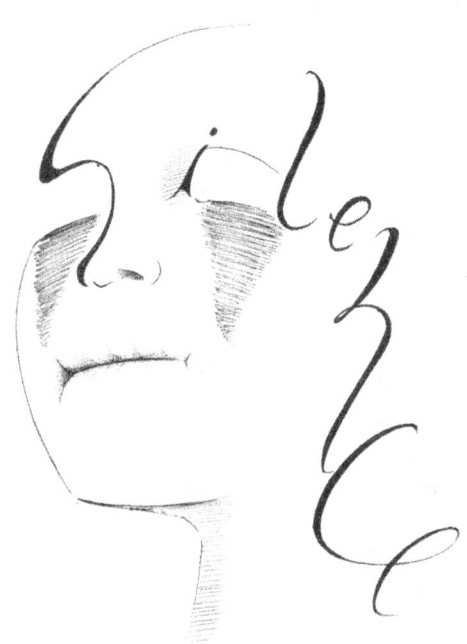

ESSAY 1 ENDNOTES

1. It is in this same sense that the World Lodge (in terms of a macrocosmic aspect), comes equipped with its own Tiler and will not permit entry until the conditions of the Divine Law have been met. As it pertains to the laws of Freemasonry, some of these revolve around moral integrity, legal age, mental aptitude, desire and intent for petitioning, and a belief in Deity.

2. In this sense of greater understanding, Darkness can be viewed as a precursor or catalyst for maturational development. There are some wisdom schools of the East that consider material light to be an illusion while darkness to be the principal means of regeneration (Truth thought to be primarily found in that which is hidden). The U.O.C. view the principles of Light and Darkness as both being aspects of the same Truth working to facilitate regeneration. In this, they both necessitate growth and maturation upon a thing, much like the Sun and the Moon does upon the Earth.

3. A descriptive term expressing the Divine Creator and governing laws by which men were fashioned and crafted.

ESSAY II

WHY FREEMASONRY?

Before going forth in exposition of some of the various symbolisms, there must be an understanding of why the men of the U.O.C. employ Freemasonry as its primary means for moral redevelopment. Freemasonry has various aspects in it's designs that allows for its members to become meaningfully engaged in a number of different pursuits. One may gravitate to committee works, or the ritualistic aspects of its ceremonies, while another may become intrigued by the historical nature of its development. Another's interest may be found to lie in the mentoring aspect of its newly raised candidates, while another to its jurisprudences. But irrespective of the different aspects that serves to hold the minds of Craftsmen, there is one that every Mason commonly shares, and that is the search for Light. No matter where that search may lead, or the nature of its revelation, the personal commitment of every Mason to seek it out is one of an universal practice, and it is one whose obtainment has mentally awakened and transformed the lives of the men of the U.O.C.

As you will later come to understand more of this term Light in this work, it suffices only to say for now that its meaning could be summed up in one word, Truth. This is not just a mere collection of information or facts, nor is it solely the study and acquisitions of the several liberal arts and sciences (even though these are manifestations of it as a result of creation), but rather it is those abstruse aspects of life pertaining to the relationship of Self; those deeper revelations that tends to awaken one to a new sense of being. The desire to know exactly what Truth is is perhaps one of the most longest standing questions presented, one that was posed even to Jesus Christ during his time when he was asked by Pontius Pilate what was truth, and again in another instance concerning the Samaritan lady who desired to drink from its wells. Although these accounts transpired hundreds of years ago, many men and women are still engaged in such quests for its obtainment, and it is this same quest that tends to draw them to the West gate asking, seeking and knocking for its discovery. This is what the U.O.C. believes both Pontius Pilate and the Samaritan lady were looking for in their questions; that spiritual fire of the Soul that constitutes the real nature of man's being (spiritual fire symbolizing the life essence and energy of all things, as well as the Divine Fire in man once fully transmuted). This Truth is One, and inexplicably, at the same time, the filling states of both material and spiritual existences in which we've come to perceive as conflicting dualities because of the Soul's descending degrees of consciousness. When the seed of Truth becomes to be planted and watered within the mind, it leads to germination which induces the Soul's awakening and subsequently the redevelopment of this consciousness. As humans, we are all endowed with consciousness from the moment we exit our mother's wombs; however, this constitutes only a particular degree of that consciousnesses which pertains to the nature of our corporal existence. To only be cognitive of this state is to be what some call the material, the lower, or the carnal natured man. It is referred to in the book of Romans, 8th Chapter verses 1-11, as the carnal minded man. All these terms are expressions that allude to the energies of the thought plane (vibrations, called by some), that reside in the thoughts we hold in mind, and in return, emanate their life essences throughout the temple until the power of its effects can be made manifest. These energies can keep one's Soul psych suspended in a death like state of sleep. On the other hand, when these same energies are transmuted into subtler and more positive thoughts of spirituality, they serve to build up one's temple, even so to the point that that which was once conceived in spirit can come to be brought into materialization.

This is what's meant when it is said that the Mind is the Builder (this being the foundation works of the temple), and is the work that the U.O.C. has come to identify with in Freemasonry. Since this constitutes a work that must first transpire within the mind, it can only be by one's True desire in the heart that this process of change begins (true initiation). It is then by the reconstructings of the Mind that the Soul gradually awakens and begins to rise to its highest potential as a Spiritual Being. What awaits every man in this is that full inception of Truth, that Light, that Fire, that supreme revelation of what God has constructed the Soul to ultimately be. This is why a Mason is said to allegorically travel to the East to receive Light, because each instance of enlightenment received (degree advancements), aids not only in the discovery of Truth concerning himself, but more of the Truth of what he is becoming. This unfolding revelation occurs from the esoteric work incorporated in Freemasonry's design.

The U.O.C. chooses Freemasonry because this work allows for the transformation of their moral character to be had both within the silent nature of themselves, while still permitting like minded men to harmoniously all engage together in this same work collectively. It has established a systematic means of conveying moral instructions using allegories and symbols that are universally applicative for any person. By doing so, it has removed the divisions we've come to see in certain religions, creeds, races, and political differences, and has set in its place an altar of universal brotherhood whose works towards one common goal are those in which all men can agree--Love and Self Betterment. This is one of the greatest benefits it has provided for the men of the U.O.C., in that it serves to repurpose their Minds and energy towards rebuilding something positive first within themselves, and then with others. Although there are certain laws prohibiting fraternal recognition among some of the more widely known Grand Bodies (it being regarded a "privilege" predicated upon the requisites of good morality and also of being a free man), there are some other bodies of occult practices that believe these laws may have been misinterpreted, whose regulations may have came to impede upon the spiritual work Freemasonry was first designed to cultivate in man. In my early stages of progression, I myself also wrestled with this, but with further enlightenment in degrees, I've come to understand that certain bulwarks are indeed needed in order to preserve the existing integrity and harmony of any work's progression. Not everyone possesses sincere motives, nor the requisites of commitment, devotion and self sacrifice required for such work. Everything has its appointed season for the person whose heart truly seeks to understand the natural signs pertaining to sowing, reaping and harvesting. But for a man who has no interests in agriculture at all, he finds no worth in the seeds, tools, nor the seasons, and as a result, would simply barter these away as Esau did his own birthright (Genesis 27th Chapter). In the face of such, there must be a Tiler in which these Landmarks then do serve. Other reasons prohibiting fraternal acceptance for one whose incarcerated is their inability to meet in a tiled Lodge together, also their inability to undergo the various ceremonial rites and customs of the degree, not to mention the inability to have free will movement (these all being primary characteristics of Freemasonry's institutional design). These alone would create a sense of inequality between the two and would no doubt come to effect the spirit of those bodies of a free society. To put this in practical terms, one, as an employee, would not hire an incarcerated man for a job knowing beforehand that he could not show up to the worksite to fulfill the duties expected of him. It would be both counterproductive and an unnecessary burden casted upon the rest of the workers. Finding themselves in like circumstances, the men of the U.O.C. are bound to the same unfortunate conditions when attempting to be on par with certain other Masonic bodies of free society. However, when strictly regarding the works of Freemasonry from a spiritual and moral standpoint of self development, it is these same inabilities that makes both the Speculative practice of Freemasonry and the discipleship of the U.O.C. compatibly one, because it is evident that the worksite is not one in which a man has to literally travel to (as with the case of an actual laborer, stonemason, or one having to drive to their respective Lodge location), but rather it is one that exists within the locality of themselves, the lodge then being the place wherever and whenever the awakening need for moral redevelopment becomes apparent to that person. And so therefore, irrespective of the locale, the men of the U.O.C., having came into the enlightenment of the values that Freemasonry provides, now utilizes its lessons in opened tabled discussions and lectures, along with the mind transforming exercises of the Rosicrucian Society, to assist in their Soul and moral redevelopment. These provisional Truths has tremendously changed their lives for the better and has became their obligated commitments to live by, not so much because their behavior predicates consideration for possible release (because most of these students are serving life sentences without the possibilities of parole), but because their wills to live as changed men, to become better than who they were, to take an active stand in both accountability and responsibility by working to right their wrongs, are all living testaments to their heart's sincerity concerning their change (irrespective of where this change occurred). These are not just mere claims, but facts supported by documentary evidences found in their institutional records and their many Annual Review Assessments. Who would then argue against allowing them to continue this moral practice, especially when such has proven to have made them better. It would be downright arbitrary to the ideals of moral reform to try and insist on such.

The building of the Temple is the building of man that requires internal development. This internal development entails the contemplation of Self and involves so much of a kindred connection to the Speculative practice of Freemasonry that there lies synonymy in the terms Consciousness, Born Freedom, Freeborn, Free man, and Freemason. This is because the allegorical lessons, symbols and moral virtues of Freemasonry inadvertently summons the powers of reasoning, discernment, understanding, emotion, and intuition to all gauge in determining what is good and bad for a person himself. By employing these contemplative works of self analysis, introspection, and cognitive thinking, the men of the U.O.C. have became better equipped to make decisions conducive to the positive changes they seek for themselves. This in return gradually frees them from the many fetters of enslavement that once limited their moral growth. It is therefore our opinion that these freeborn stipulations should be reconsidered from more of a spiritual standpoint than that of a physical one alone (it being most apparent that the actions of the body are predicated upon both the will and mental powers of reasoning first). For we see many evidences of free citizens mentally and emotionally shackled by their destructive passions, and in this sense, stand in need of being freed just as much as one who is legally bound by physical restraints. Therefore, it is the U.O.C.'s stand, that from a Speculative standpoint of Freemasonry's practice, its tenets are an all inclusive right when pertaining to the works of one's own individual development. However, (not dismissing the need for such regulation altogether), we also recognize it as being a "privilege" when it pertains to the assembling of men under their own respective banners of obediences, and in this case should be made exclusive to those of proven sincerity (the measure of ones moral character then having to be assessed in order to insure the integrity of existing work). Although these points brought to view are not intended to bring offense or disruption to any of the more widely recognized Grand Bodies; however, the subject matter of Freemasonry, as it pertains to these men's incarcerated conditions, certainly has its place in the works of temple development. If you think otherwise, imagine how John the Baptist, the apostle Paul, and murdering Moses all would probably think? They were all incarcerees themselves.

So why do the students of the U.O.C. employ Freemasonry in their lives. Simply because it works. It works to bring out the better nature of their beings. It works to further cultivate into view the moral excellencies and potentials underlying their Souls. It works to make them conscious of the greater truths of their lives and the positive benefits they can be to society. It redefines the meaning of their lives and reestablishes worth first from within and then abroad. And most of all, it works to make them more conscious of life and how to live in harmony with the Divine Laws of God and their fellow man.

Universal Craftsmen

ESSAY III

133RD PSALM

Verse 1. Behold how good and how pleasant it is for brethren to dwell together in unity.

Verse 2. It is like the precious ointment upon the head that ran down the beard, even Aaron's beard that went down to the skirts of his garments.

Verse 3. As the dew of Hermon, and as the dew that descended upon the mountains of Zion, for there the Lord commanded the blessing, even life for evermore.

This beautiful passage reveals not only the workings of God's divine order with esoteric elegance, but through symbology, those members which governs its operations(1). Upon viewing this Psalm, we see the numbers 1, 2, and 3, which aside from their implications of the many triune deities found in religions, also denotes the numerical sequence of the first three degrees of Freemasonry. In either path of respective rite, whether that be York or Scottish, one must begin their advancements with the First, Second, and Third Degree. These numbers represent, not only triple stages of development, but once all three are obtained, a point in travel that leads forth towards eternal Light, for if God is to be regarded eternal, so then must his Light be also. It should be understood that the summit of degrees in any particular rite of practice, such as 33, is not to be regarded as a definitive quantity or ending point to all knowledge to be obtained, but rather a quality or state of condition to be achieved. This understanding sheds light to the importance of Psalm 133, it being one of the 1st passages cited in the candidate's circumambulation that marks, not only the embarking of his Mind's search for Light (represented by the number 1), but also his Soul's eastward approach towards immortality (represented by the number 33), hence 1-33. Whether this play on numbers was of deliberate intent by the earlier ritualist is uncertain. Nonetheless; however, we still find its spiritual implication no less true, for oddly enough we find in each number, as well as in their overall sum, the spiritual principles of unity, triplication, and completion. This is seen in the numbers 1, 3, and 7 (1+3+3 =7).

In the first verse we are presented with the author's overwhelming sentiments of unity, unity implying the idea of many different components all harmoniously working together for the achievement of one common goal. Even though we've become unconscious to its operations, the laws of creation are perpetually working to facilitate this state of condition. The fact that the natural laws of creation all operates as one efficient whole is evidence within itself of such Divinity existing at its core. In respects to man, no greater evidence of this same truth is more transparent than in the operations of his own Soul filled body. Even our current circumstances with the Covid-19 bear witness to this. Although this pandemic has physically separated us, it has not divided us, for we find our Souls during this time being more united in Love and concern than ever before. Now if this can be done on a global scale in times of crisis, how much more beautiful would this be if it could be done without inducements, but rather of "...our own free will and accord... ." Could we not then usher in a heaven on earth? However, it stands by design that no permanent state of unification will ever be had as a whole until each individual begins to achieve that state first within himself (it being evident that each individual serves to make up a collective whole). Still, to be able to experience such, if only in measure, truly enlivens the Soul.

To further appreciate in verse 2 exactly just "..How good and how pleasant..." this unity truly is, the explanation of some symbols and biblical history must be had. In this verse, the particular Aaron spoken of is the older brother of Moses, who was the first High Priest of Israel during their exodus from out of Egypt. At his installation ceremony there were various rites prescribed by God that had to be performed before assuming his position. One in particular involved the anointing with oil. This anointing was not only to be initially performed upon Aaron as both a sanctification and purification rite, but also upon all subsequent High Priests and temple priests thereafter. This was ultimately for purposes which was to then set them aside strictly for sacred uses only for the Lord. When administering this rite, a considerable amount of oil was poured over the top of their heads which naturally flowed down upon their bodies. Now, as the head is the apex of the anatomical temple (it being also the seat of man's intellect and the point from where all thought, action, and manifestation emanates), we come to see in this verse a sequential order of purification taking place, alluding first to the Mind of man, then flowing downward in a natural course of subsequent manifestation upon the rest of the temple body. This bears an allusion to the natural order of how man brings spiritual thoughts into material manifestation. As this was the writer's choice of comparative imagery to describe unity, there lies an implication that such joys and pleasantries can not be fully had without purification of the Mind. An indecisive and divided mind that's unstable in its own thoughts can only inseminate the same seeds of uncertainty and division into the heart and thenceforth onto the body. There must be a stabilization of the mind and a sense of clarity in understanding before one can navigate the depths of their own self spirituality. This is essential for not only one's efforts in moral reformation, but for any works of development one desires to achieve, because troubles waters of the mind tends to wash away the seeds of Truth needed to find root for fertilization. It was not by coincidence that the ancient Egyptians waited until the torrential waters of the flooding Nile River to subside before sowing their yearly seeds. Nothing can grow and properly develop into an individual whole or collective body, if there is no existing unification in mind. A unified and tranquil mind flowing with calming waters of Truth will render life unto the entire body.

When looking up this word ointment in Strong's Hebrew and Aramaic Dictionary of the Old Testament, we come to see a direct connection to the olive plant, whose oil was extracted for use in the rites of sanctification for the High Priest, whose reference is being spoken of in the 2nd verse(2). Aside from its literal meaning, its connotative meaning signifies purity, healing, prosperity, an exuberance of life, and various other implications of bountifulness. Therefore, the comparison of unity to this precious ointment in verse 2 (when pouring such amount to cause it to run down off the top of his head, onto his beard, all the way down to the skirts of his garments), was in fact a sacred conferral of the blessings of health, vitality, purity, and more important, those spiritual inheritances of God upon him. This manner of anointing one from the top of their heads to the bottom of their feet was a symbolic expression that covered the whole nature of man, his Mind, Body, and Soul. This same expression shows us how both the Divine and natural order of such life giving seeds are dispensed down from the heights of God onto the temple mount. In this sense, the temple mount symbolizes Creation in one aspect, and in another, the body of man. Like the priesthood and instruments that were all consecrated and devoted for God's use in constructing and governing his temple, so should we purify our minds, bodies, and souls for consecrated and devoted purposes in building and governing our temples unto God. This actual purification process lays in the removing of those things not positive to our developmental growth (starting first with destructive thoughts of negativity in the mind). Doing so sets us forth to discover the real nature of who and what our purposes really are.

In showing even further that the divine and natural order of life is being depicted within this passage, consider verse 3, where the dew's descent upon Mt. Hermon and Mt. Zion are comparatively used to once again describe unity. Logically, it could be asked what does dew and mountains have to do with unity, and how do they pertain to the mind? In answering this, a look must be had into the significances of Mt. Hermon. Aside from the fact that this, and many other mountains were regarded sacred among the ancient Eastern civilizations (these being where many of the divine citings and revelations of God were said to have taken place), Mt. Hermon is also notable for being the highest mountain in Syria with its peak reaching nearly 9,232ft above sea level. It has been regarded by many as possibly being the "high mountain" referenced to in the 17th Chapter of the book of St. Matthew in respects to Christ's transfiguration. Although quite impressive in size, another notable geographical feature are its peaks, which remains snow capped nearly all year around, thus affording life sustaining waters for plush vegetative life of its lower plains. It is also of considerable interests that the melting snow caps of this mountain constitutes a main water supply for the Jordan River, a river most notable for use of baptisms throughout biblical history. In addition to this, this mountain's night dew condenses so thick that it not only provides irrigation to all the low land areas surrounding it (bearing in mind that this mountain range is nearly 19 miles long from north to south), but it also sustains vegetation and crops during the various drought seasons. With all of these life sustaining provisions, how apt does this mountain beautifully illustrates the life giving benefits of our Creator? Here again we see water as a provisional element being dispensed down from on high in the form of dew. As material waters give life unto the body and is vital for the perseveration of material life, so are spiritual waters vital in sustaining the life of the Soul, one providing temporary effects, the other eternal. These spiritual waters are symbolic of the lofty Truths that emanates from the mind of God. Such was also the esoteric understanding conveyed to the Samaritan lady at the well by Jesus Christ, who exclaimed that the waters that he would give her to drink would cause her to thirst no more(3). Truths that fulfills the life's thirst for growth and development gives vitality and nourishing wholesomeness to both the Soul and thenceforth the body. When there is a lack of water upon any particular area of ground, especially a mud puddle as it dries over time, it will harden up, crack, and then separate. Such are the same effects upon a mind deprived of life sustaining irrigations of Truth. It will become indecisively stagnant, or even worse, reprobate, until it's no longer able to render adequate health to the body. It is the spiritual seeds of Truth afforded to the Mind that in return induces life sustaining cohesion unto the body This is an important truth to understand in tearing down the old temple and rebuilding the new one, because when the various seasons of drought occur in our lives (hardships, crisis, and temptations), we naturally draw from the existing wells of our mental and spiritual beings in order to either cope or overcome it. When there is no new and living waters within, we tend to drink from the old waters that remain, and naturally we end up receiving the same ill results that sickens us. To do better, we must first come to know better. A lack of Truth, or weakness to employ it, are often what causes us to resort to our old choices and behaviors in life.

"...For there the Lord commanded the blessing, even life forever more." This "there" in verse 3, is still in direct relationship to the mountains previously mentioned. It should be kept in mind that God spoke with Moses upon the heights of Mt. Sinai, and that this was where the many Truths of God, along with all of the curses and blesses were given to him as commandments of the Law. It was then his obligated duty to descend back down and relay these to the remaining body of Israel. These laws were the expressed directives of God's Mind and Will for them and were given as means to establish, regulate, and maintain order by their uses. They were to instruct, direct, and guide them so that they could achieve the fullest benefits of what God had given them as their inheritance. The laws of God being afforded to the body of Israelites by Moses is comparatively like the Truths of God being afforded to us through our minds. Both have been charged with the primary responsibility of not only instructing and governing the entire body in matters of the law, but also leading the Soul(s) into that awaited promised land. Remembering that Masons anciently met "...on high hills and low valleys...," we find many parallel connections of men ascending mountain heights in order to commune with God. Abraham did so with Isaac, as well as Moses on several different occasions. Jesus also prayed to God upon the slopes of Mt. Olives in the garden of Gethsemane. When we go to that higher place within ourselves to reason, to seek guidance and proper instruction, we are in essence seeking to hear those commandments of Truth being spoken to us within so that it may render its benefits of blessings and development in out lives. When we do ascend such heights within ourselves, it is then that we begin to hear the still voice of God speaking to our consciousness with more and more clarity instructing us. Exactly how God speaks to our Minds is through the provisions of the natural law of creation, the written Word of the Law, and most important, the Spiritual Law written upon our very hearts and souls. The voice of God is the highest nature of our spiritual self speaking to the forefront of our consciousness. As law establishes order, and order promotes harmony, we then come to find that the very laws all around us all witnesses to one derivative source of origin--God, that exact "point" where unification began and simultaneously still resides. That is where "there" is in this verse. This is where the commandments of life are heard. This is where "...life forever more..." resides, and it is here, from out of the Mind of God, where all must ascend to in Truth, if ever we expect to become one and experience that true goodness of Love and Unification.

Universal Craftsmen

ESSAY III ENDNOTES

1. Although the word esoteric is often employed in terminology to describe lessons and various other ceremonial aspects of the craft considered privy to only its members. It also entails that which may lay privy to members of a particular degree, in which another hasn't yet received. Nevertheless, knowledge and Truth, in it's unfathomable range, will always serve to be esoteric to some degree or another, whether an initiate or not. For what one person may know, another may be ignorant of, but what that ignorant person does know, you'll find a totally different person also ignorant of.

2. Outlined in Exodus 31: 23-33.

3. This scriptural reference is found in the book of St. John, 4: 7-24

ESSAY IV

HOODWINK

In the various rites of practice, the hoodwink is an implement used to conceal from the candidate those things which are forbidden to be seen until their appointed time. To momentarily veil or conceal a thing to later reveal it in its due season, is a natural order of law in which we then find darkness serving as a precursor to illumination. It is by the aid of material light that the faculties of sight are permitted and consciousness is thereby increased. It has been defined by Albert G. Mackey in his Lexicon of Freemasonry that "...Darkness among Freemasons is emblematical of ignorance, for our science is technically called Lux or light; therefore, the absence of light is the absence of knowledge, hence the rule that the eye should not see until the heart has conceived the true nature of those beauties which constitute our order; Freemasonry has restored darkness to its proper place, a state of preparation." When looking in Strongs Concise Dictionary of the Hebrew Bible, we find the meaning of the word dark /darkness being rendered as obscurity, and is how ignorance finds its relationship with the hoodwink. This is because what is unseen is often obscure to one's consciousness and is therefore unknown to a certain degree. In this, we find these conditions in which the hoodwink facilitates. Now, aside from this philosophical view, when we look at the word light from a religious standpoint, we find it being associated with the idea of God and Truth, it providing conscious awareness of that which exists. Well, that's odd, haven't we been told that God and Truth exists all around us? So what stands to be obscure and hoodwinked to us? The answer is our consciousness, and subsequently, as a result, our perception. It is not our material sight or our faculties that's been hoodwinked. It is our spiritual faculties, the divine and greater nature of our inner selves. The next logical question that arises is why have we been deliberately hoodwinked into a material existence with an induced state of spiritual ignorance about ourselves? Symbolically, this has something to do with the same reason why the ceremonial left side of a candidate is considered to be the weaker side of Freemasonry. This is because the Soul had to be sown in material weakness in order to afford it the lessons of wisdom it could receive from undergoing various experiences in the body. The Soul's incarnate birth upon the earth is this weaker side that induces its own state of ignorance. Now, as darkness is defined as obscurity and ignorance, in which the conditions of the hoodwink creates by concealing, we find that it is the laws of creation that has established the hoodwink (we having been made from such). These laws, as mentioned in prior essays, are the expression of God's Mind and Will and are not arbitrary, but are for our developing maturation. How, you ask? The answer lies in what the hoodwink causes. Although it conceals when worn, it inadvertently heightens our awareness by forcing us to have to seek out and rely on other faculties to reestablish a sense of reorientation. It is a scientific fact that when we are unable to see we employ more of our other senses. We begin to rely more upon our sense of smell, our sense of hearing, and our sense of feeling. We feel a sense of awareness that registers within ourselves differently from that of sight alone. We become more attentive to what we hear, and most important, how we feel, because our other senses are compensating for those which are inoperable. As a result, this causes increased levels of sensitivity to not only those things going on around us, but more so to those things going on inside of us. All our senses become acute, our heartbeat and breathing changes, our mind becomes hyper focused and we become super conscious to our inner being and what is being communicated to it. It is no surprise that when we pray, meditate, or attempt to recollect a lost memory, we close our eyes in order to gain an increased sense of focus, as if we are summoning some sort of mental energy to aid us. I can't recall how many times in the past I have silently sat in a dark room attempting to iron out certain issues within myself. Doing so seemed to have afforded me the mental space needed to work out with clarity the steps of my intended approach without any pretentiousness. As the nature of man is constructed from the Laws of Creation (and these laws embody the powers of Light and Darkness), the Soul's dark experiences encountered during its circumambulations of life, serves to weaken the ego's identity it has came to cloak itself in, until it has to rely upon something or someone else greater in measure to its own self perception. It causes it to have to look into the mirror of self assessment only to see the true nakedness of its weakness staring back at itself. This creates a brief window of vulnerability, and to some degree, more or less, discomfort, even anger in many cases (which are all needed in the early stages of redevelopment). These momentary disruptions serves as catalyst for the tearing down of false perceptions. When stripped of all falsely apparel and left nakedly exposed, the desire to be clothed with self understanding, revelation, healing, and identity (the Truth of the Soul's being) will all begin to arise. This desire of the heart is what fuels the search of one's spiritual consciousness that awaits their Soul's discovery. This spiritual consciousness doesn't lie in open view to be sought with material faculties, but rather it lies internally within the darkness of our own lodges which can only be unveiled with the heart and mind. Until such is done, the hoodwink still remains worn. We should be mindful that it is actually the things we don't see that we should instead seek to procure in life. For what lie exposed to our material sight is already apparent.

Elaborating on Mackey's statement "...that the eyes should not see until the heart has conceived the true nature of those beauties...," this is an allusion to that place where every candidate must first come to be prepared when truly being made a Mason. It is quite unfortunate, but true, that there are some brothers, though having had their material hoodwinks ceremonially removed from their eyes quite some time ago, are still nonetheless blind. Even when the hoodwink comes to be removed from one's eyes to reveal such external beauties of the Lodge, if the heart has not been "duly and truly prepared," then there will still remain a veil that conceals the true spiritual and more glorious nature of what lies before them. The reason is that it can only be by spiritual conception in the heart that true illumination and understanding comes about in the Soul(1). In the heart's womb-like state of darkness, a divine union must occur between two institutions (the Mind, and the Heart's Desire, or Will), whereby the true evidence of such having occurred comes to reflect in the development of a third institution. The development and maturation of this third institution comes to represent in all its parts the glorious harmony between both parent institutions. Nothing more beautifully expresses this than in the union of man and woman, in which the rite of marriage symbolizes. As a bridal veil becomes to be removed by the groom in order that he may behold the beauty of his wife, in which he then kisses her after the taking of their vows, so must the hoodwink from over one's own heart be removed when taking upon himself the obligations of Freemasonry, otherwise, spiritual consummation, even though ritually performed, will not render forth fruits. The bride will remain barren. This is also the esoteric understanding alluded to in the two types of circumcisions spoken of in the book of Romans, 2nd Chapter 28 -29th verse. Therefore, as darkness serves as a preparation period for germination, much like an embryo in the womb that awaits material birthing in due season, so does the hoodwink suspends the candidate in his preparatory state of darkness, conditioning him until his heart becomes fertile enough to receive and understand the spiritual Truths that awaits him. While undergoing such conditioning, the sustainment of his life is facilitated by means of the cable-tow, the life line which enables the necessary nourishment for development to be had within in the womb until such time when the matrix becomes opened and he then becomes to be truly born and bound by a stronger tie. As a man child comes to be born into material consciousness, so must the Soul child come to be rebirthed into spiritual consciousness. This Truth has its esoteric implications reflecting in the twelve tribes of Israel in their exodus from out of Egypt and also in the birth, life death, and resurrection of Jesus Christ.

It is considered by most that light induces growth, while darkness, on the other hand, obstructs or impedes it. As this is not too far from the truth (at least from one perspective), it is both principles, however, that serves to impact a thing having been made subject to their forces. And as this Truth is very seldom welcomed, and even more misunderstood, it is not the workings of some vengeful God, or agent of evil personally targeting individuals, but rather it is the various principles of the Divine Law working together to induce further development for the greater consciousness and sustainment of life. As all things have been divinely prescribed an appointed season for its development according to its design, these two principles work under one governing order of law to bring about the necessary changes for maturation. When coming to understand the nature of these laws, we begin to operate in harmony with them, and as a result, we begin, to feel less of the impact of things we've been formerly taught to attribute to some evil entity. As it is a fact of law that nothing in its developing process can go from an embryonic state to that of maturation all at once, we come to find both the principles of darkness and light working hand in hand to further bring about its intended design. This is also the case with the development! of man's Soul. It is evident that what a man learns today about a thing can be said to constitute the receiving of light; however, what he comes to learn more of tomorrow, pertaining to this same particular thing, can be said to constitute more light, and when going further, what he may come to learn more of in two years would be considered further light. Now when looking back at each advancement, we see darkness as being a precursor to each new stage of obtained enlightenment, for if it wasn't, then there would have been nothing more existing to therefore learn. No man engages in a pursuit to recover what he's already in possession of, nor does he seeks to remember what he already remembers. The very fact that we have been endowed with the cognitive abilities to observe, learn, choose, act, and make mistakes, but more important, to be able to learn from those mistakes, are all evidences within themselves of how darkness as a deliberate design serves to foster our development. This bear witness to the powers of Light and Darkness both simultaneously facilitating the progressive development for one common cause in which the Freemason's hoodwink then serves in its ritualistic use to esoterically teach. That which we experience in the light and dark, or in moral terms, good and bad, are intended to render forth their results for the benefit of man. This is why we are admonished in the book of James, Chapter 1, verses 2-4 to "...count it all joy when we fall into divers temptation... ." Coming into the understanding and harmonizing actions of these Truths aren't so easy, and requires help the moment we enter this world by those "...who have gone this way before..."(2).

 The hoodwink is also intended to teach an incoming candidate those moralistic virtues of trust and reliance. For out of the same state of ignorance and darkness that a baby comes to be born into the world out of (having to trust and rely on others for guidance, instructions, and proper understanding), so in like conditions that a first time candidate enters the Lodge room, as he being shrouded in darkness to the mysteries that awaits. This is to remind him, as in the natural order of the Law, that in the same manner he entered into the Lodge in Darkness (ignorant), so should he also keep others until they have met the necessary requisites in order to receive such. As the candidate has been deduced to an infantile state, he comes to realize that he must rely on the aid of a brother to answer, instruct, and safely guide him to where he needs to be, so that in time, he can come to develop into Masonic maturity and be able to speak and move about on his own. This entails great implications in respects to one's moral redevelopment, because the state of darkness that the symbolization of the hoodwink also attests to, are those things in which a person is ignorant of within himself, those long forgotten rough ashlars lodged deep within the quarries of self. It is these that the individual must work to bring to light. So as we are being instructed and guided on how to properly respond, how to move, the various modes of recognition, and other peculiar mannerisms of the Craft, we must not forget that all these particulars pertain to our own temple, and that what we are really being taught is how to spiritually navigate the dark portals of our own internal lodges to that altar where lie those Great Lights found in the center of ourselves; and if our hoodwinks have been truly removed, then we will no doubt be afforded greater degrees of consciousness.(3)

Universal Craftsmen

ESSAY IV ENDNOTES

1. As the catechism states, Where were you first prepared to be made a Mason? In my heart."

2. Only those who've had their own hoodwink removed from their eyes can thereby properly assist the candidate in his travels. The blind cannot lead the blind. He, who is therefore a blind candidate, must place his fidelity in a friend who can see in order to obtain his own sight.

3. All the individual signs and symbols when properly unveiled, collectively forms a massive structure of witnessing Truths extending from the most earliest times of antiquity to our present day. Although the material form of a symbol may change, the spiritual truth of it doesn't. He who begins to see, act, and feel with their spiritual facilities, bear witness to having undergone a true initiation, wherein they were duly and truly prepared in their hearts.

ESSAY V

CABLE-TOW

The ritualistic uses of the cable-tow entails both exoteric and esoteric implications among the Craft. In its exoteric view, when the cable-tow is placed about the candidate, it is to aid in leading him around about the Lodge to the East. It also aids in safely removing him from the Lodge, if perhaps he wishes no longer to participate in the ceremony. When viewing the different variations of this device and its overall uses from strictly a trade of construction, we see that it serves to move objects of considerable weight and size from one location to another. In our modern times of construction, we employ the uses of lifts, winches, pulleys, and comealongs as well as other mechanical devices to accomplish these tasks. As these types of devices usaually incorporate the use of chains, cables, or some type of straps, the earlier stonemasons; however, were more so confined to the use of ropes and lewisis for hoisting and adjusting their stones into place. In most cases, due to the size and weight of certain stones to be used, it required several ropes manned by strong bodied men, who were not only skillful in wielding such massive weight with precision, but experienced also in tying certain knots that would prevent slippage (a skill critical in preventing damage to both the workers and stone itself). This occupation is what we now call Riggers and was dangerous back then as we still find it to be today. Improperly securing loads having to be moved about in mid air, carried potential risks of injury and even death, and was even more risky when you consider the possible language barriers of the different temple workers. The fact that in the face of such risks that these men were still all able to work together in harmony, truly attest to both their high skill levels and strong ties of trust held in each other. These same virtuous qualities are not only found in the bonds held between each Freemason, but in also the skillful wielding of every rough ashlar extracted from out of the quarry (a candidate). This is symbolically alluded to by one end of the cable-tow being attached to the candidate, and the other being wielded by a member of the Lodge. This symbolizes both the nature of work and support that's to be extended from the Lodge to that of the candidate. These connecting ties begin even before his entrance into the Lodge occurs. From the moment his petition is read and accepted into the Lodge, he is thenceforth placed under special consideration by its members, in which the contingency of him being made a Mason, is regulated by the laws of the Masonic jurisprudence. Everything from the reading of his petition, to the conducting of his interview, to the receiving of his declaration, to the due and ancient forms, all constitutes an integral part of a jurisprudential procedure that aids in gradually getting the candidate a little bit closer to that point where he eventually becomes a full fledge member of the Lodge. This comparatively operates much like a mechanical cable-tow does in moving an object closer to its final destination.

Now, in the same way a material stone has to be transported from one location to another without undergoing irreparable damage, so must Masons engaged in the works of transitioning living stones from one state of condition to another without incurring harm. These are done by the spiritual bands of love spoken of in the book of Hosea 11th Chapter, 4th verse where the ties of compassion, understanding, patience, trust, and thoughtful consideration are extended by the members of the Lodge in assisting a new candidate in their new sought development. Even though these ties are not material and certainly doesn't bring about any actual movement of any type, they nonetheless, must still be wielded with skill and careful precision when pertaining to the nature of men. For unlike the material stone, that feels not the blows of the gavel upon their surfaces, we as living stones feel the reverberations of every stroke delivered to our spiritual being. Although Freemasonry has its particular aspects of work that involves the candidate and lodge members collectively, there are still certain candidacy aspects that should only be entrusted to those possessing certain levels of Masonic knowledge and understanding. Not everyone possesses the social skills and patience for dispensing Light that incites contemplation and self pursuit, rather than sole dependency. Such ties, symbolically speaking, should be wielded by men of spiritual strength and wisdom, whose undergone levels of personal development and experience allows for their cable-tow lengths to be extended considerably longer in helping others. Like the State Farm commercial advertises "They know a thing or two because they've seen a thing or two." These generally entail the elders and overseers of Freemasonry, whose words of wisdom serve as beacons of Light unto the Craft. In the same way an infant is born needing to be fed by another, so must the candidate be given nourishment by those knowing how to properly dispense such. This will aid to mature him into the Masonic man he seeks to become. It is like the movie The Matrix, where Neo gets detached from all his connecting cables that had formerly sustained him while he was in his protoplasmic cocoon of ignorance. After he becomes to be reborn (awakened and detached from the Matrix), he then comes to be nakedly retrieved as a newborn baby, and afterward brought forth into a world of greater consciousness. This is where he began to receive the new supporting ties of his spiritual birth Mother, Zion, through the gradual instructions of Morpheus(1). This in return enabled him to develop the uses of his Soul and Spiritual capabilities. When he first comes to see, he complains that his eyes hurt. Morpheus replied its because he has never used them before. From this point he has to be taught how to eat, walk, and most of all, how to perceive things around him as they truly are. Coincidence? I leave this for conjecture. Nevertheless, this is why it is so critical that in the Foundation Degrees of Freemasonry (1-3), that the candidate comes to drink from the spiritual waters of the East. For it is upon the foundation stone(s) of Truth, having been deeply laid in the mind, that the regenerative development of the faculties begins to take place (the rest of the temple parts being dependent upon this for proper regulation and corrective instruction). In a spiritual sense, these bands of love are of divine origin in which the brothers have been endowed with for use of Temple service unto others. This brings into view another aspect of the cable-tow's symbolism that's briefly alluded to in the 2nd Degree's Obligation, i.e. "...within the limits of my cable-tow."

In former times, operative stonemasons were admonished to remain within a several mile range of their respective work sites in order to be able to report to work. During those times, such distances roughly consisted of a day's travel under normal weather conditions, they not having the luxuries of modern day transportation. As it is now nothing for one to travel from state to state within a matter of hours, even minutes in some cases, this regulation (when pertaining to Speculative Freemasonry), has come to take on the scope of one's own reasonable abilities in being able to carry out the performances of their duties. An example of this can be exhibited in the exercise of one's charity, wherein one craftsmen may be able to financially donate $500.00, but another only $50.00. In both cases the dollar amount doesn't determine the propriety of their obligation having been met in comparison to each other (each possibly having different household incomes), but rather it is the act of the charitable contribution within itself that determines such. This doesn't mean, however that there is no accountability to be had for one's deliberate derelictions, because even when man attempts to hide their deeds in the dark, there is an All Seeing Eye that holds and weighs all upon the scales of Truth and Justice, who renders to each and every individual Craftsmen his due wages.

When observing this instrument's overall use in general construction, we see that it fosters the idea of dependency and support, its purposes being employed for tying, assisting, aiding, and binding together. Considering the cable-tow from this particular understanding casts further light upon the esoteric nature of its ceremonial use. At a particular point in the ceremony, when the cable-tow has been removed, the candidate is then informed that he is now bound by a stronger tie. This stronger tie has been referred to in past times as the Mystic Tie, and is that indissoluble chain that links one Mason to another, hence the appellation of Freemasons in former times as Brethren of the Mystic Tie. This stronger tie is the Divine and Living cords of all Fraternal Souls conjoined together in spiritual Oneness to make up the Universal Soul. Although unseen, it's a pervading force that serves as a life line support for every awakened Soul. Just as there is an umbilical cord extending from one's biological mother to her unborn baby while in the womb (it having to be severed at birth in order for the next level of life's consciousness to be encountered), so is it that the candidate undergoes detachment from the material ties of the world that has long bounded and nurtured him in his mental womb of darkened consciousness. He must become awakened and attached to the new life support of his spiritual mother by opening his Mind to the Truths that are intended to strengthen him. It is like the parable concerning new wine in old skins in the book of St. Matthew, 9th Chapter 16 and 17th verses, which reads: "No man pattern a piece of new cloth unto an old garment, for that which is put in to fill it up taketh from the garment and the rent is made worse. Neither do men put new wine into old bottles, else the bottles break and the wine runneth out, and the bottles perish, but they put new wine into new bottles and both are preserved." As mentioned in other essays, there must be a relinquishing of turbulent thoughts and cares that washes away the seeds of greater life in order for a full regenerative transformation to be had. It is hard to grasp hold of the more loftier pursuits of life while still being bound by the weights of negative thinking. The material ties of the world are of different properties than that of the spiritual, and are not adhesive without undergoing transmutation.

 Another esoteric allusion of the cable-tow lies in the peculiar placement of its use. When it is placed about the candidate in its particular manner in the 1st Degree, it could be said to bear symbolical allusions to an unregenerated mind having been formerly nurtured and sustained in material unconsciousness upon this plane (Earth being the state of condition that all mankind becomes to be inherently subjected to at birth). On the other hand, its removal would imply an awakened mind to spiritual consciousness and the Soul's subsequent return to its plane of preeminence. In both a metaphysical and microcosmic sense, this lines up with many of the world's religious beliefs concerning the afterlife. Therefore, the ceremonial removing of one's material cable-tow, and the spiritual binding of the stronger one, foreshadows the necessity of death. Death in not just the symbolic manner of those vices and superfluities in our lives, but literal Death, as in one's corporeal temple. In this aspect, the nurturing life line of Mother Nature's support which sustains our mortal beings (that brittle thread of Life), would have to be severed in order to facilitate our transition over into the next level of spirituality. This should casts more light for the purposes of death, as well as the esoteric understanding of the follow scripture, "But we all with open face, beholding as in a glass the glory of the Lord, are changed into the same image from glory to glory even as the spirit of the Lord(2). These stages of glory gradually reveals more and more of the truth of our Divine Being in which the navel cord of God's Spirit serves to provide consciousness for.

Universal Craftsmen

ESSAY V ENDNOTES

1. In Greek mythology, Morpheus was the god of dreams. Hypnos, his father, was the god of sleep.
2. 2nd Corinthian, 2nd Chapter, 18th verse.

ESSAY VI

DISCALCEATION

Before expounding on how this rite particularly pertains to Freemasonry, a clearer understanding of this word's meaning should be had, it being somewhat difficult to reference without a comprehensive unabridged type dictionary. The entry found in Webster's Encyclopedic Unabridged Dictionary of the English Language renders the following tense and meaning as: Discalced (dis kal'), adj. (chiefly members of certain religious orders); without shoes, unshod, barefoot; also discalceate (dis kal' se-it-at), from the Latin word discalceatus, which is comprised of dis-, a Latin prefix meaning apart, asunder, away, utterly or having a privative, negative or reversing force, and also from the word calce(us), which means shoe or shod. When putting these two together, we can see both its implicative meaning of doing away with and the removal of one's shoe. This is a practice commonly seen in various religions throughout the world, especially those entailing offices of a priestly nature. It is one that stems throughout religious history whose evidences can be found among the Greek hierophants of Pythagoras, the priests of the Jewish temple, the prophets of Islam, the Druids, the Persians, the Ancient Mystery schools of the East(1), and many other religions and schools of ancient thought. Its practice is considered to be of great antiquity, but exactly when it was first instituted has never really been determined. Even though one finds the command for Moses to takes off his shoes in the 3rd Chapter of Exodus, it being holy ground he stood upon, it is believed by some; however, that this practice long predates the recordings of Moses. It has been hypothesized by Clarke that this rite's usage was so general among all nations that it was one of the 13 evidences that all humanity derived from one family(2). The fact that we find this observance in nearly every religion of antiquity, certainly supports the possibility of one universal origin. Even today we still find this practice being faithfully observed among some of the Southwest Asian countries, where the removal of shoes is a common custom when entering into any of their homes.

When viewing this rite from strictly a religious standpoint, its significance expresses reverence and submission before God. It declares a discarding of all pretentious attitudes and beliefs that incites or exalts egotism, thus debasing one's self unto humility by casting aside all exercising rights and preexisting claims of self entitlements. It is not only an expression of reverence and due respect, but also obeisance to another's right of overruling authority concerning whatever matters at hand. Now, when attempting to see how this particular rite pertains to Freemasonry, a look at its customary use in biblical times is needed. In the book of Ruth we are told that this rite was an ancient Israelite custom pertaining to the manner of exchanging and redeeming things in those times (property, inheritance, etc.). Here is where we see its use being employed by an unnamed man in the 4th Chapter, who gave his shoe over to a man named Boaz in the forfeiture of his purchasing rights concerning Ruth and all her possessions. Ruth, who was a Bethelamite tribeswoman by marriage, but a Moabitess by nativity, had unfortunately became a childless widow. As it was unlawful during those times for wives to receive the inheritance of their deceased husbands, it became her desire, and Boaz's obligation, to redeem her according to a particular law called the Levirate Marriage, known also as the Brother in Law Marriage. This law, which was instituted in the 25th Chapter of Deuteronomy, required that: "...if brethren dwell together, and one of them die, and have no child, the wife of the dead shall not marry without into a stranger, her husband's brother shall go into her, and take to him to wife, and perform the duty of an husband's brother unto her." Now before carrying out this law, one had to first insure that there were no male relatives closer than himself who would want to exercise their rights of legal claim (the nearest of kin having precedent over others to do so). If the nearer kinsman declined, in which case this unnamed man did, such forfeiture was then made legally contractual, in which the removal of one's shoe served as a token. By this man having done this, at what basically constituted the town square, before all the witnessing elders of the city, it served as a public proclamation of him relinquishing his rights over to Boaz. In a legal sense, this was a transferral of rights which served also as a testimony of good faith before the polity of Israel that he would fulfill his duties according to the dictates of the law (much like how contracts serve today as). Now, in the comparative understanding of this rite's use in Freemasonry, we find it also serving as a contractual expression of one's good intent, wherein one willingly relinquishes their authority over in obeisance to the principles expressed by the institution therein, and that they, with all sincerity, devotion, and serious intent, will reverently honor and duly uphold the principles of Truth expressed to them in Freemasonry to the best of their ability. Such are the understandings of this ritualistic practice from an exoteric view.

From an esoteric view, the greater spirit of this rite is found largely in Boaz's statement in Chapter 4 where he expresses before the gathering witnesses that he had just "...purchased Ruth to be his wife... to raise up the name of the dead upon his inheritance, that the name of the dead be not cut off from among his brethren." The use of the particular words "dead" and "cut off" points to a state of condition that expresses alienation and estrangement, a condition that implies separation, and therefore stands to be incomplete in a sense from the whole. Although the inheritances that stood to be redeemed in this story may thought to be only material, it alludes also to those spiritual possessions that have suffered loss due to one's separated consciousnesses from God. This same dead state could be called widowed when pertaining to God's Spirit, as we have been bereft of the understanding concerning its Truths and afforded uses. This disenfranchised state is comparatively symbolized in Ruth's condition, who, as a result of estrangement and widowhood, no longer had claim to any of the rights formerly extended to her. This is where the work of transmutation transpires by spiritual consummation which has its symbolic correlations to Self Development. For in both, we find consummation needing to occur as a requisite of the law in order for restoration to be achieved, hence the theme of rebuilding the Temple. Now when looking at the word restoration and its root, it expresses the understanding of something being made new or whole again, as well as the idea of reversing the effects or conditions of (as in doing away with--discalceate). This is important, because in order for something to stand in need of restoration, it must have been considered whole, new, acceptable, or completed at some point. This is believed by many religions to have been the state of man's condition prior to his fall, which in return, true repentance and adherences to its laws establishes his return to this state, but this time; however, with the endowments of wisdom and understanding having been obtained. This could be said to have been the case with Ruth, who, after experiencing the blessings and protection of her husband's household, unfortunately became subject to poverty, hardship, and shame. Bearing in mind that there was a long standing decree that forbade marriage between the Moabite and Israelite nations, it is certain that she was met with scrutiny and maybe even ostracism. By material standards of wealth, Ruth was nothing more than a poor foreigner who had no rights to the benefits and blessings of the Israelite nation; however, what was seen by Boaz was an abundance of her spiritual wealth, whose virtues of faithfulness, obedience, and diligence in labor, far exceeded those who were already rightful born workers among his fields, and who perhaps held a sense of entitlement as being heirs to Abraham's promise. Ruth's faithful obedience and application to the wise counsel and instructions of Naomi (Naomi being a typification of Spiritual Wisdom), led to not only the procurement of her repurchase, but the matriarchal bloodline of King David. Boaz's and Ruth's union was an esoteric foreshadowing of work in which Jesus Christ would ultimately typify concerning the redemption and reestablishing of every estranged and severed Soul from their divine inheritances as Sons of God. This beautiful union depicts a divine engrafting that would later serve to bring all nations under the Spiritual Oneness of Love.

Love is obedience to the Law, and obedience is spiritual redemption in action. Now when looking at the word redeem, its Hebrew transliteration is ga'al, which means to buy back, as in to free from, or repudiate (repudiate meaning to disavow, disclaim, or deny). It also means to reject, as in no longer having authority or binding force over, as to renounce. It is a great Truth that we are driven by the desires of our heart (whether those desires be of health or detriment to us), and that it requires a sincere change in these, followed by sought after Truths and obedience to them, in order to procure Truth's positive effects. One's true desire for change is what incites the beginning of mental work. When beginning to build or restore the temple, as it pertains to our moral redevelopment, there can be no self mental reservation. One must be willing to reject their claims of former living, otherwise there can be no advancements made in spiritual ascent due to one's preexisting claims of perfection and completion already present. There will be held in mind that no form of restoration or personal development is needed, and that the lessons of Truth are non applicable to them. It is hard for one to express true sorrow, (the kind of sorrow that results in penitent changes), if they do not see themselves having been at fault. There is no need to restore or build that which is believed to be whole or not broken. Where there is no motive, there is no desire, and where there is no desire, there can be no genuine commitment in effort. Equally, where there is no admission of guilt, there can be no remission of sins (no restoration or the reversal effects of). This reversal, or disavowal, truly occurs when a commitment to change from a material state of desire to a spiritual state transpires in the heart. Therefore, the divesting of one's shoe is also a symbolical representation of one, who from out of a true place of sincere motive to be redeemed, wishes to be repurchased from under their material state of consciousnesses to that of a spiritual one, one which facilitates the discovery of Truths and its application. In essence, what one is saying is that they no longer desire to be under the binding nature of that particular law and its effects, and therefore, they relinquish their exercising rights by willful separation and discontinuation of one's former practices (one's true denunciation in heart being shown in their actions). Where it establishes a contract of consent in one sense, it also denounces it in another. To those receiving such, they are the symbolical representations of those exercising their near kinsman rights in the performance of the Brother in Law Marriage to "...raise up the dead upon his inheritance, that the name of the dead be not cut off from among his brethren" (we all being brothers derived from one Divine Paternal Father in the greatest macrocosmic sense and it being our duty to assist our spiritual kindred to be drawn up from out of the darkness into the glorious Light of Redemption).

Universal Craftsmen

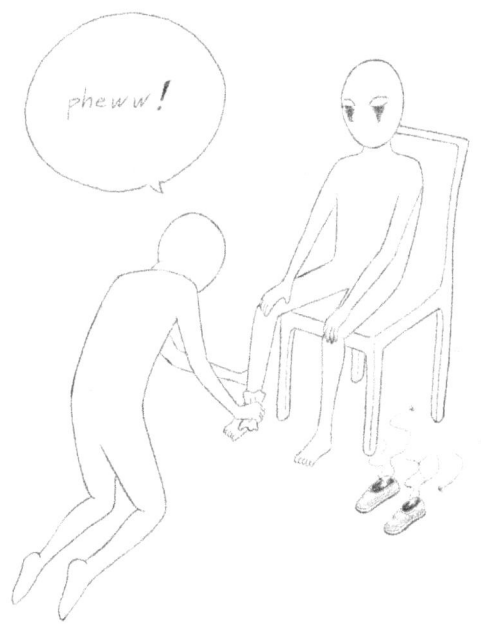

ESSAY VI ENDNOTES

1. Some of these, along with their particular deities were known under the names Bacchus, Adonis, Ceres, and Venus. They were considered paganistic by many of the leading church officials, as they were said to entail practices of magic divination, sex rites, and child sacrifices, as well as other practices abhorrent to the beliefs and custom of the then established church. Some of these schools have been suggested as being the origins of Freemasonry by some less informed of the matter, and others ignorant of its history altogether. A particular example being the Dionysia Mysteries, in which many writers in the past have attempted to establish the Hiram Abif of Freemasonry with certain aspects of this ancient group's existence.

2. As written in Albert G. Mackey's, The Symbolism Of Freemasonry.

ESSAY VII

LUSTRATION

Lustration is a rite which entails ceremonial washing and cleansing of the body. In some instances the whole body may be washed, while in others, just only certain parts. It serves as an act of devotion, as well as an propitious requisite when establishing fellowship with God. In ancient times persons were often not permitted to enter into the shrines or temple of worship if found to be unclean, stained, or defiled, this being regarded in the same sense as an act of desecration and irreverence for the nature of things holy. This rite was held in so much esteem among the Romans that they, in honor of their respective deities, went as far as to carry out its performance every five years after the conducting of their census. Even though oil is used in some cases when pertaining to the priesthood and their installation, water was, and still remains however to be the primary element employed in the performance of this rite. This has spiritual significance, because water has always had its esoteric relationship among the wisdom schools as being a symbol of the Mind whose regenerative effects brought about the renewal of life. Its understanding entails both the principles of life and death and also the primordial formlessness that existed before creation. These veiled understandings are even alluded to in the 1st Chapter of the book of Genesis, as well as in the events pertaining to the biblical Flood. Now, when looking at the events of creation in Genesis, one of the most logical questions (among many perhaps), is whether or not water was ever created, as we seem to find it's mentioning in the 3rd verse of the very 1st Chapter even before the creation of the cosmogonies, the formation of the Earth, and even the pronouncement of light itself. And if that is not strange enough, we come to see its appearance once again in verse 5 in respects to its upper and lower divisions. It has been taught by various schools of ancient thought that the very beginning of all life stemmed from waters. (the Brahmins believing that the World Egg, also known as the Cosmic Egg of Life, was hatched upon its surfaces). These various accounts of water serving as a precursor to life is a theme that can be found universally common to almost every religion in some context or another.

Although some of the esoteric understanding of this may have been lost to antiquity, there remains a great deal of its ritualistic practice found in many religions, which can be notably seen in the rites of Christian baptisms, Islamic ablutions, and Catholic christenings. These, and many more forms of its practice, depicts not only the prerequisites of spiritual purity required before entering before the presence of God in fellowship, but as expressed earlier, also the transitional states between both life and death needed in order to achieve further consciousness (a symbolic expression clearly conveyed in the immersive burial of a person in the waters and then raising them up out of it during baptism). In this sense, the use of water embodies a 2 fold aspect of regeneration, which once again, points to the transitional states of the upper and lower water's division in Genesis. These have been said to allude to the two thought planes of the spiritual and material manifestations of the Cosmic Mind. The open vastness from which the Mind creates symbolizes the waters of primordial nothingness before celestial creation, the God Mind. The division of this is believed by some to make up the planes of manifestations that came to be. It is in these two divided planes that the powers of the Spirit lies from its highest etheric expression to its lowest (the degrees or vibrations of energy descending from Spirit to Matter). There are many other symbolic correspondences that alludes also to this same aspect of cyclic life and its regeneration between the two dualities of existence. In any case, that which comes to be immersed into the baptismal waters represents the entombment of all that is impure, immoral, unstable, and chaotic (its forms being temporal and corruptible, even unto death), whereas that which comes to resurface as a symbolization of rebirth, lives to represent purity, holiness, stability, and governing order unto maturation, even unto immortality. Although such life and death transformations are symbolically represented by uses of this ceremonial rite, it is; nonetheless, a real process of regeneration that is suppose to transpire within every true aspirant. Here, in this rite's understanding, lies a Divine Truth in respects to the building of one's temple (especially when pertaining to the works of the mind's redevelopment and its coming into greater consciousness), and that is that, in order for the fullness of life to occur, so must death. For in the same moment one comes to be birthed into life, so does in this same instance he begins to die. Just as life is a precursor to our mortal death, so is death a precursor to immortality. One must die daily to the old train of thought (a sacrificial offering of the old, one would say) in order for continuous progression to ensue.

As water is also a symbolical representation of wisdom, we come to see a correlative understanding between drinking from its wells and being washed by it. Both, by their respective symbolisms, teaches transformation by its use whereby a doing away with the lesser for the obtainment of the greater is had, hence a sacrificial death of the lower waters of the mind (an emphasized point the U.O.C. attempts to convey to its students early in their pre-curriculum course before acceptance). This is important, because as it stands, everybody wants to go to heaven, but nobody wants to die. Many desire the benefits of a goal, but not the work involved in achieving it. Our mindsets have been unconsciously programmed for so long to automatically look for the most easiest way in gaining a benefit, that natural development from hard work, patience, and sacrifice are rarities, and now when seen, are treated as big foot sightings that are given all sorts of media coverages, awards and accolades. We make every attempt to circumvent the natural order and process of the law to induce faster results, not realizing that we're not only sinking down the slopes of immorality, but we are also becoming mentally and physically impotent as a people. The demands of our unbridled passions have become greater than our abilities to naturally produce; so much to the point that we alter, bend and break, if necessary, both natural and man-made laws in order to accommodate them. The reasons why so many of us are numb to this is because our consciousness have been seared by the miseducations of freedom. Our senses are constantly nurtured with the falsities of mainstream media which suggests that winning, luxury, style, and material success are what constitutes American liberties and the value of life. This has been embedded deeply in our psychs, and has became the gauge by which we measure ourselves and others by. The desire for material quantity, rather than spiritual quality, has became our "pursuit of happiness" spoken of in America's Constitution, and has became the lower waters of our thinking that has given life to our ambitions which brings about materialization, but at what profound costs? I write about this from 1st hand knowledge with experience as my teacher (having to pay three life sentences of 600 years a piece in prison, and 60 more for good measure as my costs). To transcend beyond this requires a baptismal immersion and washing away with spiritual waters of Truth. It is not easy, and it certainly takes time, but it is most necessary for our redevelopment. In rendering forth a more figurative depiction, consider a precious stone (gold) that is extracted from out of the earth's quarry, whose true value and worth is to be appraised and then given over to the purchaser. In doing so, it is necessary that certain sequential stages of preparation be had before presentation, (one being washing). The requisite of using actual water in washing away the elements of rubbish that lessens and desecrates worth, are comparative to the washing away of the immoral corruption accrued upon one's mental state by the spiritual waters of Truth. Just as it is essential in bringing forth the best quality of stones for material building, so is it even more essential to use sound Truths when constructing the temple made not with hands (not weak and partial virtues).

As this rite points to the necessity of change by means of purification, it's imperative that one's work as an individual, as well as those of a collective body, witnesses to that change. Therefore, we the U.O.C., employ this rite (along with both a written and verbal declaration from the student), as a proclamation of their heart's sincerity to employ changes in their lives. Knowing; however, that such true evidence lies not in one's speech alone, but in the evidence of their works, we also assess our students efforts and monitor their subsequent development for evidence of this change. We take our work serious as we wish for others to take us serious. The work that one chooses to engage in, no matter what that may be, should always be performed, assessed, and presented in its best light, as it serves as a reflection of the laborer himself.

Universal Craftsmen

ESSAY VIII

STONE QUARRY

In Masonic discourse one may hear use of the word quarry. Quarries are excavation sites comprised usually of mountain ranges where the extraction of stones are obtained for purposes of building. Although the exact quarry location for the building of the Temple hasn't been made definitively conclusive, past explorations show many large sized stone extractions having been made northeast of Jerusalem near the Damascus Gate. When considering their vicinity and sizes, many contend that this location more than likely may have been the site where such stones were extracted. Traditionally speaking, the craftsmen employed in the building of King Solomon's Temple were not only highly skilled in extracting and hewing stones needed for erecting, but were able to do so without damaging them during their removal and transport to the temple site. According to Rev. Oliver, in his Historical Landmarks of Freemasonry, the quarry grounds and construction site were in two different locations, where caste workers were assigned to each according to their particular skill set. He goes further to indicate that the primary workers assigned to the quarry grounds were general laborers and apprentices, who for the most part, were engaged in the more laborious works of cutting, lifting, and carrying of the stone (all such works pertaining to its extraction). The Fellow Craftsmen, who were more so responsible for the precision hewing and squaring of them, were said to be located at the temple site along with the fitters and setters. As all the different aspects of temple building required manual labor to some degree, it has been said that the work among the quarries was the most physically exerting, and is why these particular class of men were distinctively known as "men of burdens." Now, whether all the details, as written in Oliver's chapter concerning the classification of workmen, can be considered accurate, Masonic scholars have questioned. However, what is veritably no less true, is that the rigorous works of any quarry are those which indeed can be demanding upon the body.

As stone acquisition from the quarry is essential, it has been asked why such emphasis on stone use rather than brick? Aside from its abundance as being one of nature's first usable building materials, it witnesses to the Great Architect's Trestle-Board design in instructing man how to build an edifice on a sure and lasting foundation. These evidences can be found in the Hebrew meaning of the words Stone and Truth themselves, both having synonymy in the understanding of building. The meaning of the word stone is to build. Its transliteration is eben, and derives its meaning from the root transliteration banah, which means, in both the literal and figurative sense, to build. In its further figurative sense, the word stone (eben), is also derivate of ben, and it means also son, as in one's seed. It had its archaic understanding to what is anatomically termed now as men's testes. It was used to express the organs by which a man was capable of producing seeds for "building" up a lineage, whether in quality, condition, family, or nation. An example of its use can be found in Deuteronomy, 23rd Chapter, 1st verse, where one was to be prohibited from entering into the congregation of the Lord, if "... wounded in the stones or hath his privy member cut off... ." Now, when looking at the word Truth and its transliteration, we find the word emeth, which means stability. Its figurative meaning is to be firm or faithful, to be permanent. Morally, it means to be certain. It also means to build up, or to support, as if to foster by parent or nurse. It also has its association with verily, truly, veracity, and faithfulness. Now when looking at how both the words Stone and Truth pertains to building, we find that they share like processes in development in that they both have undergone and withstood long periods of development that serves to forge their strength and abilities to hold up when tested; one by the natural elements of geological conditioning, the other by the proven conditioning of the Spiritual Law. It is the underwent process of them both that determines the lasting permanency of the structures they build (material or spiritual). Now, when seeing how such process of earthly stones undergo geological transformations over time to one day develop into a hardened stone, even to become a massive size mountain at some point, symbolically compares to our own developmental process we undergo as living stones to be be built up as One Spiritual Body unto God. Although we are materially crafted from earthly minerals, (it being biblically taught that man was formed from the earth), we are also Soul seeds of God that's being crafted and spiritually developed. The Soul's experiences in this body is the underwent development that forges its permanency so that it may be set in that spiritual edifice. In both instances, it is the Great Architect of The Universe that tries them both. If we are to understand that Time is the great Leveler, which subjects everything to a beginning and ending, then Truth, which preceded even Time, is coeval with God and has no ending or beginning, and can be the only true permanency of the Eternal Spirit of Life as a constant. This is the reason why in our works of Speculative Freemasonry, a work embodying the developmental erecting of the Soul, the requisites for stone use is so critical, because they are the symbolical representations of Truths that extends beyond mortality and quickens the Soul with spiritual permanency. Once done, it comes to have its permanent place of service in the Spiritual Temple as being a symmetrical part of a governing whole. Morally, this is also to say, that when internal Truths are discovered and thenceforth exercised, it then comes to render their beneficial health to the members of the whole body, and thenceforth to collective society. A desire for self and community betterment are the most noble purposes for why anyone should seek to build, in which the quality of materials for achieving a lasting result then becomes a factor. Therefore, the first stone to be extracted from out of the quarry for building such a structure should be the Foundation Stone of Truth, and thereafter, stones of moral and spiritual virtues. All stones for use must rest upon this Foundation Stone in order for the temple to operate as one harmonious whole for its betterment. This understanding is alluded to in the particular lesson rendered to the candidate concerning the explanations of Truth: "Truth is a divine attribute, and the foundation of every virtue. To be good and true is the first lesson we are taught in Masonry. On this theme we contemplate, and by its dictates, endeavor to regulate our conduct. Hence influenced by this principle, hypocrisy and deceit are unknown among us; sincerity and plain dealings distinguish us; and the heart and tongue join in promoting each other's welfare, and rejoicing in each other's prosperity." What better quality of materials are there for use in building such a spiritual edifice? Bricks, on the other hand, are man made fabrications which symbolizes the deviations of Truth's natural design. They are inferior in substance and quality, being mixed with straws of falsehoods and untempered mortar, which at best, can only exemplify an exterior fleeting beauty while lacking the substance of interior permanency. When such becomes to be tried and tested, it is certain to break, because it has not been properly tempered (a process by which the proper working mixture brings about the correct consistency for hardening, hence Love).

Whereas stone extractions from a rock quarry in Operative Masonry pertains to the nature of a material work, we are to understand that in the nature of Speculative Freemasonry, it pertains to a spiritual work of moral and Self development. Therefore, when understanding that the use of the term quarry in this spiritual sense, is a site for extracting Truths, a quarry would then come to signify the physical being of man. It is within the nature of one's own being that the speculative quarryman is to dig and chisel away for the extraction of Truths to be hewn and used for the building of his foundation and moral redevelopment. What lays within is hidden from ourselves, in which our Creator have implemented the Law to aid us in both its revelation and cultivation. Just as the candidate was aided by an experienced workmen in his search to discover the symbolizations of Light upon his first entrance into the Lodge, so does the workings of the Law aid in developing us to become skilled enough to independently navigate within the grounds of our own bodily quarries to discover Truths. The speculative works of extracting stones from out of the quarries of Self involves learning, training, and reconditioning our faculties to become cognizant of those spiritual signs of the Law that points to those precious Truths. To extract these is to unveil them from our concealed states of subconsciousness to our revealed state of consciousness. This process of bringing Light from out of Darkness can be seen alluded to in the W.M. coming forth from out of the depths of the East to dispense Masonic Light upon the candidate, who has traveled from out of the West in search of Light. This is to say, that much like how the Sun dispenses its life giving rays upon the Earth, so does an illuminated Mind dispenses its regenerative effects upon a searching Heart. Although these extracted Truths surfaces to mind in their rude and rough state, they have to be worked and smoothed in order to be made effective in our lives. In our efforts of self redevelopment, we must be willing to travel through our own portals of ignorances and prejudices to discover the real nature of not only the problem, but more important, those solutions of Truth needed to resolve them.

These life possessing minerals of Truth (precious gems and stones) are also symbolic of those Divine energies concerning the Soul. These energies are what gives the corporeal body its animation whose essence stems from God (termed by some as the Divine Spark). We possess the potential to exponentially generate more of this fire like spark by the cultivating works of the Law; however, on the other hand, we can also decrease this energy by the negative works we cultivate in our lives, even to the point that we can extinguish the fire like properties of our own Divine Spark. This is why the fairest gem a Mason can be said to boast of is Love, because it's a powerful source of energy (especially when collectively employed), that counteracts the negative effects of the dross elements that has came to attach itself upon the aspects of the Soul. To reverse such effects is what constitutes the regeneration of the Spirit. Now, as we can see from one angle of view how the extraction of earthly gems and stones, such as gold and diamonds, contributes to the regulation of material life, so can it be seen from a spiritual standpoint that such living stones of God extracted from out of the bowels of the Earth contributes also to the regulation of Spiritual Life. In a cosmological aspect, this would then render this planet as one huge quarry from which God is extracting Souls as a consecrated priesthood of Spiritual Temple Workers.

Universal Craftsmen

ESSAY IX

WHOLE STONES (PERFECT YOUTH)

Among the symbolisms of Freemasonry, various stone types are used to convey different lessons of spiritual truths, such examples being the Foundation Stone, the Cornerstone, and the Key Stone. One of particular interest to the U.O.C. studies is the Whole Stone(1). This stone was requisitioned for use by the command of God to Moses in the 20th Chapter of Exodus regarding the manner of how the altar of the Tabernacle was to be constructed, and as "...King Solomon's Temple is said to have been a representation of that tabernacle," and that "...every well and regulated and governed Lodge is, or ought to be a correct representation of King Solomon's Temple," we come to see a regulation symbolically pertaining to petitioning candidates termed as the Perfect Youth(2). This regulation stipulates that all petitioners of Freemasonry must possess sound minds and whole bodies when being considered for candidacy. This means that they should neither be mentally inapt, physically dismembered, or maimed; that they should possess an overall healthy state of condition in both their physical and mental beings. This regulation is believed by some to have had its possible derivatives from the laws of the ancient priesthood concerning the governing of their temples (particularly the Egyptians). As these were said to have been decreed by their respective deities, these ordinances pertained to everything from the instructive rites of ceremonial tool usage, to the physical qualifications of the men selected for temple service. An example of this can be found in the book of Leviticus where such laws were given to Moses in order to prevent anything blemished, impure, defective, or irregular from being brought to the Tabernacle for use (believing that doing so was a defilement of its pure and holy nature). So stringent were these laws that there was instances where individuals were slain for even touching certain consecrated objects used in relationship to the Temple. Therefore, in attempts to gather a better understanding of this regulation, let's consider the necessity of its use among Operative Masons in former times, as well as the possible basis of its Speculative enactment.

Now, naturally one can easily see where the need of having a whole and fit body was necessary for the kind of physical labor required for operative stonework, but let's not forget that even though there was Operative Masons that were engaged in the actual working of stones, there were those among them that were not a part of the fraternal class of Masons that constituted the speculative nature of its practice (and vice versa). This was the standing difference between the two types of craftsmen during those times, where among their records, we find some of the most earliest manuscript writings of their stone guilds outlining the principles of their conduct. Also, it should be kept in mind that the craft of one of these practices (the speculative form of Masonry), drew its designs and symbolisms from the other (the operative trade). This is significantly important, because many of the regulations in these early manuscripts that pertained to things of an Operative element were also part of the Speculative, the following being a few examples. "The Master must be steadfast, trusty and true, provide victuals for his men and pay their wages punctually." "A Mason shall not be obliged to work after the sun has set in the West." Every Mason shall cultivate brotherly love and love of God, and frequent the holy church." "If a brother see his Fellow hewing a stone, and likely to spoil it by unskillful craftsmanship, he shall teach him to amend it with fair words and brotherly speeches." Other charges found to have been given at the making of Masons during those times states: "That every Master Mason do reverence to his elder, and that a Mason be no common player at the cards, dice or hazard; or at any other unlawful plays, through which the Science and Craft may be dishonored or slandered." And ye shall keep truly all the counsel that ought to be kept in the way of Masonhood, and all the counsel of the Lodge or of the chamber. Also, that he shall be no thief, nor thieves to your knowledge free, that ye shall be true to the king, lord, or master that ye serve, truly to see and work for his advantage"(3). These show, like in today's time, that with any job, morality and self circumspection (the practices in which Freemasonry embodies today), all play an integral part of any aspect of an operative work. Everything, from the quality and performance of one's work, to one's reliability and truthfulness in dealing with another, are all points that could be said to constitute a general code of moral ethics.

However, with the growth of Speculative Masonry retaining some of the elements of their operative regulations, the continued disqualification of candidates with blemishes and "...those not having the full and proper use of his limbs; for a maimed man can do the Craft no good," began to raise concerns of whether some of these were still in line with what had now became strictly a speculative practice. As Speculative Masonry had taken on its own distinct identity as Freemasonry, the prohibiting of such candidates, who were otherwise considered excellent potentials, seemed to be contrary to a system intended for the betterment and advancement of humanity. This was in the face of servicemen who had loss limbs in defense of their country, fighting for the beliefs and principles of freedom found on par with Freemasonry, not to mention the firefighters and police officers wounded in preserving those freedoms. This did not sit well among the consciousness of many brothers and caused the Grand Lodges to have to contemplate the basis for what this regulation was intended to speculatively serve (its purpose under former operative practices having been well understood(4).

Now, when attempting to consider this, we must revisit the viewpoint mentioned earlier of those believing this regulation to be of religious origin and take a look into the meaning of the word "whole" as used in these earliest regulations and biblically found in the 27th Chapter of Deuteronomy. Its transliteration in Strong's Hebrew and Greek Dictionary of the Bible is shalem, which means in both its figurative and literal sense, complete or completed. An example of these are heard in such statements as, "I would like a whole piece of cake," or "Her love makes me feel whole," or as used in the Antiquity Manuscript, that a "...Apprentice freeborn and of Limbs whole as a Man ought to be... ." It derives its basis from the root word shalam which means to be safe (in mind, body, or estate). Its connotative meanings are requite, recompense, restitution, to restore, to reward, to repay, made ready, made good made peaceable, made friendly, to deliver, made well, made prosperous, made PERFECT (emphasis on the word Perfect, as it pertains to a descriptive condition of a completed development). This same transliteration is also rendered for the word salem as found in the word Jerusalem, Jeru meaning City, and salem meaning Peace. Its variations reflect in common greetings among both the Jews and Muslims as "Shalom" and "Es Salmu Aleikum, Aleikum Salaam," meaning "Peace, be with you," and "With you be Peace"(5). Now, when further viewing the meaning of this word whole, we find that it is not only a descriptive condition that can be attributed to the materials, workers, and overall final state of the Temple design when completed (there being a desire to employ and present no less than the best unto a sacred and perfect God), but it bears witness also to a requisite process of work to be employed in order to achieve that state. Evidence of this reflects in the nature of the word itself as it is a causative word, meaning that the conditions of its meaning are those which can only be brought about by the course or process of something, or someone else. The conditions of its word meaning are predicated upon a direct or indirect involvement of action by means of a cause. Now, when further considering this in relationship to Jerusalem, a city or place of Peace (the place upon Mt. Moriah where all the materials were BROUGHT to for purposes for erecting), it becomes quite suggestive that the requisites of "whole" stones mandated for use (the word whole having the same figurative meaning of salem as a condition), are ones which are to be made whole, meaning they were made "good," "complete," and "ready," and therefore made PERFECT by a causative process in their transition to the Temple site (that being Jerusalem). That it has been recorded in both biblical and monitorial accounts that the stones selected for Temple use "...were made ready BEFORE brought thither..." prepared by Solomon's and Hiram's builder, "...underwent hewing, squaring, and raising in the quarries..." (capitalizations the author), indeed witnesses to a causative process that was employed in order to bring about the resulting state of wholeness. This certainly harmonizes with the requisite purposes of an operative process, but how so much a speculative one, you may ask? Let us further consider.

In our Speculative practice, we are to regard ourselves as living stones when pertaining to the work of Temple building, in which we are to then consider the working tools, the materials, and manner of their uses, all from an allegorical and symbolic aspect of moral and spiritual application. This also includes the various regulations pertaining to an operative process of work, its specifications of stones to be used, its completion, and that part of the Temple placement in which it belongs. Therefore, the descriptive process given above of how such stones were made whole, completed, and perfected, and then set in place for use would then pertain to one's inner aspects of self development, rather than anything pertaining to a physical one (as the ancient builders of men's Spirits greatly emphasized in their religious texts and historical writings). It must be remembered that the Temple that is said to be under erecting is the "... temple made not with hands, eternal in the heavens," and if ancient Masons practiced BOTH Operative and Speculatively, as we are told in our monitors, then they (like we), were also building a Temple made not with hands eternal in the heavens. Therefore, in the Speculative aspect of their practice, what would physical hands, testes, or any limbs at all, serve in the constructing of an immaterial and spiritual Temple (other than for their instructive purposes of conveying signs, symbols, and modes of recognition between members, for which then they would still only point to those virtuous lessons of morality incorporated in its speculative practice). Remember, Spirit recognizes Spirit, and there are many who see, feel, and hear the Truth in each other, as well as all around, having not eyes, hands, nor ears to see the signs, feel the grips, or hear the words. Therefore, this regulation from a speculative point symbolizes those virtues of Truths to be brought forth from out of a candidate by means of a causative process, and thereby made whole and perfect for use in the building of his Spiritual Temple (a process of mental development followed by subsequent exercise, that establishes the perfecting of his Soul). Even though we are craftsmen upon this corporeal plane of existence, our materials for building; however, are stones of virtuous Truths and mortar of Love, by which use of the working tools of self applications, we build what is eternally incorruptible. This causative process, which ultimately serves to bring about a state of wholeness or perfection within our being, is veiled in the resulting conditions of the meaning salem, which can be looked at in a couple of speculative ways. Masonically, it would serve to mean that as much as in the same way that a material stone is selected from out of the quarries to undergo a process that would make its addition symmetrically whole to an existing edifice, so must an individual candidate come to be extracted from out of the quarries of society to undergo a Masonic process of development that would make him a part of a collective body that's already operating and functioning as a harmonious and peaceful whole. In another sense of application, it would also convey one undergoing a constructive work of mental, moral, and Spiritual self redevelopment, whose results bring about that state of internal peace (that sense of fulfillment and completion that renders a person to feel whole and adequate). It would also signify that the stones that are to be made whole by a causative process are our own Souls undergoing extraction and development here on Earth, and that Earth would then serve as the Ground Floor from where we begin to build in our process to be conveyed to that Spiritual Jerusalem, that city of Peace where rest is found and we are whole and One with all things and the Creator. In all these understandings harmony is now found in its speculative practices of today. Today most Grand Lodges, if not all, do not incorporate the wording as formerly written under the Ancient Charges and Constitutions of the past, but rather have instituted a wording that allows for a case by case basis under a dispensation when considering individuals with physical injuries.

In summing up this particular essay, it should be noted that there are some who hold to the belief that Freemasonry's origin, as a Speculative practice, derives from the earliest religions and their priesthoods, while others believe its origins stems from an operative trade, as far as its developing organization concerns. It is the U.O.C.'s belief; however, that Masonry has always been a work of speculative nature that has been afforded to us for the purposes of Moral, Soul and Spiritual development. Its lessons are embodied in the various practices of some of the most earliest religions, Mystery Schools, Sciences, it's working trades, and many other studies. But even without these, we would still find the vast Trestle-board designs of Operative Creation serving to instruct us in its beautiful Truths of morality that would inspire us to reverence and emulate it for purposes of our own self betterment. When viewing the meaning of Speculative Masonry in its rendered monitors, does it not convey this same understanding. Therefore, what the U.O.C. believes that makes us extractable for use as living stones for Temple use is our spiritualized efforts of Love, that mortar that binds and fills the imperfections of mortal weakness. To assume in any way that man is not acceptable enough to better himself (the works of building his own temple), because he is not on par with God's perfection, whether that be moral or physically, truly undermines the deeper understanding for why we are to worship God in Truth and in Spirit, and for why we are building spiritual temples in the first place. To attempt to gauge the standard of perfection by a ruler of carnality, which is corruptible under time, renders every single man wanton (all having sinned and fell short of the glory of God). But to gauge perfection by the eternal Spirit of Love, constitutes that Christic essence of man's Soul that bridges the gap between Matter and Spirit and makes the Temple truly Whole, Complete, and Perfect. As builders, we must never forget that even though it's a causative process of the Law that aids to develop us, it is the Love of God that works within us to Perfect us.

Universal Craftsmen

ESSAY IX ENDNOTES

1. Whole Stone is not a term particularly found employed in the Degrees of Craft Masonry. It is a symbolical viewpoint having been derived from the interpretation of the book of Exodus 20th Chapter, 5th verse, and Deuteronomy 27th Chapter, 6th verse, in conjunction with those requisite qualifications pertaining to a petitioner's moral, physical, and mental conditions, the basis of which are amply discussed in Mackey's Jurisprudence of Freemasonry, Pgs. 59-79.

2. This is a candidate qualification, whose basis stems from one of the oldest regulations of the Operative Masons, which states: "A candidate must be without blemish, and have the full and proper use of his limbs for a maimed man can do the craft no good."---Old York Constitutions; 5th Article (more widely accepted as the Halliwell Manuscript under the publishing of James Orchard Halliwell).

3. These are various regulations found within the Regius Manuscript the Grand Lodge of 1353, and the Antiquity Manuscript. Many of the subsequent regulations that came to be enacted in further draftings later Masonic Constitutions stemmed from these. This was the case concerning the Constitutions of 1723, when the Grand Lodge of England had just recently established themselves in 1717/

4. It is now evident that Freemasonry's speculative design concerns it self with only the applicable lessons of the inner morality and spiritual development, whose precepts are in keeping with some of the oldest religions and philosophical practices of history. However, evidence of this nature of practice (as it entailed their laws of morality), can still be found within the Operative stonemason's regulations with the 15 Articles and Points of the Gothic Constitutions.

5. There are many other names and places in which this word can be seen to be used, and when properly understood, serves to provide greater revelation surrounding biblical events and their esoteric implications.

ESSAY X

PERAMBULATION

As man is admonished in the holy scriptures to walk by faith and not by sight, the unseen is seemingly ever before him with each new step. It is in this same way that Darkness is ever seemingly a precursor to Light. In both instances we find the nature of these two principles inescapably present along the diurnal course of the Soul's travels. In the conferring of some degrees, this diurnal course is referred to as perambulations, which means to walk through, about, or over. It aids in the inspection of the candidate as he walks around about the Lodge to determine if he's been "duly and truly prepared." It also allows for the candidate to be asked certain questions concerning his reasons for petitioning and the various aspects of his qualifications. This practice in Freemasonry is believed to have had its derivative ties to the ancient Rite of Circumambulation, which is said to date back to some of the most earliest religions and Mystery Schools of Egypt and India. In imitation of the Sun's rising and setting, the neophyte was instructed to walk in this same diurnal course, where along his journey, he would then come to encounter various obstacles and trials that would serve to test his fortitude and moral integrity. The staging of this course was often accompanied with enigmatic riddles, depictions of different deities, symbols, and even constellational designs intended to teach Truths both spiritual and scientific in nature. Even though no one knows with certainty when this rite was first devised and employed as an instructive means for conveying wisdoms, it is believed; however, that it came by way of man's first observational studies of nature and how he came to notice the cyclic course of the seasons that effected everything around him, including himself. With the diurnal rotation of the Earth causing its equinoctial and solstice effects, it was these he noticed that seemingly correlated also with other reoccurring events. These events were the annual inundations of the Nile River, the annual fertility spikes in both livestock and agricultural productions, the course of various star patterns as seen from the Earth, and even more noticeably, the positional changes of the Moon and the rising and setting Sun. All these pointed to an unseen force seemingly at work in which his continued study of these would bring about the revelation of many sciences that would enhance and further develop his existence. Now, as the most primitive wisdoms would first revolve around man's basic provisional needs, such as food, water, lodging, and pastoral acquisition (these being foremost and demanding), it would be of no surprise that much of the rhetoric later found to be used in their sacred writings would be astrological, architectural, and pastoral in nature. We can see this in their common use of words such as builder, stones, grapes, stars, lambs, and bulls when describing certain events of their men and deities. A biblical example of this lies in the agricultural metonymy pertaining to Jesus Christ when being called the first "fruit" unto God, or in other instances when referred to as being the "lamb" of God.

So with further contemplative studies, more revelations of the sciences came not only to be had, but a greater understanding of the laws that also governed them. He quickly learned that the forces of the governing law impacted not only the aspects of all that he saw, but all that he couldn't see, including the internal nature of himself. And so the cold and blistering effects of Winter came to impact his physical being, so did it come to impact his mental and emotional states as well. With the degeneracy of life and its death-like state of appearance upon the Earth, it is certain that man's morale and his sense of hope slowly diminished along with nature's provisional resources. Only by the confirming evidences of Spring's regenerative effects would his hope begin to be restored. This would come to reflect in the early sproutings of seedling growth and budding vegetation until it would then give way to Summer's strength and developing maturation. Summer's closing would then reveal the first fruit reapings from their earliest plantings, which was indicative of the full harvest they could soon expect to yield in Autumn's approach. When the bountiful provisions in which they had hoped for had indeed became a reality, the joy of their abundant reapings were often expressed with festive celebrations and time honored traditions. Now, as there were many festivals that were agriculturally related and were unmistakably keyed in to a specific produce, it is of no coincidence that these crops beared esoteric and spiritual correlations to not only the four major seasons, but also to the various types of sacrificial offerings that had been mandated to be presented by their respective deities (such notably seen among the Hebrew nation). Now, even though these may have appeared insignificant, but what was veiled within; however, were the many esoteric Sciences and sublime Truths of the Law pertaining to man's Soul development. It was these designs of both an earthly and spiritual nature that became employed for Temple use to thereby instruct the sincere aspirant in his search for Truth.

And so, as our primitive parents continued forth experiencing the re-occurring effects of seasonal changes while discovering more Truths, an increase of faith and hope began to be built up upon their respective deities for the annual reestablishings of their provisional resources. This is how the provisional aspects of the Divine Law and its workings became to be regarded as blessings and favor, and when negatively felt, as curses and punishments. It became established in many minds that these seemingly malevolent and benevolent forces of nature, whose conditions became to be given earthly and cosmic deifications, were therefore rewards for their obediences and disobediences. Whereas the masses generally regarded this as a standing truth, the more intimately instructed; however, were afforded deeper understandings of both the material and spiritual workings of the Law, whose effects, as it pertained to science and nature, had unfortunately became idolized. While many sought not to pierce the veil, it was the initiate who sought to gain more spiritual insight of what these rites, observances, pantheon of gods, and designs really meant in their religions, while many, as still today, only venerated the material provisions of the Law's workings, rather than its Spiritual. In respects to these designs, Freemasonry has not only preserved many of them in their Lodge structures, such as the All Seeing Eye, the Mosaic Pavement, and the Blazing Star, but also certain rites, such as the rite of circumambulation, as a means for conveying various lessons and precepts of morality. And since Freemasonry is not a religion, it does this while excluding those particulars that promotes worship to any one particular deity, past or present(1).

Now, as with many of the designs used in those times, there may lie layers of understanding for one symbol, for which those, who are able to arrive at such, will come to discover significant Truths within Truths. An example of this is found in this rite. For just as one may consider the use of circumambulating a symbolical means for degree advancements by progressive circuits, it could also be looked at as being the seasonal changes of Earth circumambulating around the Sun. Still, another view could also be understood as the candidate's Soul traversing the perambulatory course of World consciousness to encounter its various experiences of both its diurnal and nocturnal seasons of life. In this case, every lessoned learned, every obstacle overcame, and every new law understood, would be more wisdom obtained to further maturate it from a Soul seed of man to a Soul seed of God (every seed, whether material or spiritual, having to undergo this course until its full development). If viewing this strictly from an engineering perspective, we can arrive at another suggestive law of science which witnesses to the workings of centrifugal and centripetal force. These workings are depicted in the coiling like circuits of perambulation made about the Lodge in their several degrees, where the principal officers occupying their respective stations, could be depicted as terminals that facilitate generative and regenerative paths of energy. This, in a deeper sense of symbolic comparison, would then make the components of the Mind, Body, and Soul conductor points of this energy (Spirit) that aids in its power and regulation. Another view to be considered is that these same principal officers, along with their respective stations, could also symbolize the state of conditions in which Light (Spiritual Energy) travels as a circulatory path from immaterialization to materialization, and from materialization back to immaterialization again (a depicted work of the Mind's process of thought to its Bodily manifestation, and once manifested, back to its thoughts again to be thereby assessed, or as biblically expressed, judged). In this understanding of immaterialization to materialization, further allusions can be seen how ancient civilization's wisdoms progressed from the ancient East to our now current West, and, as it now appears with the reemergence of many

Eastern philosophies and meditative practices being sought out, a return back towards the spiritualistic wisdoms of the East. This entails several esoteric implications that harmonizes with the motif of building the 1st Temple, its destruction, and then the necessity of rebuilding the 2nd one. Primarily, what it points to is the state of our own fallen consciousness, the tearing down of our current one, and the works of reestablishing a greater one. In this, we find the stations of the three Principal Officers symbolizing the three states of Time (Past, Present and Future). It's been hypothesized by certain researchers specializing in the field of neural studies that the laws of energy and its effects upon the brain, may very well hold the key to unlocking man's psychic abilities which could possibly permit the recollection of such past, present, and even subconscious existences (believing such states and conditions of time to be only matters of distances in which energy travels along its points). Although this may sound like something from out of a science fiction movie, the idea may not be too far fetched when one consider patients who have awakened from out of year long commas with a sense of having only slept an hour or so, not to mention the conditions of our subconscious states while dreaming. It is a scientific fact that our bodies undergo more rejuvenation and healing during this period than any other time. Could it be because during this time the internal nature of our being (our Souls), are not subjectively conscious to the constructs of time? In considering this, this would witness to how the symbol of the Hour Glass is not only a symbol of Time, but also a symbol of Mortality, which allows one's Soul to transition from this Westerly world of corporeal confinement back to its Spiritual Providence of Eastern immortality (a liberation from the laws of time and distance). This would make the rite of circumambulation a symbolic means that would enable such. Now when one Masonically considers that every Lodge is a symbol of the World, and that every bodily temple should be considered a symbolical representation of a Lodge, thus making himself a microcosmic world, then such understanding gives greater revelation to what appears to be the coiling like nature of the universe revolving around one central point while it's said to be expanding at the same time. This center point would constitute the perambulatory origin from which all of creation has stemmed from and seemingly is returning to. This diurnal course, along with its central point, finds its ritualization in the perambulatory circuits conducted by the candidate with its altar being at the center, the point where he then finds himself receiving light before the East. When taking into account that a candidate receives light from the Master of the Lodge, and when further considering God to be the embodiment of the World Temple Himself, then the point in the circle would then symbolize the Omniscient Mind of God where all Divine Law and Order stems from, and where division comes together a One (Harmony). Therefore, the increase of perambulations in one's degree advancements would not only symbolize further descent into the depths of one's own individual mind, but also further descent into the Consciousness of God's. This spiritual progression is believed by some religious adherents to endow them with various Christ like faculties that exceed natural capabilities, these being the gifts of prophecy, healing, psychic abilities, and even astral projection(2). Whose to say that this doesn't constitute those mysteries in which Christ spoke of in his statement to Nicodemus in the Gospel of St. John: "If I have told you earthly things and ye believe not, how shall ye believe if I tell you of heavenly things (the book of St. John, 3rd Chapter, 12th verse).

Although much can be spiritually gleaned from this rite, the only way to receive its benefits for the Soul is by its moral application. It is then that one will come to see how its particular manner of use in Freemasonry is intended to be personified. By doing so, it allows for introspection and self examine and cross examinations to then be conducted. Just as in the ceremony, where the candidate encounters the three Principal Officer's stations in his perambulatory circuits, where certain questions and responses are then had between them, so should in likewise manner a mental discourse be formulated to be asked of his own 3 aspects of being until he can successfully reach the center point of his own lodge, that spiritual East where lie the Light he so desires (revelational Truths and instructions). When his true desire for betterment, for change, for positive development leads him to knock at the West entrance of his own being, questioning the actions of his body, seeking to know why he does what he do, the correct answers returned to him will then lead him on towards the gate of his own heart asking himself what makes him feel the way he feels which seemingly incites him to act and react the way he does. If having been most honest in his previous questions and answers, and if having came to grips with such Truths, then he will indeed be permitted to pass on where he will then find himself before the altar of his Mind, seeking to discover and have removed the veil of ignorance that has long served to forge the basis of his reasoning (his learned experiences that served in formulating his thinking and standing beliefs). Eureka!! It is here where the crux of the matter will be found and another whole stone of Truth extracted. In employing such methods of internalization, it may take several circuits or more for one to descend to the depths where lie some of the most hardest stones of Truth to be unveiled about Self (some being too heavy to lift without help and repetitive effort). Even though one is certain to meet with various obstacles along his course, as the material and lower nature will attempt to retain its dominance by employing false projections and tactics of distraction, a commitment to faithful persistence however, will no doubt bring about the necessary stone for building. This depicted process is one of many exercises that the U.O.C. employ as a tool for Self development. Masonically speaking, this is the speculative work of excavating and extracting stones (Truths), whereas the subsequent hewing of these stones are a symbolization for one's progressive efforts to apply them until they become structural placements in the temple (that which becomes to be the permanent moral character that defines a spiritual being).

Universal Craftsmen

ESSAY X ENDNOTES

1. The Rite of Circumambulation, which is considered to be a very ancient practice, is said to have been employed among many of the Ancient Mystery Schools. Although a variation of such is employed in Freemasonry, it is not in worship to the Sun, Moon, or any other cosmic body, or related type deity, as some have claimed in their slanderous accusations against Freemasonry. Rather, it is the abstract and speculative nature of Truths extracted from this rite's practice that Freemasonry has moralized and serve to now instruct its candidates with.

2. Astral Projection is not a prescribed belief or practice taught in the principles of Freemasonry. It is one that was held under certain practices of the Hermetic designs of other occultic Orders.

ESSAY XI

THE RIGHT HAND

 As the candidate renders forth this particular hand to be led about the Lodge, his doing so is further presented evidence of his trust and commitment to pursue that which his heart desires, despite whatever unforeseeable circumstances and dangers that may possibly await. The extending of his hand in blind trust over to another conveys a couple of great moral lessons. One, is that mankind's search for Truth will require faith, trust, and guidance. And that two, the lack of these in no way negates its existence. Whether a person chooses to believe a matter or not, doesn't make its existence any less a reality. It may, on the other hand, remain veiled to that particular person until the season in which his faith comes to germinate, but that certainly doesn't make it nonexistent. If this was the case, then light would not exist due to darkness, progression would not occur due to stagnation, and wisdom would never have manifested due to ignorance. However, we know that such is not the case, for history vividly displays all of man's evolutionary advancements where he has had to blindly grope along the path of darkness towards the awaiting ages of enlightenment, overcoming the many unknown obstacles and unforseen dangers that laid before him. This, in like manner, aptly depicts the pending journey that is to be undertook by the candidate, who steps upon the precipice of the unknown, and in an open display of faithfulness and trust, dives off the cliff into the sea of uncertainty. Great is the virtue found in man who is able to yield over what he has already laid claim to in order to reach for the unknown. Such actions attests to man's capacity to hope, for it is this virtue of the heart that sparks and fuel man's Will to employ those dexterous expenditures called hands. Although what he seeks lie in the spiritual clouds of obscurity (mental envisionment), its procurement is still there waiting to be discovered and brought to light (materialization).

Faith and Trust are the substances of Fidelity and are the forerunners of labor and commitment, for nothing can be accomplished without either. Therefore, the Egyptians, when choosing to depict an industrious man building, did so by the hieroglyphic carvings of a hand, because, as Harpollo M. Goulianof commented in his work of Archeologist Egyptienne, "the hand proceeds all labors." It has been wisely said "...the head conceive and the heart devise in vain, if the hand be not prompt to execute the design." This euphemism conveys a beautiful Truth concerning the relationship the hands bear with that of Heavenly and Earthly concord. The hands are the deacons of the Mind and Heart that labors to bring that which was conceived in the realm of Spirit into the world of materialization. Unless such dualities are brought together by means of exertive effort, that which was first envisioned, will never come to be had. The evidence of one's spiritual and material concord is beautifully played out in the manifestation of labor (one of Love's many outward exhibitings). One's response to a summoning call for action lies in their hands, limbs and other members of the body, as these are all what's relied upon in carrying out the expressed intents of the Mind and Heart's expressions.

It is of considerable interest that the word heart has etymological connections to the word concord (concord meaning agreement), whose symbolization among the ancients was depicted as a hand. Some scholars believe that the nature of this understanding was inherent with man's Creation in which he became cognizant of in the first instance he sought to procure something for himself. His natural instincts automatically summoned the uses of his hands in efforts of its obtainment. With such being seemingly true, even among infants, then it is of no surprise that the early development of communication would reflect hieroglyphic depictings of the hand to convey this same idea. So prevailing was the sentiments of the hand among the ancients that it became to serve as a summoning invocation of their deities for sealing whatever contractual matters undertook between two parties. This is where the clasping of the hands came to serve, not only as a token of mutual agreement to whatever terms proposed and settled upon, but even more to the binding penalties of its breachment. Although there are some monitorial explanations that references the association of the hand to Fides (an ancient Roman deity of Faith, Honesty, and Truth, who in some cases was depicted by two right hands joined together, and in others, by two human figures holding each other by their rights), it dates back; however, to even further times, with some of its earliest depictings surfacing around 2300 BCE as an Egyptian hieroglyphic of an extended right hand(1). Another depiction can be seen in an ancient Mesopatamia painting dating back around 1800 BCE that's referred to as the Investiture Panel. It is believed to depict the Babylonian god Marduk transferring the governing power of kingship to a man through the grasping of hands, his right appearing to be engaged in an oath taking gesture. Whether in these most ancient times, or in the patriarchal period of Abraham when he lifted up his hand unto God and swore that he would not accept anything from the King of Sodom, or the apostolic times of Christianity when Paul had received the right hand of fellowship from Cephus and John, or even today in its utilizations for court swear ins and officer inductions, its sacred use has always been a standing expression of fidelity. On the other hand, it has became so much of a common use that it has unfortunately lost much of its spiritual and moral fiber, it being nothing for one to now shake your hand to curry favor with the intent only to scam you. Where the shaking of hands was once mandatory and held sacred and integral meaning in contractual affairs (a time when men looked each other in the eyes when conducting business), it has now came to be replaced with just a simple click of the mouse.

In viewing this word hand in its Hebraic transliteration, as far as it pertains to the right, we discover the word yamiyn, whose meaning, aside from its literal anatomical rendering, figuratively expresses both direction and exalted states of condition and position. It is used to denote positions of prominence that's often associated with power and due recognition associated with priestly and kingly authority. An example of its use to express direction is found in the the 3rd Chapter of 2nd Chronicles,

17th verse, where it refers to "...the pillars before the Temple on the right hand, and the other on the left." An example of its use as an expression of condition can be found in the book of Colossians, 3rd Chapter verse 1, which depicts Christ as one "...who sitteth on the right hand of God" (this being an anthropomorphical expression). An even further example of this can be found in the 110th Psalm, verse 1, wherein the Lord remarks to "Sit thou on at my right hand until I make thine enemies thy footstool." In further revelation of this word, we also find its meaning being figuratively used to denote the cardinal direction of the South, the South being on the "right side" of the body in relationship to one facing the rising Sun of the East. This should cast more more light to the understanding of why Hiram is associated with this particular location, and also the manners of preparing a Fellow Craft candidate. As the course of the Sun travels from left to right (as it so seems to appear as a result of the Earth's rotation upon its own axis), its heat producing rays increases in strength until it reaches its zenith at high meridian in the Southern Hemisphere (the Earth's position in relationship to the Sun). While this is transpiring on the side of the Southern Hemisphere, the gradual declination of the Sun is occurring on the Northern Hemisphere, whereby the waning effects of the Sun's vitality can be felt in decreasing temperatures and loss of light's visibility. It is believed that it may have been this observational study of the Sun that led the ancients to associate their right hands with the South, and with it, the attributes of life's maturational strength and divine authority, whereas the North (with its degradation of light), became to be associated with obscurity, ignorance, and weakness, and therefore came to take on the left. Keeping in mind that the learned ancients regarded themselves as a microcosmic world, it is not hard to see how they would analogously regard the left side of their own nature the weaker in comparison to that of the right. And so it was for such reasons, in imitation of what seemed to be the apparent course of the Sun and its effects rendered upon the Earth's temple, that not only the right became employed in making oaths (it being considered the more bindingly stronger), but it also became to be employed in the rite of circumambulation(2). The candidate, who was placed under hoodwink, was taken by the right hand and was guided in his travels by one who had already proven skillfully apt in navigating those in such course. Now, with the meaning and scriptural uses of this word having been afforded, the esoteric implications of him who sits in the Southern part of the

Lodge should be considerably revealing to all those having been Raised (an allusion to that Divine state of the Soul's awakening and its potential Exaltation).

In the extending of one's right hand of fellowship, there is another virtue of importance to be considered (especially when pertaining to a person's moral redevelopment). That is the exercise of Prudence. If we are to keep our badges unsullied, we must be mindful of those places and people we choose to engage ourselves with. This is not to say that we should carry ourselves in a better than thou attitude. No, this doesn't "...conciliates true friendship among those who might otherwise have remained at a perpetual distance," but what we should do is be mindful of fellowshipping with those who compromise our moral integrity. The best way to do this is to be a living example of your practicing belief. Our choice to live in a manner so as to be beacons of light unto ourselves and unto others, especially in places and circumstances where there is darkness, speaks volumes and further witnesses to what Freemasonry truly is. We should not be afraid to be different in the name of righteousness, as this is what distinguishes us as real men and real Masons. The integrity of a virtuous man should not change with his location or with the encountering of different people and circumstances(3). The unyielding virtues of faithfulness and fortitude, even in the face of temptation and violence, are beautifully exemplified both in Hiram and in Jesus Christ, and are those examples in which we are admonished to follow. This high degree of virtue, as with any virtue, comes with gradual development, and is something that initially requires help. In doing this, it is critical that we surround ourselves with those things, places, and people who are conducive to the conditions we are seeking to aspire to. These serve to fortify and support us in our efforts of self betterment. It would be unwise for an alcoholic to hang out in bars, if he is struggling to quit drinking. It would be a counterproductive strain on his efforts. Such should be the same stand taken when working to change whatever aspects of ourselves desired. We must allow ourselves the best nurturing conditions for development by removing those things that obstructs our growth. The effort of clearing away the existing rubbish is enough counterweight within itself without having to add on more for one's personal conditioning and strengthening. There are some boulders laying among every temple's ruins (many which require assistance in removing). One extending their right hand of fellowship to assist another in such work is one who can truly be called a brother. In this aspect, one's right hand is that extension of brotherly love and assistance that recognizes and supports the laudable pursuits of his brother and desires for his well being and successes as if they were his own. He rejoices in his brother's achievements, aids in his brother's endeavors, and mourns for his brother's losses. In this sense, the attributes of this practice brings us in close relationship to that tenet called Relief, and reminds us that the work of Temple building is one of both an individual and collective work, where we soon learn that one hand serves to washes the other.

ESSAY XI ENDNOTES

1. Fide is also depicted with a key in her hand and a dog alongside her feet. She is also shown in some depictions holding a heart in the palm of her hand.

2. Concerning the Rite of Circumambulation, the candidate's course of turns and movements were always conducted with the right side facing towards the altar.

3. This is one of the hardest challenges often encountered by the students of the U.O.C. The conditions of prison society are not conducive to true moral reformation despite the many programs offered (which only provide outward certificates of course completion, but no real evidence of internal change). Truly standing up for the principles of true righteousness can be met with stigmas that often result in physical harm and even death in some instances.

ESSAY XII

THE RITE OF INVESTITURE

In Freemasonry there is a particular point where the candidate comes to be ceremonially clothed with what will probably be the most significant piece of Masonic garment he'll ever come to wear. This rite is known as the Rite of Investiture and is where the candidate receives the badge of a Mason. This badge is commonly referred to as the Lambskin Apron, which is said to be more ancient and honorable than the Golden Fleece, the Roman Eagle, the Order of the Star, and the Noble Order of the Garter. In providing some historical insight of these, we find the Noble Order of the Garter, and the Order of the Star being chivalric orders dating back to 1351 in France and 1348 in England with King John III and King Edward III. The Golden Fleece was a knighthood that originated January 10, 1430, in honor of the marriage between Phillip III and Princess Isabella of Portugal. Phillip III, also known as Phillip The Good, was Duke of both Burgundy and Netherlands. Now, as we know that the Golden fleece that's monitorially mentioned in the candidate's lecture of the E.A. is certainly not the fabled one made of pure gold which was taken by Jason and the Argonauts, the adventuresome exploits in this classic mythical story, however are believed to have had some influence in the naming of Phillip's order (as evidence show many particulars of the main character, Jason, having been attributed to another character named Gideon). The fact that ram's wool was one of Burgundy's major commodities tends to also lend evidence that all of this may have had some contributing influence in his choice of name. In regards to the Roman Eagle, it was represented by a black eagle on a gold background as the imperial arms of the Holy Roman Empire and was a symbol also associated with the Order of the Black Eagle which was formed in honor of King Friedrich's crowning in Prussia (Prussia at that time still being a part of the Holy Roman Empire). This symbolization, which was infamously depicted on their shields, underwent various changes in appearances until it eventually became a double headed eagle which came to denote the East and Western empires of Rome and Constantinople. In Freemasonry, it most notably appears in the 33rd Degree of the Scottish Rites.

With these Orders all being quite old indeed, what attests to the apron still being the most ancient and honorable among them all, finds its basis in the sacrificial ordinances pertaining to various priesthoods, where lambs and goats without blemishes or defects had to be presented up as offerings. These were used as propitiations in sin offerings, purifications, and various other religious rites and observances in which the ritualistic imparting of purity and innocence would be transferred upon such items as altars, doorposts, and people by the application of blood in exchange for immunity and the expiation of punishment and curses. In other instances they would be used for the transferral of man's sins upon the goat or lamb (as in Passover and Yom Kippur). With Yom Kippur, one of these would then be offered to God as an sacrificial atonement on behalf of the nation while another would have the sins of the people placed upon it and then banished out into the wilderness. This event was associated with Azazel in connection to its statutory law concerning the use of goats, hence the name "scapegoat." The particulars of these observances are found in the book of Leviticus, 16th Chapter, and Exodus, 12th Chapter. Because of the lamb's meek and gentle nature, along with its white coat, it was an apt typification to morally symbolize innocence and purity when used for ceremonial observances. Ceremonially transferring purity and innocence onto an object or person(s) for sacred uses is a form of transubstantiation, and can be seen performed in such rites as the Eucharist, where bread and wine become holy sacraments representing Christ as the slain lamb that expiates men's sins. Although these rites and observances are in many ways traditions and customs that were mandated to be perpetually observed, they are only effective when spiritually understood and morally applied. One who seeks to engage in such sacrificial works of their "...own free will and accord," must become the living sacrifice themselves. The ransoming exchange of man's sinful nature for that of the lamb's purity, occurs when one's belief in Truth incites obedience to its practice. This is the death and banishment of the goat, (all that could be represented as the Wintery season of the North), which undergoes transformation by workings of the Divine Law to be born again and resurrected with greater Life and Consciousness of Truth in the East (the Lamb). Obedience is an expression of Love. The symbolization of the lamb is a figurative type of the Soul and Love which has been invested to us by God. It is the only sacrifice that's worthy enough to be presented to Him (this being the same sacrifice He gave of Himself to the world when He began to create). In this sense, the Spirit of purity, perfection, and innocence, are all symbolizations of the eternal expression of God's Love as a slain lamb of himself, in which Christ not only esoterically depicts, but also all those who follow his like example in the offering up of their Soul. Our greatest offering is our Souls to be shepherded back to its spiritual residency by the regenerative power of God's love and his Truth. This whole understanding is alluded to in 1st Peter, Chapters 1 and 2: "Because it is written, Be ye Holy for I am Holy...Forasmuch as ye know that ye were not redeemed with corruptible things, as silver and gold, from your vain conversation received by tradition from your fathers, but with the precious blood of Christ as a lamb without blemish and spot; who was foreordained before the foundation of the world, but was manifest in these last times for you... Seeing ye have purified your souls in obeying the truth through the Spirit unto unfeigned love of the brethren, see that ye love one another with a pure heart fervently. We must remember that the allegories, practices, and various observances are all representations of these "...conversation received by tradition... ," and are indeed vain if the Truths in which they are suppose to symbolize are not lived out. As plainly made by Peter in his passage, its "...obeying the truth through the Spirit unto unfeigned love... ," that purifies the Soul. This is equally true concerning the ceremonial investiture of a Mason's apron, whose bestowal is to serve as a perpetual reminder to him of how his conduct should be of purity and innocence, in which, not only the color and material from which its made symbolizes, but also that illustrious Master who exemplified these virtues in character (Jesus Christ). To employ this in our moral conduct and in all the workings in which our hands serve to engage in, is the sacrificial exchange from the mortal to the Divine when accepting this investment at the altar of Freemasonry. Although in some Grand Jurisdictions the gloves are not always presented at the same time of the ceremonial investment of the apron itself, these honorable attires are; nonetheless, both reminders of the obligating duties of a Mason to remain cloaked in the garments of moral Righteousness and Truth whether in or out of ceremonial dress.

In deeper view of the apron and its esoteric relationship to the sacrificial lamb, there are some who hold the opinion that when the Lord made coats of skins for the covering of Adam and Eve's nakedness, as recorded in the 1st Chapter of Genesis, it was of direct consequence of their fall (the word fall being indicative of a descent from an elevated state of position or status). It is believed that this was not only a prophetical allusion to the sacrificial offering of Christ as a mercy covering of innocence and propitiation for mankind's sinful state and his subsequent redemption, but that it was also a metaphysical representation for their Soul's awakening inception into their own lower natured selves (such evidence being alluded to in their new found cognizance of their nakedness and fear mentioned in the 7th verse of Chapter 3). It appeared that their conscious descent into materiality inadvertently induced the unconsciousness of their own divine states of spirituality. This can be seen alluded to in not only their attempts to hide themselves, but also in the anthropomorphic idea that God had somehow lost their whereabouts in verse 9. As a result of this autonomous separation of spiritual consciousness, duality ensued, which severed harmony and brought about discord and irregularities in the government of the temple. Now, in Hebrew the word skin means to be made naked, bare, hide, leather, to awake, while the word light means in its connotations, illumination, East, flame, brilliance, radiance, and wisdom. It is of particular interest that the transliteration for the Hebrew words skin and light are both identically rendered as owr (and in another written variation as uwr, minus the aleph and ayin sounds for pronunciation). From the connotative meanings of these words, many suppositions have been drawn that the coats of skins weren't just provisional clothing for the covering of their physical nakedness alone, but were symbolic for the cloakings of all the illuminating wisdoms and Spiritual Truths that were inherently embodied within their own beings, which had now became veiled until such point in time that they would come to be rediscovered by rebirth of the Mind. In a greater sense, this was the veiling of their spiritual consciousness (their communal Oneness with Him), which resulted, as some believe, from the Soul's incarnation. This understanding could very well have been the reason for why a Tabernacle and Temple was first commanded to be erected in almost every religion, so that the material representations and designs would not only teach and witness to what was spiritually True, but had been veiled, but also to intruct them as to how such Temples were one and the same nature of themselves.

This same speculative idea finds further credence in the allusions of the zodiac animal associated with Spring., that being the Ram of Aries., whose cognate variation of the word lamb is transliterated as kebes. Now as Spring was anciently, and still is regarded in symbolism as the season of birth, life, enlightenment, and the rising of the Sun, this automatically draws to mind the idea of one coming into awakening consciousness (these same ideas being implicated in the meanings of the words light and skin). Therefore, if such Soul was divested of its purity of innocence, which brought about its spiritual unconsciousness into material consciousness (incarnation), then it stands by reason, that this same Soul (in its intent to engage in the works of reestablishing its spiritual consciousness), would then need to be reinvested with what it had initially lost, that being its purity and innocence (a state of condition symbolized in the lambskin apron). No labors, offerings, or specimens of work can ever be presented without it as such within itself outlines the requisite standard by which all propitiations are accepted. The admonishments to every newly made Entered Apprentice to keep his apron spotless, alludes to this one and the same Spiritual Truth, which was taught by Christ in his instructions of how to obey the law in the book of Matthew, 22nd Chapter, 37-40th verse: "Thou shall love the Lord thy God with all thy heart, with all thy soul, and with all thy mind. This is the first and great commandment. And the second is liken into it. Thou shall love thy neighbor as thyself. On these two commandments hang all the law and the prophets."

There is another correlation of particular interest that symbolically coincides with this same witnessing Truth which is alluded to in the lower extremities or private parts in which the apron tends to cover when worn.

In the seemingly warring states of our spiritual and material natures, one finds himself succumbing to the ruling influence of one or the other, where the evidence of the victor is seen played out in subsequent actions. This correlation is seen in the contrasting nature of man's penis and his mind which are both capable of issuing out a seed of life; one generating material existence unto corporeal death, the other spiritual awakening unto everlasting life. The transitional development of not being under the ruling authority of the head between one's legs, but rather the one upon their shoulders (the spiritual), can never transpire without willful obedience to the principles of the Law. This brings us back once again to the regenerative purposes for which the lambskin apron symbolizes, which in this aspect, Temperance, Self Control, Prudence, and all the virtues of Love and Truth embodied in obedience, are what brings about expiation as a Love offering of the Soul. To merely believe in Christ alone without efforts in applications to what he followed and prescribed as law will not clothe, cover, nor procure blood as a mercy seat covering to one's lower, weaker, or less virtuous side of themselves.

Now, aside from its monitorial rendering, the importance of the apron's use in Temple building should become more transparent as it symbolically shows to cover the imperfections of one's lesser nature and inadequacies (as Love covers a multitude of sins). A dirty and blemished apron symbolically reflects the immoral tarnishings of one's Soul, as well as the body of the Craft. Even though every Soul must individually stand before God to be judged, this doesn't mean; however, we are to cop out and wallow in filth just because we are not sparkling perfect. No man is. We are still responsible for working to cultivate the virtues of Love as best we can while willingly allowing the Divine Laws of God to work in us to properly develop and maturate our Souls. Understanding the difference between what is God's work and what is man's, keeps us focused in insuring that we are using tempered mortar at all times when building. Now, when equating the Lambskin Apron with the innocence of one's Soul, one can truly see where its value far exceeds any other badge of honor or merit which could ever come to be presented to them, it showing to be an investment coeval with man's very created existence. Now tell me, what linen could be said to be more ancient or nobler?

Universal Craftsmen

ESSAY XIII

THE RITE OF DESTITUTION

The Rite of Destitution is conducted at a candidate's initiation to impress upon him the important tenets of Relief and Charity. This rite conveys a reminding lesson that no one lives independent of each other; that the common stock of provisions that facilitate life are those which are to be shared among each other as one family species, recalling to mind the conditions that he himself was in when he underwent this rite, and if he were to ever find someone in like circumstances, it would be his duty to tend to their needs as much as his abilities could permit without incurring detriment to himself. We do not live to ourselves, neither do we die to ourselves, meaning that we neither experience life or death exclusively aside from others. We all share, more or less, in the same commonalities of life's misfortunes, its successes, its joys, its pains, and its love. Charitable regard for one's well being, both individually and collectively constitutes the moral basis of this rite's practice.

When delving into the ritualistic aspect of this rite, I draw your recollection to that particular point in the ceremonies where the candidate is solicited to render something of metallic nature in keeping with a time honored tradition. However, having been divested of all his possessions prior to entry (especially those items of metallic nature), he now finds himself completely destitute, which renders him unable to present anything of value when asked. As this is intended to invoke embarrassment and shame, it is meant more so to deeply impress upon him the lesson of Charity and the effects of its practice upon others. Now, aside from the immediate lesson of morality afforded, there can also be found traces of alchemical transmutation with elements of the Masonic Ladder being hinted to in this rite(1).

In some of the Ancient Mystery Schools, precious stones (ores and jewels) were esoterically assigned to the rungs of ladders ranging from lead to gold. These ladder designs were found depicted in some of the Hermetic Rites of practices, as well as in those pertaining to Mithraism, where various other symbols were also assigned to these rungs, such as planets, gates anatomical limbs, and other esoteric particulars of interest(2). Understanding that Freemasonry also employs a symbolic ladder for instructions, it has been conjectured by some that the early composers of the Masonic rituals may have drawn some of their symbolic designs from these institutions. Whether indeed true or not, one common understanding that can be clearly arrived at in both their uses is their purposes to teach the lesson of transition and change (whether that be symbolically expressed using virtues, planets, or metals). Among some of these symbolical expressions depicted upon the ladder was the virtue of Charity, which was chief among the Theological Virtues. This particular virtue bears so close of a relationship with that of Relief, that the two are synonymously inseparable in their nature of practice (one bringing about the result of the other). This virtue was held in so much esteem, that it was often symbolized among the practices of antiquity as either the Sun or the element of Gold, both of these being chief among their classes of cosmogonies and metals. Now, as these were all arranged from least to greatest, the virtue of Charity was depicted topmost upon the ladder's rungs with Gold posted alongside it so as to equate its esoteric analogy of standing importance. This manner of classification was assigned to several different virtues so as to symbolically convey the progress of one's moral development transpiring from one's rung ascent to another. With this progression, the dross materials of all the lesser metals depicted along with their virtues would undergo removal until only the highest purity of the final element was left at the topmost rung. Although it may have started out as lead, by the time one's final ascent was reached, there would exist a totally different element altogether. This is what was known as transmutation (the science of converting base metals into greater value), and was a major theme among the Hermetic practices, it being attributed to Hermes Trismegistus by the Greeks, and to Thoth by the Egyptians. Now, when hypothetically attributing this ladder's extent from the West to the East of the Lodge as a means for the traveling candidate to morally ascend, then what can be found to be divested from him upon his entry (that which would be spiritually offensive), are not only those metallic ores of copper pennies, nickels and jewelries (man's material standards of wealth), but in a more spiritual sense, those metallurgic passions and vices of immorality accrued upon his Soul (metallurgic, meaning the scientific process of separating metals from their ores). The divesting of these from one's being must occur before entry into the Temple and full ascension up to the East is had (that Sanctum Sanctorum), the place referred to also as the oracle in the book of 1st Kings(3). Now, when continuing to consider the bottom end of the ladder to symbolize the West, and the top end extending to the East, then what is also being asked in a spiritual sense when the candidate is being solicited to render something commemorative in keeping with a time honored tradition, is actually the presentation of that spiritual ore of Love (Charity), whose possession thereof, should be the only imperishable ore remaining after the Soul has bean metallurgical disrobed of all its earthly garments of flesh. The removing of these are an allusion to those prerequisite conditions that the Level imposes upon all men when having to enter into that Eternal Lodge (that being the prerequisite of Death as the great equalizer of all men).When one considers that our physical bodies are composed of such minerals as magnesium, zinc, and iron that returns back to the earth during its decomposition, this alchemical process of removing material ores of the flesh, while the spiritual ores of the Soul ascends back to God, becomes to be seen as a work of the Divine Law that must inevitably transpire with Death. Understanding that the immortality of the Soul is one of the bedrock beliefs of Freemasonry, divesting oneself of their worldly passions (metals), should provide greater clarity in the esoteric understanding of how the Masonic Ladder of Faith, Hope, and Charity (Love) facilitates the Soul's development in that ascent.

Now, as the symbolization of this spiritual ore was depicted as the Sun or Gold among the ancients, we also find it being used to symbolize the covering of man's earthly works. When the material works of all

Master Masons have undergone deterioration under the weaponry of the 24 Inch Gauge, the spirit of Love will still continue to ascend forth as an indestructible force that mercifully imbues the Soul as it's crowning works before God, just as gold so covered the finishing works of King Solomon's furniture (all underlying material's such as wood, copper, and bronze being of lesser or inferior quality and subject to decay)(4). And so, as some of the lesser metals and materials are symbolic representations of the external and lesser nature of man, so are the more precious and virtuous ores symbolic representations of the greater and internal nature of man's Soul and Spirit. By extraction and progressive cultivation a candidate learns to employ them for the services of God as a co-builder of the Spiritual Temple. Such allusions are deeply veiled in the Urim, Thummin and jewels of the ephod, which were worn and employed for use by the High Priest(5). As ores are forged within the bowels of the Earth by pressure and the surrounding conditions that contribute to their development (some serving as excellent conduits of light and energy, especially diamonds), so must all incarnated Souls undergo this same symbolical process of alchemical cultivation in their own development. The spiritual ore of Love that serves to develop one's Soul does not consist solely in the expressions of monetary alms, but resides also in those forces and energies that find their expressions in kind words, a shoulder of support, comforting advice, and silent prayers. These are those commemorative substances of metallic kind that are to be "...laid up among the relics of the Lodge," while all other dross materials are to be discarded from oneself. These types of energies are the spiritual vitalities that enables the Soul's ascent. This whole idea finds its symbolical expression in the virtues and monitorial explanation of the Masonic Ladder, which in a truer sense could be rightfully called a Ladder of Regeneration, because this is certainly what occurs from its use. Having shown the spiritual congruency of this rite's esoteric understanding with that of both the Masonic Ladder and Alchemical Transmutation, the following author's comments have been additionally afforded for further enlightenment.

"Man, since his fall from the heavenly--undefiled state is one of the earth, earthly. His beginning toward heaven (upward) must naturally commences on, or with the earth (physical), but his desires must ever be upwards. Consequently when he enters the Mysteries, he must at once raise a ladder (hopes and desires). If he is sincere, then gradually and laboriously, with many denials, sacrifices, aye mishaps, he climbs, builds step by step, until at last, the final rung, which is symbolized by the mystic number seven, is taken, and his ladder (spiritual or soul self) reaches to heaven, that is to say, he has attained the spiritual termed conscious immortality.-illumination of the Soul--his spiritual birthright, if earned."----Dr. R. Swinburne Clymer, The Mysticism of Masonry.

The Masonic author Albert G. Mackey writes: " Charity; therefore, takes the same place in the ladder of masonic virtues as the sun does in the ladder of planets. In the ladder of material we find gold, and in that color, yellow, occupying the same elevated position. Now St. Paul explains charity as signifying not almsgiving, which is the popular modern meaning, but love--that love which suffereth long and is kind; and when, in our lectures on this subject, we speak of it as the greatest of virtues, because when faith is lost and hope is ceased, it extends beyond the grave to realms of endless bliss," we there refer it to the Divine love of our Creator. But Portal, in his essay on symbolic colors, informs us that the sun represents divine love and gold indicates the goodness of God, that if Charity is equivalent to divine love, and divine love is represented by the sun, and lastly, if Charity be the topmost rung of the Masonic ladder, then again we arrive, as a result of our researches, at the symbol so often already repeated of the orb, the natural sun or the spiritual sun--the sun, either as the vivifying principle of animated nature, and therefore, the special object of adoration, or as the most prominent instrument of the Creator's benevolence--was ever a leading idea in symbolism of antiquity."----Albert G. Mackey, Symbolism of Freemasonry.

Universal Craftsmen

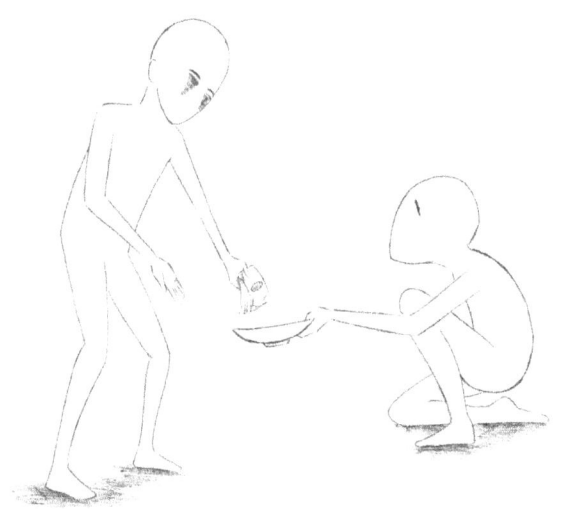

ESSAY XIII ENDNOTES

1. Although alchemy is not flat out taught in the Masonic lessons, it is still hard to ignore some of the philosophical congruences shared in both their objectives towards a future state of Self betterment. In the strictest sense of the word transmutation, does it not entail the applicable works that brings about the transitional changes of one's mental, moral, and spiritual states of being, those which are also found in the lessons of Freemasonry?

2. This is not the case concerning the rungs of the Masonic Ladder. The congruency here to be understood are not those in the symbols alone, nor so much in the manner of how they are ceremonially depicted as a design in their respective schools or religions, but rather in their derived at Truths for spiritual and moral application.

3. This place is where all things come together under Truth, in which only Oneness (Harmonization), is had. Here is where we commune with T.G.A.O.T.U., and come to be revealed the instructive designs of the Trestle Board (those silent Truths pertaining to our own personal temples and works of development).

4. 1st Kings, 6th Chapter, 15th and 16th verses.

5. The meaning of the words Urim and Thummin in Hebrew means Lights and Perfection, whose transliterations are owr and teman, meaning further to make or cause to shine or illuminate, and to complete. It is of considerable interest that the same transliteration owr has its connection to the word uwr (meaning to awake), it having its further association with the words East and Chaldea (origins of the ancient Magi's).

ESSAY XIV

THE CORNERSTONE

Webster's Encyclopedic Unabridged Dictionary Of The English Language renders the following definitions for the word cornerstone:
1. A stone uniting two main masonry walls at an intersection.
2. A stone representing the nominal starting place in the construction of a monumental building, usually carved with the date and laid with appropriate ceremonies.
3. Something that is essential and indispensable or basic.
4. The chief foundation on which something is constructed or developed. In all these definitions, the cornerstone in Freemasonry can be seen to embody like understandings. To appreciate these in their symbolic connections, a brief look at its uses in operative building is necessary.

A cornerstone is a building stone made up of two expenditures which intersects to create a 90 degree angle that allows for two opposing directions to be united for building purposes. When four of these are laid in their respective corners (N.E., S.E., S.W., N.W.), it further enables one to build both horizontal and perpendicular in all four directions, thus allowing for the erecting of walls(1). Among the stone guild masons of former times, this stone was usually laid in the Northeast corner to mark the orientation of works to be thenceforth constructed. Now, in the laying of a cornerstone, which is a public ceremony performed to commemorate the construction of a new building, this stone was, and often still is, anointed with corn, wine, and oil, it having inscriptions of dates, names, and erecting purposes sometimes engraved upon it. In some cases today it may be hollow wherein commemorative items are placed in it by the owner, architectural, designer, or builder. The ancient stonemason's placement of this stone in the N.E. corner had not only spiritual implications, as the many edifices in which they built were places of worship and were always dedicated to God at this particular beginning point of their works, but it was said to also have practical uses. For it would be by the rising sun heading Eastward from out of the North, that the first rays of light in the Northeast would provide visibility for their work. In the writings of C. Mertz, titled Guild Masonry In The Making, it is said: "At six o'clock in the morning, the Grand Master Mason Solomon began to lay the great North East cornerstone, because at that time, the sunlight was on the outside of that cornerstone. That stone having been "well and truly laid," he proceeded at ten o'clock to the south east corner and laid that cornerstone, as the sun at that time was shining at that corner. After refreshments, he proceeded to lay the south west cornerstone...at which time the sun was shining from the South West and finally...he proceeded to the north west corner and laid that cornerstone. It will be seen that the course of the sun was the reasoning for commencing the Temple at the north east corner and then working around to the North West." This is particularly interesting when considering Light to be a symbolization of Truth in Freemasonry, and that it was by the aid of the sun's first light that the cornerstones were said to have been laid. This would imply that it can only be by the first casting rays of Truth that we can begin to erect our own spiritual temples. This is the underlying understanding found in both the basis of Dedicating a Lodge, and the placement of a newly made Entered Apprentice. For it is in this same Northeast corner, subsequent of taking his Obligations, that he is placed and then given his first set of instructions pertaining to the building of his own temple edifice. This is one of the Divine most pivotal points in his forth going quest, as this marks the definitive point of his own commencement of temple works. For even though he may have been previously declared duly and truly prepared, made in due form, and underwent various performances of rites and customs, these were all requisites that relied, for the most part, upon the aid of others for their execution. After receiving his Charge, it stands from that point on, that it will be of his own individual actions that serve to assess his real apprenticeship (as the responsibility of living out the dictates of his given instructions now becomes primarily his own). Although he has the wise counsel and host of brothers of the Lodge ready to assist him in his new found light, it will be by his own efforts in application; however, that will determine the resulting quality of his stone specimen. Just because he's been Obligated, Charged, and have been afforded various lessons in Truth, doesn't mean he will employ them. Many have been afforded ample light by the graces of God to begin working in the most earliest part of their lives (6:00 a.m.), and have found the sun still setting upon them in their later years (9.00 p.m.) with not even one stone having been laid. As the saying goes, "you can lead a horse to water, but you can't make him drink." So as a candidate stands between the North and the East, neither fully in light, nor fully in darkness, no words more befitting than those of Christ's could be used to describe the spiritual implications of his then present state---"Choose this day in who you will serve." Although unspoken and unheard, the internal evidence of that silent question presented and one's decision made, will come to be seen in his efforts. The virtues of Discipline, Commitment, Execution, and Obedience are all requisites for self development that serves to constitute the real evidences of one's journey having begun. As the setting of the stone in the Northeast corner in operative masonry establishes the first point towards progressive building, so does this cornerstone marks the point of one's orientation of works towards Self Regeneration. From this first point established, all the candidate's subsequent works are to be for the culminating purposes he mentally envisioned. Morally speaking, this first step is Faith, which serves to summon the Will in efforts towards accomplishment. This is the basis of man's beginning point that requires germination in order for progression to occur and fruition to transpire(2). In more of a metaphorical sense, the candidate become this cornerstone when he begins to engage himself in the works of temple development. In doing so, he is to utilize all the given tools and instructions to sculpt himself into the designs in which the angle of the cornerstone morally symbolizes. As a cornerstone's angle is 90 degrees (the same degrees of a Square), an apprentice choosing to emulate this design, symbolizes one engaged in the foundational works of right judgement, right thoughts, right actions, and right speech required as the basis of erecting their own temple. Just as the tools of the Square, the Level, and the Plumb are applied to an operative stone in order to bring it into specifications, so must the living stone come to be tried in order to determine whether he is square, level, and plumb (of moral Truth, Equity, and Upright Integrity). If not, he is expected to correct his character in line with Truth's dictates. The libations of corn, wine, and oil are those provisional blessings that have been bestowed upon him from his Creator for aiding, not only in the accomplishment of his work, (those sustenances that nourishes the body, refreshes the Soul, and brings joy unto the Spirit), but for those which are to God, his Lodge, and his fellow man. In this aspect, he's to consider himself having been "dedicated" for use in God's Temple, and is to live in a way that morally exemplifies such.

Now, in viewing some other ways in which this stone can be symbolically contemplated, consider the lines that form a square box. We see that in the same way there are four corners that make up it's geometrical design, so can it be seen that these same four corners reflect in their designs four cornerstones. From its appearance, it's not hard to see that when these are all conjoined together, it establishes the outline perimeter of a squared foundation to be laid. This is the Ground Floor from where one begins to work (as the working tool of the Square being depicted in the four corners symbolically denotes). Along this same line of thinking, we see that if the four Cardinal Virtues were to be assigned to each one of these cornered squares, and if this floor was to be circumambulated, then what would be seen to exist would be an entire squared perimeter of moral virtues circumscribing and morally governing the basis of all our progressive development (see diagram A). After such virtuous Truths have been well laid as a foundation in the Mind, one can then begin to build upward upon these (the symbolical construction of building walls). Now, as walls deals with the aspects of vertical heights, so would four of these being erected and conjoined together then deal with volume, volume alluding to those things which are to be held within or inside the conditions of internal space (like the heart and Soul being housed within the cavity of the body). The perpendicularity of these walls rests not only upon the plumbness of the first stone laid, but also upon the Plumbline in all subsequent building (the Plumbliine being a working tool familiar to every Past Master that is used to establish the criteria of rectitude).

If such was not to occur then the structural stability of the walls upon its foundation would be compromised even while undergoing erecting. Biblically referencing, it would be equivalent to building a house upon sinking sands. This is to say, that it is not just enough to be imbued with the knowledge of squared Truths in the works of erecting a moral and spiritual temple, but that in its progressive building, the stoneworks of internal application are to be laid with the same scrupulous care as all other stones of Truth. There can be no deviations or leaning favoritism in one's practice. Simply put, one must, with willful determination and effort, live what they know to the best of their ability, not just being hearers of the Truth , but doers of it as well. Executing the Truth without prejudice, insures, much like walls, the plumbness of the Soul, as this determines whether it is perpendicularly ascending upright in moral excellence or leaning downward in immoral depravity.

Another symbolic view of this stone's moralistic use can be seen reflecting in the symbol of the Cross (see diagram B and C). When we look at where all the lines converge at one single point in the center of this diagram, one can see four right angles, which could be regarded by some as four cornerstones, not because of their arrangements on the outer corners (in which they are not), but because of their inverted placements in the center. From this view, these could be symbolically attributed to the creation process, where the four lines of the cornerstones seen extending forth, could be looked at as emanations of life flowing from one central point working to bring about material existence along their progressive movement. Geometrically symbolizing, this would once again allude to that "point" of origin which is monitorially spoken of as being "...from a point to a line, from a line to a superfice, from a superfice to a solid." In a theological perspective, this same point from which these virtuous emanations stem, would constitute God as the Great Cause, or that cosmic expression having been called by others as the Big Bang. In a moral sense, it could be looked at as that moment of truth, or what could be called by some as an epiphany.

In further consideration of these cornerstones, it can be easily seen that they consist of 90 degree right angles, which when multiplied by four, equals 360 degrees, hence, denoting in further symbolism, either an open circle of consciousness (that which permits light by the open space it affords), or a completely closed circle of consciousness (that which restricts light). Therefore, when considering the process of gradual evolution from a closed point to an open circle, we see the Masonic, expression referred to as: "From Darkness To Light." The birth of the Soul into the Body, and its resurrection upon death, correlates with this understanding(3). Such esoteric allusions lie in Christ's statement in the 32nd verse of the 12th Chapter of St. John: "And I, if I be lifted up from the earth, will draw all men unto me." Whether the cornerstones within the cross symbolically depicts the Soul's consciousness being crucified from a spiritual state to a material state of creation, or rather its crucifixion from a material state to a spiritual state of recreation (or maybe possibly both in their successions), they nevertheless, allow for the means of greater development to be had by the Soul's underwent experiences in the Body (the deeper understanding symbolically conveyed by the works of conjoining the Square and Compasses). Morally, this shows that we must be conscious of both natures of our being, that we must consider what we do externally, as well as what we feel and think internally. These two aspects which embodies one and the same Temple, are symbolized in the geometrical designs of the Square and Circle, which are formed by the working tools of the Square and Compasses. These are also alluded to in the four cornerstones of the the Ground Floor symbolizing Earth, and the three angles of the Equilateral Triangle, symbolizing the celestial and Divine Heavens, thus when consummating these together, (4 +3), we obtain the number 7, which symbolizes completion, perfection, Divine Providence, and God.

Universal Craftsmen

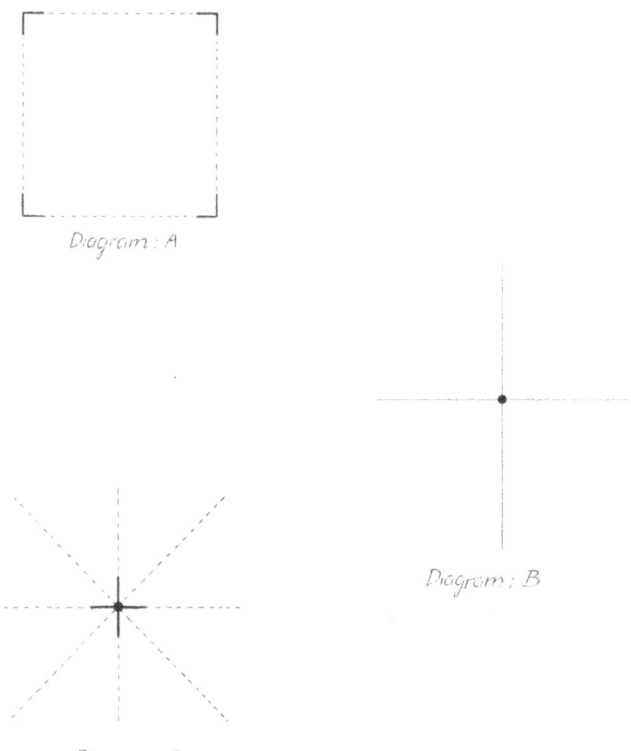

Diagram: A

Diagram: B

Diagram: C

Universal Craftsmen

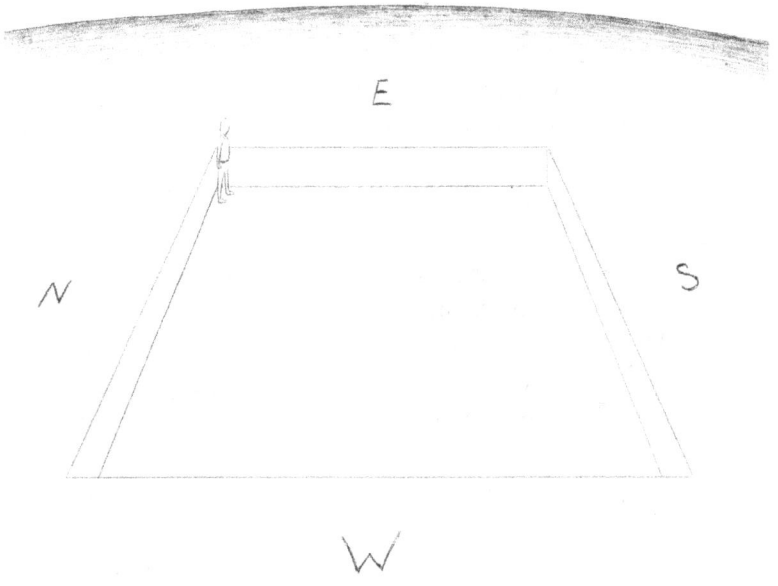

ESSAY XIV ENDNOTES

1. In this statement, and its forth going explanations, it must be kept in mind that the nature in which this stone is described for uses are to be speculatively viewed from a symbolic standpoint for purposes of bringing about further moral elucidations. This will account for the differences of this stone's employed uses in actual building, verses its uses as herein described. For as it stands, the cornerstone, in respects to the rules of architecture, is technically not a part of the foundation of a building structure.

2. This is to say that the Mind orientates all works for subsequent operations, as well as its instructive steps that facilitates manifestation (the Mind possessing both within itself the seed and envisioned end). This is the symbolization of Temples being situated due East and West which correlates further to man's own temple. For that which has been envisioned, duly begins in the East of the Mind, and then must subsequently travel Westerly seeking materialization through means of the Will and Body. Such is the greater understanding of the Cosmic Universe having came into existence by a Triune God, still evolving under the laws of progressive evolution, or as viewed by others in a theological sense, God's Mind bringing about what he Spiritually conceived within Himself until it fully becomes manifest.

3. An achieved state of the Soul's consciousness of God in which Christ depicts. It is the bestowal of divine sonship, along with all the inheritable rights that entails the conditions of being born again. Its spiritual maturation is the full oneness of Man with God, in which the pillar of Beauty in Freemasonry esoterically typifies in its greatest macrocosmic aspect of existence. The evidence and conditions of obtaining such inheritable rights was alluded to the 17th Chapter of St. John, particularly verse 11, and verses 19-24.

ESSAY XV

WHAT IS A LODGE?

By monitorial definition, a Lodge is "A certain number of Masons duly assembled furnished with the Holy Bible, Square and Compasses, together with a charter or dispensation from some Grand Body empowering them to work"(1). In respects to what that number may be, there are constitutional regulations that outlines the requisites for whatever degree a Lodge is to be opened on. However, monitorial wise, it is said a Master Mason's Lodge consists of a minimum of 3 Master Masons, a Fellow Craft's of 5, and an Entered Apprentice's of 7, (these entailing further implications of Divine Order and its process of development). If asking one who is not a Mason what they think a Lodge is, you may hear such responses that it is a building where Masons meet to do secret things. Some may say it's some type of fraternity house or club resident, while others may even say they believe it to be a place for worship. Although a Lodge may entail a few of the elements found in all of these responses, such as comradery and works of philanthropy, it is still sacredly so much more, especially when engaged in its degree works, in which it then serves to teach some of the most beautiful and mind astounding Truths concerning man and creation.

A Lodge is a microcosmic representation of the World that uses figurative types, designs and symbols to afford greater understanding of moral and spiritual Truths. Although many are unaware, they will be surprised to find, with little research, that most religious institutions are microcosmic representations of this macrocosmic World, and that their designs should be deliberately patterned so as to bring their practitioners in closer relationship, to not only their respective deities, but with themselves in relationship to all things under the Divine Law. Unfortunately, many institutions today have lost this understanding due to time, usurpation, and in some cases, even flat out falsehoods, and is why, when in times where the Lights of the World should be casted abroad and not shut up behind walls, these Lamps, which could be illuminations unto many darkened feet, have instead became dim and even extinguished in their ability to bring about new Life. But, for those having retained this Truth unsullied, having risen from out of the ashes like the Great Phoenix, what remains to still be offered to their devotees are those evidences of Truth that God is indeed One, just as the Temple, the Lodge, the World, and Man are all One. These evidences displays all its designs in the governing operations of the natural law seen in creation. Man, having his divine connection to this world through creation, came to seek and understand these and gradually discovered that they brought him more into a interactive and harmonious relationship with all around him. This was the first religion that was, which is, and will always be (Order being heaven's first Law). Therefore, when taught in some monitors that a Lodge is a symbol of the Universe, this is by no means imaginative, but a standing Truth that's based upon some of the most earliest evidences of scientific laws and discoveries revealed to man.

In preservation of these discoveries (for the sake of posterity), man built sacred temple structures that served to teach these by means of various ritual practices, sacred writings, oral traditions, and the esoteric operations of their sacred priests. These discoveries entailed the various educations of the 7 Liberal Arts and Sciences, various Trade skills, the Celestial Wisdoms of the Cosmogonies (Astronomy), the advanced study of Medicine and Architectural Sciences, and even more, those Metaphysical studies of spiritual Truths pertaining directly to man's mental, and Soul development. As the Earth served as a habitable Temple for man and also an instructor of wisdoms, so did man erect temple structures for the indwelling spirit of their deities and then made these centers of learning for their devotees. It was within these sacred structures that the neophyte learned the true nature of himself and his latent abilities of being both a Mortal Man and Immortal Being(2), as the phrase "Know Thyself," inscribed above the entryways of some of their temples, alluded to. For it would eventually come by revelation to the student that his travels within the portals of the temple, was not only a discovery of himself, but also an inexplicable journey towards Supreme Consciousness, which was the underlying Truth that was to be unveiled in their chief deity. This full discovery, among many of the ancient mystery schools (as written by the Masonic scholar Albert Mackey), was called the autopsy, which by medical implications of the word itself, permitted the aspirant access to explore the deepest recesses of the temple cavity that retained all of its sacred Truths. The lessons of Truth taught within these conveyed the means of obtaining Oneness with God and the Divine Law (one being a reflection of the other), and as Masonic Lodges are said to be representations of such temples (particularly King Solomon's), so do we find such corroborating evidences of this type of instructive work being symbolized in the theme of the Master's Word, and the Recovery of it in the Royal Arch Degrees.

So aside from the administrative labors of the Lodge, which allows for its several orders of business, a Lodge, in its spiritual aspect, is a microcosmic temple of man where he is afforded the lessons of how to bring himself into Soul Consciousness of God, or in a theological sense, erect a temple of Self so that the indwelling Spirit of God can come to live in. This is what the presence of God in the cloud of smoke filling the temple represented at its Dedication by King Solomon. For God and Man to become One has always been the purposes and primary understanding to be had for erecting temples. "Know ye not that ye are the temple of God and that the Spirit of God dwelleth in you?" (1st Corinthian, 3rd Chapter, 16th verse), and further again in the 2nd book of Corinthian, 6th Chapter, 16th verse: "...for ye are the temple of the living God, as God has said I will dwell in them, and walk in them, and I will be their God, and they shall be my people." These are pretty clear understandings of how the temple was to be viewed. However, if any skepticism remains, it should be emphatically dispelled by evidence of Christ's statement: "Destroy this temple, and in three days I will rear it up. Then said the Jews, Forty and six years was this temple in building, and wilt thou rear it up in three days? But he spake of the temple of his body," (St. John,

2nd Chapter, 19th and 21st verse). This particular passage shows within itself, that even in the fledging stages of what would later come to be the religion of Christianity, how both the Jewish and early Christian practitioners had already lost the understanding and spirit of what the temple was meant to signify in design and purpose. Evidence of this was even emphasized way back among the prophet's time as referenced to in the 7th Chapter of Acts, 47th-50th verse: "But Solomon built him an house. Howbeit the most High dwelleth not in temples made with hands; saith the prophet. Heaven is my throne, and earth is my footstool: what house shall you build me? saith the Lord: or what is the place of my rest? Hath not my hands made all these?" So in understanding that a Lodge is a symbol of the World that's been patterned from King Solomon's Temple and has its symbolic correlation to man, the statement of Christ destroying the temple is therefore understood among the initiates to be the tearing down of one's nature of lower self, the passions and vices of immorality that suspends the Soul to the lower aspects of its conscious existence (that being Earth in a metaphysical sense, and the Body in an anatomical one). The rearing or raising up of the temple, spoken of by Christ, is the progressive establishment of higher levels of consciousness by the Soul's advancings within the World Temple. Even though this World Temple is unfathomably vast, ironically, this can only transpire by the works conducted within the aspects of one's own Self temple first (in which the degree advancements in the Lodge are symbolical instructions of). Now, as the inner being of one's temple is not composed of the denser or heavier aspects of elemental matter, but of those lighter substances associated with the cosmic and etheric Spirit of Life, the implications of the Soul's highest potential in ascent, is therefore God Consciousness (the Soul becoming consciously and harmoniously immersed in the Spiritual Life force of all); the same Life Force that was imparted to us from out of Himself in which we return to with Consciousness.

    The moral and esoteric practices of this development, which is called the Great Work by some, and Temple Building by others(3), was first embodied in the earlier religious systems of the Hindus, Ethiopians, and Egyptians, who veiled in like manner as the Laws of Science and nature, their designs within the attributes of their gods, demigods, geographical landmarks, material signs, and symbols. They did this to further protect them from the vulgarly corrupt who had no true interest in the harmonious compliance and purposes for which they were intended to effect.

What a heart truly seeks is evidence of what it really wants, which will eventually come to reveal itself. This will bear witness to one's own worthy or unworthiness. If it's an idol his heart seeks, he will no doubt be led to one. The Spirit of Truth, in which Earth serves as an esoteric Gate for, comes equipped with its own Tiler, so that even with the symbols of materiality laid ever before the most profane of men, the veil of her spiritual promises still can not be pierced and seized by the unworthy, the tyrant, the thief, or anyone unwilling to meet the requisites set forth by the Divine Law, for God is not mocked. Only an earnest and integral heart seeks to achieve what is good by means of a just and integral way (adherence to the Law)(4). For all those who attempt to enter into this Lodge by any other means other than the Master's Word (Truth), then it will be by this same Word, that will serve as a "...two edged sword, piercing even to the dividing of the soul and spirit, and even of joints and marrow..." that will purge them from out of the Lodge (Hebrews, 4th Chapter, 12th and 13th verse). This is why the Speculative element of Freemasonry's origin has been arguably said to date back to the first man and his erecting of civilization, not because of a Temple, a Lodge, a Tabernacle, a Shrine, a Crypt, or any other material representation of a building structure having ever been erected for sacred purposes (all these at some point having undergone decay), but because the true depository and archives of Freemasonry's Spiritual Truths has, and will always be, well preserved in the eternal Lodge of the Soul of Man. Even when the material Lodge goes dark and the broken column of this existence has transpired, the Light of the Soul will continue to shine forth.

ESSAY XV ENDNOTES

1. As a Charter is needed in a legislative sense to establish ties of acceptance and fraternal recognition by some of the more widely known Grand Bodies, it is the U.O.C.'s opinion that the speculative practices of moral and spiritual development in which Freemasonry embodies as a work, is one that does not require a parchment of legal validity, as we believe that such charter was divinely instituted with the Soul's design and its incarnation, and becomes commissioned to work once it's been awakened to its own Divinity within its corporeal body. In this aspect, the right to employ oneself in the regenerative works of Temple Building is an all inclusive right for each individual to exercise. However, in the works of Temple Building as a collective fraternal body with others, it is then an exclusive privilege, whose rights of selection for admittance should be retained among members of those Grand Bodies and their jurisdictions. Not everyone possess the right interests or moral character for building, and whether deliberate, or unintentional, their works may be detrimental to those already laboring. Immorality, crimes, and transgressions against the same community and society that Freemasonry is seeking to uplift is totally inconsistent with its purposes. This is one of the main reasons why it's rights of exclusivity regarding membership and fraternal ties are needed (as all should possess the same common interest in mind for why they are working together). Still, it is quite unfortunate for those who has truly undergone moral reform, and have been brought to Light within (such now reflecting in their characters), that there are no existing legislations that accommodates the acceptances of their temple works. Withstanding these barriers, the U.O.C., not only work to assist such men truly engaged in erecting their spiritual edifices, but teaches them to extend their labor to both free and incarcerated societies (irrespective of a charter). Nevertheless, we still understand that while in the corporeal body upon this plane of existence, the order and governing law demands that one should "...render unto Caesar what is Caesar," so it has been with this understanding that the U.O.C. seeks adoption by some of our preexisting Grand Bodies, who in seeing the sincerity and true spirit of our works, may be willing to sift through the bureaucracy of legislative red tape to incorporate our labors of Charity with those among their own.

2. The true and purest aspects of Self lies in the existence of the unveiled Soul along with all the discovery of its Truths, Powers, and Wisdoms. By the removal of superficial materials does it then gradually comes to shine through to reveal itself.

3. The Great Work is a term often used by the Rosicrucian Society. Although not spoken of in Masonic literature, nor its monitors, its effects establishes that same state of Oneness in which Freemasonry symbolizes in the pillar of "Beauty."

4. That is to say that all things are under the ever watchful All Seeing Eye, whereby the Divine Laws that governs creation has its own requisites for those seeking to obtain its Truths, as well as its justice for those who seek to pervert its requisites. Its operations are embodied in what some term as Cause and Effect, and others, as the Karmic Law. To take that which has not been given or earned is unlawful, and in return brings upon such person the Lawful demand of restitution.

ESSAY XVI

FORM OF A LODGE

The Form of a Lodge is an oblong square, oblong, according to Webster's Encyclopedia Unabridged Dictionary, being:
1. elongated, usually from the square or circular form.
2. in the form of a rectangle, one whose dimensions are greater than the other. As a geometrical figure, this is what also constitutes a parallelogram, four lines being grouped in two pairs facing opposite sides of each other. In respects to its appearance, it would look like a flat rectangle. On the other hand, when all four of these lines triplicate as a result of building, they then become what is referred to as a parallelepipedon, which looks like an elongated or rectangular squared box. This strange looking word is composed of the Greek prefix para, meaning alongside of, and the word epipedon, which means ground or flat surfaces. The appearance of these two designs are found both in the Lodge from two different perspectives, one from a flat surface (see diagrams D and E), and the other from a polygonal figure (see diagrams F and G). This is because the floor of one (the parallelogram) naturally serves as a flat foundation for the other (a parallelepipedon). In both aspects they are oblong in nature, meaning that they are an extended elongated square, which in

simpler terms could truthfully be called a rectangle or rectangled box. To show how this oblong form of a Lodge is made spiritually applicable, its symbolic implications must be further considered.

Monitorial wise, the word oblong first comes to be mentioned in the 1st Degree were the form and dimensions of a Lodge are therein given. As a building structure alone, the Lodges of an Entered Apprentice, Fellow Craft, and Master Mason's are all individually oblong in appearances, as they are all made up of one and the same actual building that's being used, but in their symbolic nature of degree work, they are considered distinct and separate Lodges(1). Just as the body serves as one vessel which houses all the distinct organs for their operations, so does one building allows for the 1st, 2nd, and 3rd Degree works to be done all under one roof. In this architectural aspect, the entire building may indeed be oblong, but in its symbolic and speculative aspect, all of the Lodges are not. Only 2/3 of the Lodges can be considered "oblong," while the addition of the remaining 1/3 can only make it whole and a perfect square. This is to say that the E.A. Lodge and the F.C. Lodge are both oblong squares, or as alluded to in its esoteric work, "...angle of an oblong square...", which is 90 degrees, while the M.M.'s Lodge is a perfect square, or "... angle of a square..."(2). Now, as the word perfect in this sense means to be just, complete, make balanced and centered, or finished without inadequacies, the 3rd Degree symbolically represents this state in its crowning works of final development. In this aspect, the completed works of the 3rd Degree embodies the works of the 2 Degrees prior to it, as the only way one can get to 3 is by the successful completion of having gone through 1 and 2. Although the 1st and 2nd Degrees are both working steps towards achieving a whole, they are still not just in respects to the relationship of the entire temple(3). Even though, the individual work within themselves may indeed be exact and completed, they are still; nonetheless, oblong in comparison to the remaining edifice to be established as a whole. For a house cannot be called a house simply because it has completed floors, nor can it be considered a house because it has erected walls.

From a geometrical view, this same 2/3, 1/3 ratio is also true of this oblong square (a rectangle), for we see that its dimensions are not equal on all four sides, 2 of them being shorter than the other. Now, if one was to cut this rectangle in half diagonally, what would then be seen in appearance, is two huge squares as working tools, each one having an elongated arm (the elongated arm consisting of the long sides of the rectangle). When these are viewed as a pair, they are found to be of the same size and dimensions, both individually being oblong and depicting the nature of a 90 degree right angle having been executed. When looking at this from this standpoint, it can be seen that the language of "...an angle of an oblong square..." monitorially used to describe the 1st two advancing steps, is really quite apt in that they both symbolize a work completed within themselves that hasn't been made equally proportionate on all 4 sides as a collective whole, but has yet and still been made exact. Now, the language used as "...an angle of a perfect square..." to express the 3rd, is no less apt, for we see by its geometrical design it depicting equality and just proportions when cut diagonally down the middle, and when looked at as an whole, has 4 equal sides. When one considers the just and equal dimensions of a perfect square, does this not symbolize that state of condition that the Third Degree Lodge symbolically depicts. Now, compare the various arms and angles previously mentioned to their appropriate degree steps, and what will be seen by geometrical designs will be found right at your feet. These dimensions entail further symbolic allusions as to why an E.A. is not permitted in a F.C. Lodge or a Master Mason's Lodge, but how a Master Mason is able to sit in either one of these two. For it stands by reason, that if one is a builder of houses, he should not lay a roof, nor erect a wall, if he hasn't laid the foundation and the cornerstones, for these are necessary in the order of things (all parts being predicated upon each other in the works of achieving a just and symmetrical whole). With some of these symbolisms having now been brought to light, we can now consider the moralistic approach of how these pertain to the temple of Self.

 In the approach of building the temple of Self, the various aspects of one's own being must be brought into employment as these are what the lodge of man are made of (Mind, Body, Soul, and Spirit). Therefore, every degree achieved is to be regarded as another "advancing step" towards becoming a just and perfect man, whereby the works conducted in these facilitates this. Although this work is conveyed by means of ritualistic expression, it is by the mental acquisition of Truth and its practicing application that brings about this Self development. In respects to a completely finished temple that comes to represent the crowning works of a whole design, its requisites are to be leveled on its foundation, perpendicularly upright in its erecting(4), just and squared on all its faces, and symmetrically harmonious in all its parts. When the temple parts of self are tried and are not found within the boundaries of these requisites, then there stands to be an angle not square. This means that there are particular virtues of Truth, whether pertaining to the Mind or the Will, that are not being understood or executed precisely, and in this sense, requires further cultivation in order for it to be brought into just symmetry (moral virtuousness). As Freemasonry deals with 90 degree angles when pertaining to the stones of the Craft Degrees, this symbolizes that the execution of Truths are to be lived out exactly as displayed upon the Master's Trestle board. When this is not done, the angle could be geometrically called an oblique or obtuse angle (an angle ranging from 1 to 89 degrees, or from 91 to 179 degrees). These are stones that are neither upright, level, nor square, and are therefore off course from the exact measurement (goal). This is to say that if a person's way of thinking is morally off course (oblique or oblong), eventually his temple actions will come to display immorality as well. This pertains equally also to the heart, the seat of one one's Will, which can also betray the Mind. Even when one knows what is right and true, they still find themselves doing contrary because of the desires of their heart. Only when one's mental acquisition of knowledge and Truth (90 degrees) becomes combined with one's Willful application of it (another 90 degrees) does a 180 degree change then comes about. Speculatively this means that in the perfecting of the temple, the works of both the Mind and Will's development are indispensable steps necessary for erecting one's temple, and will continue to be so until all individual parts of the temple are finally raised to One unified whole. It is for such reasons why Freemasonry has been called a progressive science, for it can only be by such progressive steps that the advancements of the Soul can come into Light, more Light, and further Light. The more light that's obtained by the Mind, the more it is to be applied by the Heart's Will in order to progress forward. This is a universal Truth that applies to anyone's works of development, for one can not discard what he has obtained in education, and then simply not apply it in their efforts of future learning, but sadly how many of us actually do just that? This is evidence within itself of the oblong nature of our own beings that requires reconstructive works in order for it to be made whole. It matters not if you possess the mind of an academic genius or the body of a body builder, the perfect and whole state to be achieved lies in the Soul, and is a work of regenerative change that can only be brought about by conciliation of 2 opposing principles of polarities.

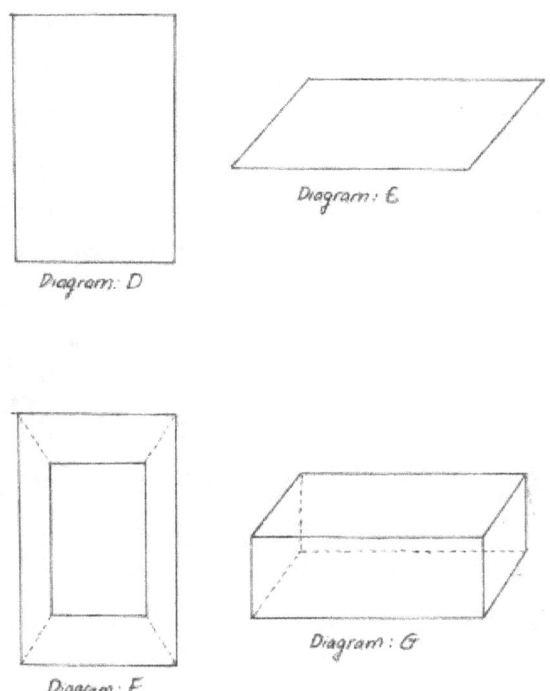

Diagram: D

Diagram: E

Diagram: F

Diagram: G

Universal Craftsmen

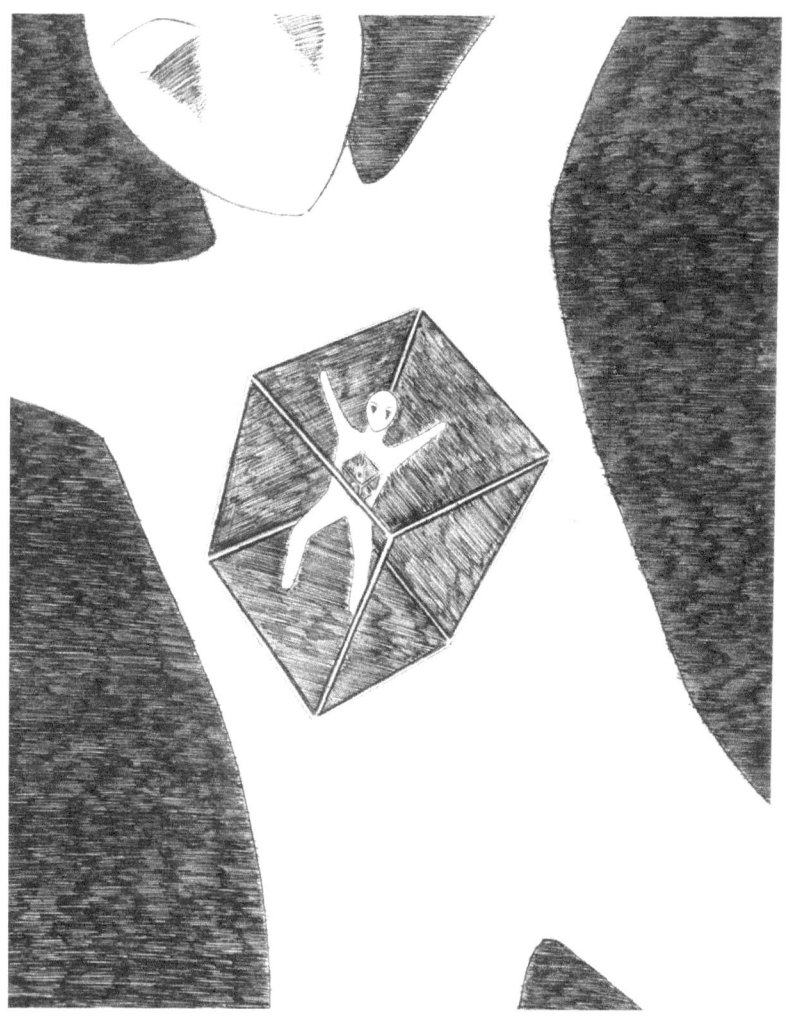

ESSAY XVI

1. When ritualistic work is done in any particular degree, it is opened and called a Lodge of that degree, meaning an Entered Apprentice Lodge, or a Fellow Craft Lodge, so on and so forth. Although these are three different Lodges in their operating designs, when conferring the Craft Degrees, they are still nonetheless conducted under the same roof of one building.

2. This alluding to the manner of how Masons are taught to approach the East.

3. Individually, each degree is distinctively whole and complete within themselves, just as much as our anatomical organs are within the body (the brain, heart, and lungs being examples). However, in their purposes and functioning relationship to all of the other organs, which all collectively serve to make up one temple body, they stand incomplete or inadequate, or symbolically speaking, oblong, each then being predicated upon each other for the vital existence of a perfect and whole system of operations.

4. The falsehoods of preexisting rubbish must be cleared away from one's mind, otherwise it will result in an unstable setting of knowledge and understanding. That which encumbers the Mind, disallows for the addition of new Truths to be had.

ESSAY XVII

EXTENT/DIMENSIONS OF A LODGE

It is written that the Dimensions of a Lodge extends from the East to the West in length, between the North and the South in breadth, from the Earth to the Heavens in height, and from the surface to the center in depth. These vast dimensions symbolically depicts the universality of Masonry irrespective of race, religion and political beliefs, and is to teach practitioners, that just like these dimensions, "...a Mason's charity is to be equally extensive, or as rendered in some of the older monitors "...that a Mason's charity should know no bounds except those of prudence." Although these dimensions are unfathomably vast, when considering them under their delineations, an actual location could be derived at that would symbolically express both states of universal and individual consciousness (as the virtue of charity also alludes to).

Theoretically, if one was to travel from the East to the West and continue forth from there, they would eventually arrive back at their same eastern point of beginning. Speculatively, this would be seen as a line extending forth so as to make up a massive circle. This would also be the case along any given point of a cardinal compass, which, if in doing so, all points and their extended lines would serve to construct a globe like sphere. When proceeding forth to incorporate the dimensions given between the North and the South, this would place a person somewhere within the perimeter of this sphere (as far as it would pertain to breadth); however, the dynamics of its magnitude would still render one's location uncertain as the dimensions of its height (from the Earth to the Heavens) would extend pass the outer limits of space and man's perception. It is only when one factors in the dimensions from the Surface to the Center does this limitless globe like sphere comes to provide one with a "point" of orientation, as one would then find themselves directly in the middle of a 360 degree circumference, irrespective of its size or location. Even with such vast measurements, a person would still be equidistant to all things, as a sense of his own cognitive existence would come to be established by discovery and interaction with all that would be afforded to him in this sphere (Creation). Now, as we know that time and space is beyond our ability to circumscribe, it has been by the use of Geometry that man has learned to bring the imperceivable into view by first establishing a definitive "point." This simple, but all important geometrical wonder, has not only mathematically contributed to the advancement of civilization, but has always entailed spiritual implications among the various schools of thought that alluded to the development of one's being.

The Point, or what could be regarded as a closed circle, has been thought by some to represent the initial fire of Life. Some have thought of it as an embryonic Soul having became unconscious of its latent Divinity, and in return, requires awakening and subsequent development unto godship. Other representations of this symbol finds its conveyances in various god types and other depictions such as the Egyptian deity Ra, the Solar Disc, the Seed, the Brahmic Egg, and the Sun, all of these expressing the embodiment of Life that brought about materialization. This same point has also been regarded as the Soul of the World, whose preeminence was consciously One with God before creation itself(1). When viewing this point as an open circle, it has esoteric allusions to the all circumscribing Law around us, which serves as a womb like matrix that fosters the development of Life. When one takes this point, or dot, and encompasses it with a circle, it conveys the idea of consciousness, which has its spiritual understandings veiled in the depictions of an open Eye (referred to by some as the Mind's Eye, the Pineal Gland, or the Third Eye). The delineations herein, pertaining to the dimensions of a

Lodge, share these same premises of understanding and could also be synonymously attributed to the center of the Lodge where the candidate finds himself being brought to Light (becoming more conscious in degrees of Life and its Truths). It is after he has circumambulated "around about" the Lodge (depictive of a circle), does he then find himself in the middle of that same circle receiving his sight. Ceremonially reflecting, it could be thought that his arrived at point, versus the direction he had been admonished to travel (the East), are contradictive to each other; however, conciliation is had when one comes to understand that the Center is synonymous to the point of one's own Soul Being, whose mental illuminations of Spiritual Truths in the East facilitates its advancing development. So when these boundless dimensions of a Lodge are symbolically attributed to the moral virtue of Charity (Charity being rendered as Love in Greek), one can retrace these dimensions, along with all their points, back to a definitive location within the anatomical lodge of Self (every act, word, and thought stemming first from a single point within ever before proceeding outward). This centering point is the Soul, that core essence within that has been imparted to man as an ultimate expression of God's Love. It constitutes the underlying motive behind every deed and is regarded as the center of man, not because of a physical location, even though there lies an esoteric connection to this, but because everything revolves around its developing condition as a temple in which the individual can feel. The admonishments of traveling Eastward is an expression of the Soul's progressive development which becomes more and more Spiritualized under the instructive guidance of the Mind's acquisitions of Truth. It is from such divine depths of an Omniscient Mind of the Grand East that the center point of man (the Soul) receives its imprint of identity and sense of Self Existence (its Be-ing), in which it then becomes to expand itself into an open circle (Spiritual Consciousness). Now, when considering the vast dimensions of a Lodge and all the points that serve to construct Creation, an inward converging of all these would be like an imploding star bringing forth Life (an expression of Divine Unification). What would issue forth as a Spiritual elixir is the very substance from which the Soul is composed of---Love, the substratum of all.

Upon further view of this point and circle, it shows itself to be singular and innumerable, as well as fixed and transitional (transitional by means of geometrization). This is to say, that this same centered and fixed point that serves as the nucleus of Life, is also the infinite point that makes up the substances of all matter seen and unseen. Even though it's regarded as One (the conceptualization of God being the First and only Self Existing), it is also incorporated in all things existing. This duality is symbolized in the two distinct parts of the point and the eternal circle that surrounds it, one typifying fixation and the other transition. Although time and distance imposes the idea of two different expressive states, they are actually of one and the same existence which are only separated by one's veil of consciousness. This is to esoterically convey that the conditions of the East (as well as every other cardinal point of existence), is a fixed point whenever and wherever conscious illumination is actually had. One's condition of cognitive discovery will always be found within the centering of one's own temple, while at the same time, its state of condition will ever be expanding. God increases in us as we increase in God. God is fixed, and in this sense, represents the point, while our consciousness is ever expanding and therefore represents the open circle. This is why in every degree advancement, further Light is sought by the candidate in his traveling pursuit towards the East, where he seemingly finds himself once again at the center of the Lodge before the altar desiring to be made more conscious of Truths that has always been around him, but he was blind to. It serves well to remember that this is why the letter G sits in a fixed location in the East in the most deepest recesses of the Lodge, but is still able to be most notably seen everywhere within the Lodge (it being the symbolization of both an independent and fixed character within itself, but also transitional by its power to cast Light). We clearly see this evidence reflecting in the duty of the W.M., as he is charged as a primary officer to dispense Light in the Lodge, but is also a recipient of it as well. God dispenses the Light of Life upon all his creation as an expression of Life which is the highest representation of Love.

This same indefinite and nondimensional point is the same microcosmic representation of a dimensional and definitive point embodied in the Soul of Man. In a macrocosmic aspect, it entails all of creation as One Life of the Spirit whereby man microcosmically begins to identify with through the experiences of his own Soul's encounterings (man finding him self circumscribed within the perimeters of these vast dimensions, and therefore impacted by its Laws). Therefore, when considering man's relationship to the whole, every time he expresses acts of Charity (Love), the vibrations of energy from within his Soul, he shares a metaphysical kindred with that of the source from where it derived. By labors of Love, we are actually developing our own fixed point of conscious Beings to become Universally in tune with God (that all encompassing Law expressed in Life itself). When this occurs, then can the words of Christ, spoken of in the book St. John Chapter 10, verse 30, come to be understood from conscious experience "...I and my father are one."

Universal Craftsmen

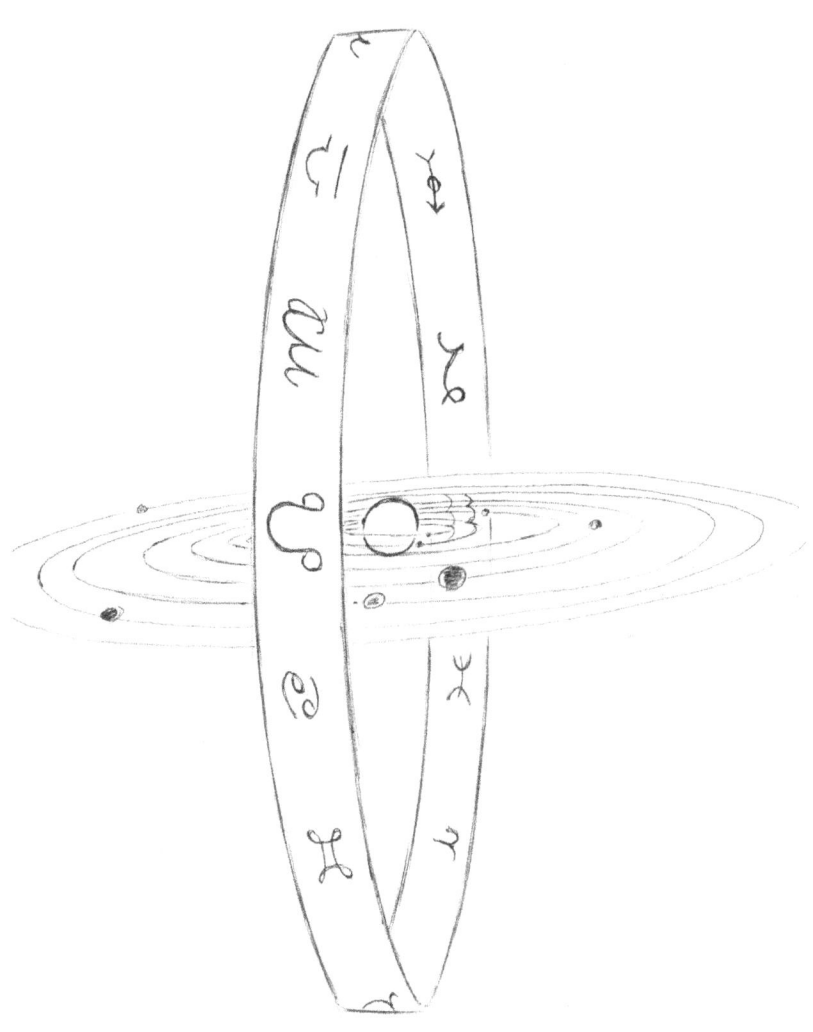

ESSAY XVII ENDNOTES

1. It is Christ as a typification of the Soul Life of the World and its Divine Light (as depicted in Genesis, 1st Chapter, 3rd verse,"...God said let there be light, and there was Light." In respects to man, it is the Divine Spark which came to be incarnate in Genesis, 2nd Chapter, 7th verse: "...And the Lord God formed man of the dust of the ground and breathed into his nostrils the breath of life, and man became a living soul."

ESSAY XVIII

PILLAR OF WISDOM

It is stated that "A Lodge is metaphorically supported by Three Great Pillars which are denominated as Wisdom, Strength and Beauty, because there should be wisdom to contrive, strength to support and beauty to adorn all great and important undertakings. The Universe is the temple of the Deity whom we serve. Wisdom, strength and beauty are about his throne, all pillars of his work, for his wisdom is infinite, his strength omnipotent, and His beauty shines forth through all his creation in symmetry and order." Such is the rendering given in the monitorial explanation concerning the pillars of a Lodge. It is these three great aspects that supports the vast dimensions of the World Temple of God that functions as one efficient whole in maintaining governing order and balance. In another sense of terminology, these supports could easily be called the Divine Attributes of God, as they vividly witness to an architectural design found pervading all of creation. It is these same attributes that attests to our spiritual origins as Divine Beings (we having derived from Terrestrial matter and Terrestrial matter having derived from Celestial space). In respects to the monitorial description of Wisdom, one will see the word contrive being associated with it, contrive meaning to devise, to plan, to invent or come up with. In view of this word one can see how knowledge and the importance of its acquisition serves as an immediate link to wisdom. Hardly could one carry out, or properly execute a plan without possessing some degree of knowledge. Knowledge alone doesn't make one wise, but rather its judicious use.

The root base of the word wisdom is wise, which according to Webster, has its etymological connection to the word wit, meaning keen perception, powers of intelligent observation, ingenious contrivances, a person having understanding, mental faculties and sense of knowledge. In archaic times it meant to know. One may hear use of this word in such expressions as, "I'm at my wits end...", or "Have you lost all your wits?" (meaning one has lost all their senses, knowledge, or abilities to reason and understand). As it stands, whenever this word is used, it automatically bears a relationship to the Mind or the faculties thereof. In respects to the word wise, it pertains to a certain state of one's measure of perception, judgement and reasoning abilities which comes not only by means of both the mental acquisition of wisdoms, but also the proper understanding of their uses (wisdoms in this sense being synonymous with education and learning, whether that be of a scholastic or moral nature). When looking at how the words wise and wisdom was used in the biblical passages of Hebrew and Greek text, this same sense of understanding appears to have been also the prevalent idea among the ancients. For we find the word wisdom in Hebrew being chokmah, which is rendered as a noun, it being derivative from the word wise; whereas the word wise is rendered as an adjective, its transliteration being chakam. Therefore, the word wisdom is something or a state that can be obtained or had, whereas wise, as an adjective, is descriptive, and is depictive of one who attests to having reached this state by exemplification (showing or displaying this). It is written in the 4th Chapter of Proverbs, verses 5 and 7: "Get wisdom, get understanding forget it not, neither decline from the words of my mouth. Wisdom is the principal thing; therefore, get wisdom, and with all thy getting get understanding." This passage alone stresses the acquisition of wisdom (knowledge), and even more, its sought understanding. This is most critical in one's pursuit of moral and spiritual redevelopment. It was one of the key Truths that was well taught and understood in all the ancient religions and esoteric schools of thought, it being conveyed to their practitioners in various emblematical ways. Examples of these conveyances can be seen in such depictions as the Kabbalah's Tree of Life, which is said to be a symbolization of creation, as well as an allusion to man. Here it shows the first three Sephiroths grouped together in a triad nature, whose names are called Keter, Chokmah, and Binah, which translates to Crown, Wisdom, and Understanding (Chokmah representing Wisdom). The Egyptians, having this same regard for Wisdom and Understanding, depicted these attributes in the personification of such gods as Isis and Aset, (Wisdom), and Djehuti and Saa (Intellect and Understanding). Such personifications also rested with Athena and Minerva, the Greek and Roman gods of ancient times. The Greeks went so far as to have a school of philosophers called by the name Sophist, (meaning, one who has became Wise), who were strictly devoted to the contemplative studies of various wisdoms and other matters of high sciences. Among others, were a group called the Gnostics, whose name derives from the word gnosis which means Knowledge. There are many other sects and schools found in the records of both secular and religious history in which the world is indebted to for some of the most pivotal discoveries that has contributed to man's development (astrological, geographical, and medicinal being just a few examples). In this aspect, history shows well that the basis of knowledge and its employed understanding has, and will always be, a vital requisite for the advancement of civilization.

When looking back in ancient times, it was understood that being wise was never a single or definitive point of accomplishment, but rather an ongoing state of condition as a sought way of life. This came with two implications of practice, one, the acquisition of material wisdom as it pertained to certain occupational trades, skilled abilities, and the basis of education which now reflects in our several liberal arts and sciences, and two, the spiritual as it pertained to not only man's inner nature, but his sacred obligations and duties to God, family and society. For a spiritually awakened man who sought to live out his vows, there was no distinction between his secular and religious life in respects to his application of wisdom, for he was bound by one circumscribing law which governed all his affairs, versus those who were not, who instead lived by a standard of governmental law that wasn't always in line with spiritual morality. In the spiritual sense of practice, the virtues of love, temperance, prudence, just reasoning, discernment, spiritual foresight, intelligence, and contemplation, were all paramount wisdoms for the spiritually inclined. For it was not just enough to seek out and learn these virtuous Truths, but daily adherences to them were requisites in their personal development. Today, the disparity between the two is more present than ever, as there are many among their fields of education who are quite academically accomplished, having been deemed smart and wise, but on the other hand, have proven themselves to be morally and spiritually depraved. They have a thousand degrees and letters beside their names, but no virtuous character or moral wealth.

When asking in what way the acquisition of wisdom and knowledge serves in temple development, the answer is that it serves for the building of the Mind as this is what facilitates the means by which the internal aspects of works are to be implemented and then conducted. In man's present state of condition, we know that experience is perceivable only with consciousness, a condition in which the Mind serves as a conduit for. We also know that Soul Consciousness (in order to be perceived), must be given a vessel with faculties. These faculties, which entail the five senses that comprises the Body, aid in relaying transferrable knowledge and experiences to and from the Mind and thenceforth to various other parts of the temple (just like the operations of the Senior and Junior Deacons do when relaying information to and from the W.M. and Wardens in the Lodge). In both these scenarios, the Mind and the W.M. are chief in coordinating and assigning out the work designs having been contrived. The Body, which has came about as a result of the materialization of the Spirit, carries out the designs of the Mind by means of the Will, in which the resulting experiences then comes to be imprinted upon the Soul as part of its development. Now, as the awakened Mind of man is cardinally represented in the East as the seat of intellect, it is the remaining parts of the temple that must rely upon its guiding light as an instructional blueprint for its proper regulation in building (especially the Soul in its early stages of candidacy). This blueprint actually comes to be imparted and spiritually contrived first in the brain as researchers have shown that it is in areas of the cerebral hemispheres of the cortex (the right and left halves of the brain), working in conjunction with the front and temporal lobes, that are directly responsible for the cognitive development of reasoning, memorization, judgement and understanding. These studies show how high levels of neuronal activity travels back and forth along these regions during the process of learning much like how electric current travels through fiber optic wires when transferring information. These traveling charges passes over wave like fibers called axons and myelineated nerves that retain bits and traces of recordings each time a thought occurs, until what comes to be formed, as a result of this repetition, is an imprint upon the part of the cerebrum responsible for long term memory. It is like repetitively walking an exact route everyday along a field of tall brush, in which energy (one's effort), meets with resistance each time. It is at first arduous and slow; however, over a period of time a worn path develops in which it becomes easier and easier to walk through to one's point of destination (there becoming less and less obstruction as energy travels the least path of resistance). This process, although not apparent to many, is inherently embodied in one of Freemasonry's aspects that has unfortunately taken on a lax adherence in some jurisdictions, this being the full memorization of the lectures and catechisms. It is both the mental and audible recitations of these that facilitate the inner working of the Minds transformation and development. The repetition of these is meant to leave deep impressions of Truths upon the Mind as instructional designs for the Will's employment. Incorporating these builds the Soul from a state of infancy of a Divine Spark to the fires of Blazing Star, a Sun which is able to cast Light and bring about life. When acquisition and proper application is employed, it begins to establish equanimity upon the Soul much like how an embryo is developed by both the father's seed and mother's egg(1). This is why it is so important that spiritual baptism occurs first in the earliest stages of one's candidacy as proper growth and development rests upon the seeds of Truth for its Wisdoms. There must be a raising up out of the waters a reborn Mind, and death to the old by its submersion, while at the same time allowing education and its application to be the ladder which enables this raising. As this is the same esoteric purposes that the W.M. in the Lodge represents in his duties as a dispenser of Light, knowledge, and instructional lessons, so should this transpire within the lodge of every Mason whose temple is also to be erected to God wherein Wisdom is sought and then had at his own Spiritual East.

Universal Craftsmen

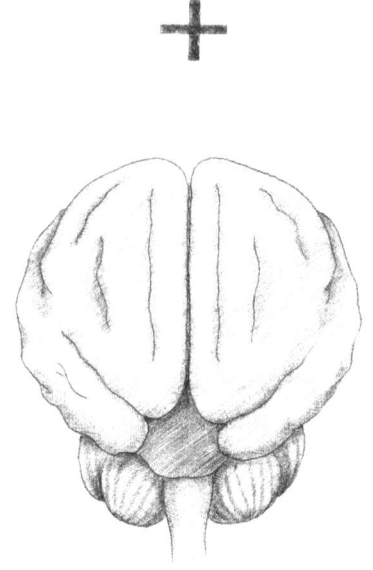

ESSAY XVIII ENDNOTES

1. As the Mind is like a King, who is the crown source for the government of its kingdom (temple), so must the Prince (Soul) ascend to the throne of Glory and receive the inherited possessions of the Father in due season. Whether the exalted Prince has came to understand those dictates afforded to him by both his Parental King and Queen, or whether he'll ever come to be called a Wise King, will come to eventually reflect in the rule of his kingdom (by either a beautiful and harmonious one, or a war torn and divided one).

ESSAY XIX

PILLAR OF STRENGTH

As there should be "...wisdom to contrive," so should there be "...strength to support," support meaning to sustain or withstand, to corroborate, to provide for with the necessity for resistance, to serve as a foundation for, to assist and aid in. Further meanings in Webster are: the quality or state of being strong; bodily, muscular, mental or moral power; force; the inherit capacity to manifest energy; to endure and to reside; potency. When used as a verb, it means to increase or grow stronger; to fortify or reinforce. As an adjective, it means showing or being able to exert great bodily or muscular power or force; especially abled; being competent or powerful in a specific field or aspect; well supplied or rich in something specific; willful; having powerful means to resist attack or assault; unyielding. These are just some of the many meanings and attributes in which strength embodies, each having implications that all harmonizes with its practices in speculative Freemasonry.

Strength is one of the Three Great Pillars that upholds the macrocosmic Temple as one structure. And just as it can be seen that man's force is fueled by his Will, which is made expressible by the employments of his anatomical body, so can the forces and power of God embodied in the

Law be seen in the expressive works of his Creation. When this force is unseen it constitutes his Will, whereas the display of this Will constitutes his Power and Strength. Creation is evidence of this, it being the embodiment of himself having been interwoven in all its designs. Now, as the "...Universe is the Temple of the Deity whom we serve...," all things created are therefore expressions of His Divine Mind and Divine Will. Therefore, as the Master of the Lodge personifies King Solomon as a representation of the Pillar of Wisdom (the spiritualized Mind found in the East), so does the Senior Warden personifies King Hiram of Tyre, a representation of the Pillar of Strength (the materialized Will of this same Spirit found in the West). From out of the dictates of Solomon's Mind, to the executions of Hiram's Will, symbolizes, not only the process of Creation having stemmed from a Divine state of spirituality to a state of materialization (from the Heavens to the Earth), but also how man's Mind is to carry out the designs of God's blueprint in building the temple. As the heart and lungs are found within the pectoral cavity of the body, or symbolically speaking, the "Middle Chamber" of one's own temple, so does the Will stand in mid-support of the Mind's contrivances and its materialization. This is to morally say that no matter how much one knows, there still must be the presence and enacting of Will Power as provisional support in order to bring about fruition. A thought will continue to remain a thought (spiritual energy) until made employable by the Will. The Will is the strengthening support of the Mind that serves to execute its designs. This is well alluded to in the material provisions given to Solomon by Hiram in support of bringing his Grand design into fruition (stones, cedar, as well as abled bodied men that were skillfully strong in their trade). What King Solomon spiritualized in Mind, King Hiram crafted by Will. In an esoteric sense, pertaining to the works of building Self, this is the transmuting of spiritual thought into material manifestation by the work of consummating differences. When the forces of the Mind and Will come together like the Brain and the Heart, like the Solomon and Hiram, like God and Spirit, like Man and Woman, like Wisdom and Strength, what results is the developing works of manifestation. This development requires a vessel to operate in like a caterpillar needs a cocoon, a chemist a flask, an alchemist a cauldron pot, a baby a womb, and as it pertains to man, a Soul a body. All created vessels are derivative of matter which operate as provisional matrixes for the cyclic process of life, death, rebirth, and further Spiritual development. The word matrix is deliberately used here (it archaically meaning womb) in allusion to the movie The Matrix, as every reborn Soul is truly a Neo upon awakening (the word Neo in Greek meaning revive or new).

    All matter is the result of condensed Spirit under its operating Laws of God's Power. When considering God's Will as a Spiritual Force of power-like gas, it being the lightest combustible of unseen force ever, it becomes perceivable how Spirit became visible in form by the ignition of a Divine Spark (such bringing about cosmic matter, galaxies, solar systems, and planets). So, when now looking back at these two contrasting ranges (spiritual and material), the highest or furthest aspect of Spirit would be the Life Force of God's Will which lies in and beyond the etheric planes of cosmic existence (what has came to be termed as Heaven), while on the other end, it is this same force made visible here upon our Earthly plane of existence that represents his conscious creation. In this respect, the unfathomable expanse of creation is an extenuation of God's Will Power operating in support to carry out the contrivances of His Mind (an autonomous operation of immutable Laws designed to perpetuate eternal perfection). This best reflects in the harmonious operations of the Law, which are fixed in purpose towards its goal of perfection, but ever evolving in the works of maintaining equilibrium and perpetual order. And since all things within the scope of the Law displays unfailing Order as a governing principle, this raises not only the idea of a Omnipotent Being that exemplifies "Fortitude" and resistance against inconstancy and chaos, but also one that is Omniscient (the regulation of this power appearing to be exercised by Divine Reason and Foresight). In this aspect, his Spiritual Omniscience could be Masonically attributed to the East, and his spiritual Omnipotence to the West (the Universe indeed being his Lodge). Even within ourselves we see the dualistic nature of this pillar at work, for in the aspects of the Mind we find the Will aiding to contrive and draw out its designs by formulating mental projection, while at the same time, we find the designs of that same projection coming into existence when our Will power summons the Body into laborious operation. The state of this dual condition is also crafted in the very core of our two-part circulatory system in which the heart, it being composed of four chambers (two on each side), anatomically witnesses to. In this operation, one side works in conjunction with the lung's air intake to oxygenate red blood cells to be carried to the remaining organs of the temple body, while the other side simultaneously receives blood returning from these organs and removes carbon dioxide during exhalation in exchange for more life supporting oxygen. This rhythmic balance of breathing attests to both our spiritual and material states of origins and how we are suspended between Life and Death, Spirit and Matter, Heaven and Earth with every single breath. This should impress upon us the importance of living life today as what we do in the here and now is what matters.

In further study, we find that the idea of strength also had its symbolic association attributed to the virile and fertile potencies of certain animals in earlier religions. This is especially notable regarding the bull, which served as an expressive representation for strength because of its procreative abilities. This was also the case concerning the cow, as it was an expressive representation for having great generative abilities. Both were highly venerated in Egypt as we find such deities as Amon, Asar, Hapi, and Serapis all hieroglyphically depicted in some form of a male bovine or another, while Hethru, in feminine form, was often depicted as a cow (even seven in some instances). The representation of these each had their own aspects of powers related to the workings of the natural Law, but still always retained their understandings as either the male enactor, or feminine supporter of Life. It is not surprising at all that the fostering of creation has always been genderfied throughout the ages as a woman (evidences being seen in the naming of some of the ancient fertility deities such as Isis, Ceres, Cybele, and Venus). This idea was long derived at in seeing the correlation of how Mother Earth and women both possessed the self inherited ability to produce offsprings from a seed within themselves, not to mention their facilitation of life sustaining provisions for its growth and development. These are testaments to the maternal principle embodied in the Spirit of Life and the nature of her Strength. It is of considerable interest that the Holy Spirit is always referred to in the bible in feminine terms whose operations exemplify not only power in many biblical passages, but also new life as a result of its endowment. In the writings of the New Testament, there are many references of it having came down upon religious converts after having been baptised (there existing an esoteric connection to it and water). It has been stated by many historians that the early Egyptians often referred to the Nile River as Isis, and that it was only by this river's annual flooding and the subsequent settling of its waters that the earth's soil was then able to withstand seeds for implantation (it being afterward then rich and fertile).

Now, as water is a principal element that facilitates Life and Death, the esoteric understanding of how both must occur in order for cyclic life to continue forth unto maturation (its full potential Strength) can be seen in the flooding of the Nile. In this aspect, its rising would symbolically correlate to baptismal death as its waters would cover the earth (the realm of existing Truths that are veiled), while the settling of its waters would symbolically correlate to one's state of rebirth and a new awakening to more abundant life. This natural occurrence was just one, and is among many that bears witness to this Truth. Other evidences lies in a woman's water breaking before birth, the daily incoming and outgoing water tides due to the Lunar effects upon the Earth, a woman's menstrual flow, which after its subsidings (like the waters of the Nile), there comes to be an over flow of eggs in which she then ovulates for a short period of time (being then most fertile).

In respects to these two Pillars of Wisdom and Strength, there are many other contrasting principles that witnesses to their dualistic natures intended to generate Life, this being: the Sun and the Moon, Fire and Air, Earth and Water, Protons and Neutrons, the Upper and lower Delta's of Egypt, the upper and lower geometrical triangles of the Star of David, Light and Darkness, even God and Satan. All these bear witness to the dualistic principles reflected in the operations of the Law needed to establish unification. Although they may appear to operate under two different aspects of purposes, they are still harmoniously One in working to bring about the full Light of the Soul's Consciousness and its maturation of Divinity. It is these natural designs found upon the Trestleboard of Creation that Freemasonry has moralized in the pillars of Wisdom and Strength which serves to intruct and reveal our own dualistic nature under the Law. In further esoterics for all F.C.'s and M.M.s, it is to show that as these pillars support the World Lodge (the Universe being the Temple in which our Deity lives), building a spiritual temple made not with hands in which we seek our Deity to also live in, requires also the recasting and erecting of these earthen clay pillars, placing within them as archive containers, the Spiritual Truths that will all withstand conflagration and inundations. Otherwise our spiritual temples will never come to be erected.

Universal Craftsmen

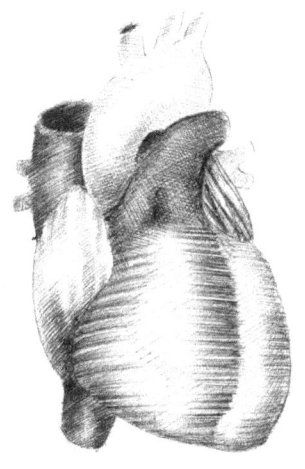

ESSAY XX

PILLAR OF BEAUTY

This word Beauty in Masonry is not merely the idea of visual attractiveness, but by its esoteric implications, it conveys the summiting addition of crowning works that establishes value and lasting quality. As mentioned in prior essays, it has been written that "...Wisdom, Strength, and Beauty are all about his throne, all pillars of his work, for his wisdom is infinite, his strength is omnipotent, and His beauty shines forth through all his creation in symmetry and order." This Beauty, which constitutes the third Great Pillar that supports the Lodge, is a symbolic representation of the crowning glory that results from Wisdom and Strength having came to together (the Omniscient Intellect of God's Mind and the Omnipotent Power of his Will). This resulting glorification is the Omnipresent force of Life as the Soul(1). To provide a better view of this understanding, a look into the word adorn will be had as this is the descriptive word used in most Masonic monitors to express this pillar's function, i.e., "...Beauty to adorn."

The two meanings for adorn in Webster are: 1. to decorate or add beauty to as by ornament. 2. to make more pleasing, attractive, impressive, etc.; enhance. Aside from these, it's synonymous with bedeck, elaborate, lavish, and showy. It is composed of the Latin prefix ad (a preposition meaning to), and the word ornate, meaning to dress (orn being the Latin basis of the word ornament that means to equip). When something or someone has been decoratively imbued or donned with ornaments, it conveys the idea of being well dressed or equipped so as to bring splendor, honor, glorification and appeasement upon both the bestower and the bestowed. It is in this particular manner that the pillar of Beauty has its symbolical comparatives to the Soul. For it can be seen how the contrivances of the pillar of Wisdom, pertaining to the Mind, and how the supporting pillar of Strength, pertaining to the Heart's Will, both bestow the nature of their essences upon the Soul. In this sense, the Soul is the crowning work that exemplifies the qualities of both the natures of the mind and heart as a new and more perfect design of order which Beautifies the whole of man. This understanding is also alluded to in the designs of the first three Classical Orders of Architecture, the Ionic being among the first. The Ionic is located in the East of the Lodge, and is said to display the clever invention and ingenuity of the Greek Ionians. The Doric pillar is attributed to the West of the Lodge, its supporting strength being depicted in its stout and robust size that allows for the absence of its base. The Corinthian, being third among these, depicts not only the function and strength of the Ionic and Doric pillar together without the massiveness, but is also equipped with the crowning works of a highly adorned capital that is composed of acanthus leaves, olives, and various other ornamental designs which serves to display the high level of craftsmanship possessed by Masons during those times. Now, as the Doric pillar is said to have been "...formed after that of a strong robust man," the Ionic, on the other hand, is said to have been designed "...after the model of an agreeable young woman of elegant shape dressed in her hair." Interestingly, it is said that the Corinthian's design was conceived from the resemblances of a child's basket of toys having been left near a young lady's tomb where the roots of an acanthus had overgrown it. Now, in all these we see the evidences of the active and passive principles being alluded to in their symbolical genderfications along with an offspring having derived from the two. These alludings symbolically point to the same three principles of Law that's been moralized in the pillars of Wisdom, Strength, and Beauty(2).

When further considering these pillars as it pertains to their respective officers, they allude to the different workings of the Law that maintain equilibrium and Harmony in all its parts. In this respects, they are one as God is One even though they work in three different capacities within one Lodge (like God works in three different capacities within one Temple of Creation). This manner of operation exists in every design of creation. From how an embryo of life is forged by an egg and sperm, to how the realms of both the Celestial and Terrestrial facilitates life for mankind. From how one's accomplishments are predicated upon their Mind and Heart, to how the precipitation of rain upon the Earth derives from the basis of two variables (the warming temperatures of the Air within the clouds, and the Earth's oceans and seas). No matter the design, the state of dualistic principles made symmetrically one under the governing order of a third, can be found as the embodiment of Life's Grand design, and is the reason why these pillars are said to be "...all about His throne." These have been afforded for our contemplative study in understanding the harmony of Life and the works of our developing consciousness. These various stages of consciousness have been referred to by some as Soul, God, or Cosmic Consciousness whose maturation is depictive of the Soul's Oneness with God (that state symbolized in the pillar of Beauty). When looking into the Greek rendering of the word adorn in Strong's, like sentiments of this same idea can be found alluded to in it's transliteration, which is rendered as Kosmos (from where the English word Cosmo comes from, meaning World). In Webster's Cosmo is defined as 1. the world, or universe regarded as an orderly harmonious system; 2. complete orderly harmonious system; 3. order and harmony. It is found in such words as cosmogony and cosmology, which is the branch of philosophy dealing with the origin and general structure of the universe with its parts, elements and laws, especially of such pertaining to space, time, causality and freedom. It is also that branch of astronomy that deals with the general structure and evolution of the universe. Therefore, in view of such understanding, we see space, time, earth, law, mankind, and all components of life seen and unseen, is what makes up this system of governing order regarded as the cosmos. This is important because many generally tend to consider the cosmos as the realm of outer space only from an Earthly standpoint of view (man naturally being more cognizant of the terrestrial laws of governing order more so than the celestial). This has inadvertently came to trump many awarenesses that the terrestrial globe itself is not only a constituent planet that comprises this governing order of comic space, but that they themselves are naturally composed of the same stellar and celestial matter found within the cosmos (Earth itself having been made from such). Both the celestial and terrestrial spheres of existences makes up the cosmos of one world in which we are to develop our Souls to become consciously harmonious with. This is why being born again is necessary because this begins the discovery of the true nature of our Beings. This is of particular importance when understanding the nature of Temple development, for it is the forging of the Soul between these two sphere's of Celestial Spirit and Terrestrial Matter that enables the crowning of its full state of illumination (the state of Oneness with the Father as the fully enlightened Soul of Christ so represents). Without these contrasting realms of duality, Divine Mastership cannot be attained, for growth cannot come about except by effort, and effort cannot be exercised without the presence of resistance. This is to say that the kingdom of Heaven can only be had by the affordings of the Law's design of Light and Darkness upon the Soul. These embody the experiences that induces development for one's Soul's ascension from out of the confinements of material consciousness. This is done by rising above the grosser elements of Earthly passions. Not by obliteration, but by Mastership. For without such opposite polarity of resistance, growth could not be achieved and the Soul could not establish its homeward ascent, nor could it ever come into its own realization of Divinity. This is allegorized by the story of the prodigal son, who after having became lost, and after having suffered the experiences of his worldly encounterings, awakened in Mind to return back from whence he came, his father's house (a symbolization of his first spiritual state of existence). It was then that he was crowned with the best of his father's "ornamentals." This same esoteric understanding is veiled in Christ's earthly Soul journey whose spiritual return is said to now sit on the right hand side of the Father (an anthropomorphic expression among the ancients depicting maturation, power and favor). Such adorning of the Soul is not limited to just Jesus Christ, but is one that's afforded to every Soul who comes to die to the lower nature of their material consciousness and awaken to their higher spirituality of Being. This work was symbolically referred to by Christ as the tearing down of the Temple(3), and is where man's Soul comes to be crowned with the glory of God's Being(4). So what would be the real work of Masons? The answer goes without saying, the building of the Soul. With the biblical account of Jesus, it is true that many see him as the epitome and grand archetype of an exalted Soul, but unfortunately they are still unable to identify themselves as being the recipients of such same honors, even though it was Christ who actually taught such understanding. For many, such fullness of God is at best imperceivable, and at worst blasphemy. They believe such was only exclusive to Christ, truly not understanding the 3rd Chapter of Galatians, 26th-28th verse that "…all are one in Christ Jesus."

Now, as the pillar of beauty entails esoteric implication alluding to the Soul, let us therefore look into the meaning of the word Soul as understood and used by the ancients. The word Nephesh has been universally translated in English as Soul, whose meaning has been rendered as breathing, animal vitality. It is derived from the primitive root word naphash, which means to breathe, but because of the difficulty of the English language in having comparative words to properly convey its different connotative meanings, it resulted in a one word use to be employed for all its text occurrences, which unfortunately didn't always convey the clearest and most accurate meaning of its spiritual understanding. Evidence of this is seen in Strong's Exhaustive Concordance which renders the same 5315 entry meaning for all instances of this word's biblical appearances even though the meaning of this word has different abstract understandings that falls, for the most part, under three main aspects (each having their respective relationship to Air and its facilitation of life). One is 5315, which means animal vitality, or in another aspect of understanding, the sentient of life (sentient meaning having the power of perception by the senses). This is the carnal aspect of life's consciousness with all its attributing passions associated with it. In this respects it is dependent upon Air (oxygen) for it's breath of material consciousness. In an esoteric sense, its the soul's consciousness of mortal existence, having only a sense of corporeal identity (it being unconscious to its divinity). The 2nd use of this word's understanding constitutes the rational being of Self, that aspect of Life pertaining to the awakened Mind and its Spiritual perception which renders itself conscious of its Divine Spark of Life. It is the cognitive awareness of one's inner being, their emotions, understanding, reasoning, feelings and dispositions of their Soul in relationship to the governing Law surrounding and instructing it. As an esoteric representation of Air or Wind, it is that breath of Life in which God "…breathed into his nostrils the breath of life and man became a living soul." It's entry is enumerated 7307 and 7308, and is rendered as Ruwach in Strong's transliteration. The third aspect of this vital force constitutes the Life energy found in all things animate and inanimate. It is the atmospheric nature from which all Life is suspended. It embodies and envelopes all. This is the all encompassing space that fills and surrounds everything from galaxies, stars, planets (Earth), rocks plants, microscopic organisms, gases, molecular and atomic energy, and anything else that lives. It is the totality of Life. The rendering of this translation is Chay, which means alive whose entry is 2416. It derives from 2421, which means to live, or in a figurative sense, to revive or give life. All of these renderings (by their connotative meanings and implications) individually makes up nature of the Kosmos previously mentioned, and collectively as one Temple, is that Cosmic Consciousness or adorning state of one's Soul having became no longer separated by these. These understandings constitutes the three aspects of the Soul's Consciousness as One, the fleshly passions of one's lowered natured self (mortal consciousness); the higher nature of oneself (that aspect of Life Consciousness that has became mentally awakened to its Divinity as a Spirit Being), and, thirdly the all pervading Life Force in all that sustains both the above and below (the Universal Consciousness that constitutes the expression of God being within in all and of all). This same understanding is also conveyed in the Greek transliteration Psuche, Pnume and Zoe, their entries being 5590, 4151, and 2222 whose meanings correspond to the three aspects of the word Soul in biblical Hebrew just before mentioned. Just as there is one Spirit working on different planes (God's Will), so is there one breath of Life working in different aspects of oxygen, wind/air and space.

When seeking to apply this pillar's design to one's aspect of moral development, we come to discover a virtue found on par with that of the boundless expanse of Life, that being Love. And as the virtue of Temperance also has its symbolic relationship to this pillar, we come to see where both Love and Temperance are indispensable adornments needed for temple building. For in the word Temperance, we find the root word temp and temper, which in respects to stone masonry, is the process of dressing the stone. Dressing or equipping the stone (works of adorning) requires mortar as material mortar fills in the cracks of man's imperfections and serves as a binding agent between the spaces of two stones. Now, just as the application of material mortar enables two stones to be joined together as one harmonious mass, so does Love harmoniously bridges together the space between two separated states of consciousness (that disconnect between Man and God, Heaven and Earth). It is the spiritual mortar of Love expressed in its labors that serves as the medium between the realms of consciousness that enables its ascent unto Divine Providence. Morally this is the same adorning Beauty that The Grand Architect Of The Universe gave of Himself at the instituting of Life, and is the same Divine and Universal Life Force that lies within every Soul which has to be offered back unto Him in order to regain such consciousness.

Universal Craftsmen

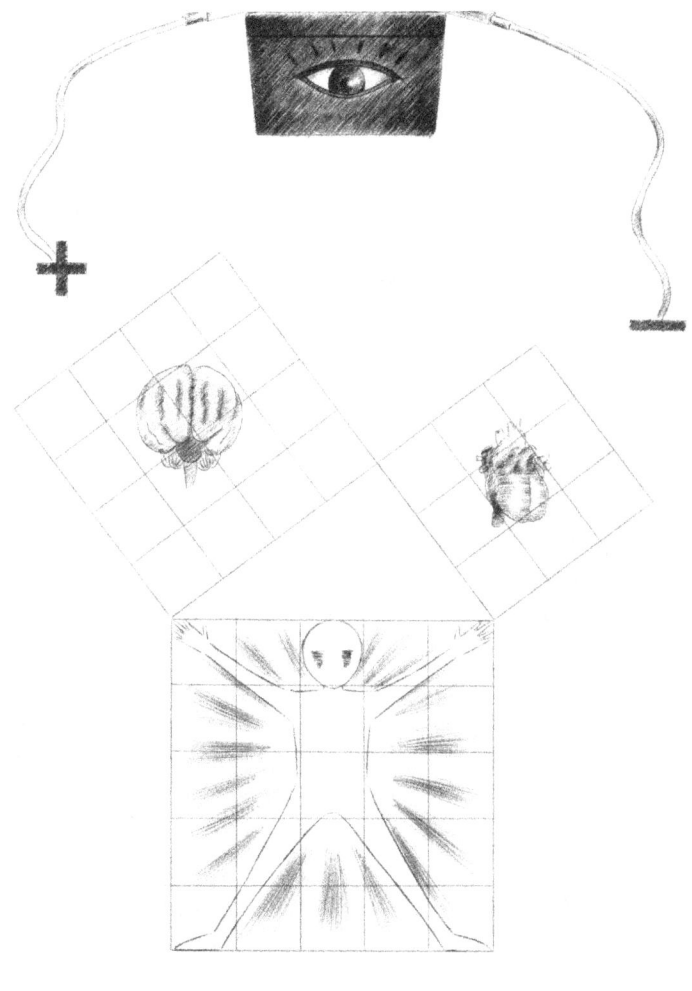

ESSAY XX ENDNOTES

1. It is in this sense that the Three Pillars that supports Creation constitutes a triune Oneness whose harmoniousness preserves the Light of Life (all three constituting the fabric of Law that governs Creation). Remove just one of these from an existing object and chaos and disorder will immediately follow.

2. As the pillars within the Lodge are attributed to the East, West, and Southern quarters (these further corresponding to the Master, Senior, and Junior Wardens), we come to see allusions to a triune aspect commonly found in many different religions, especially in their deities and in their accounts of creation. Bearing in mind that the Universe is God's Temple, then it becomes quite suggestive that these same three pillars are the symbolic representations of a Divine Force which reflects the nature of Himself in all things seen and unseen. This makes God the Temple and the Temple God, a Deity of One and One Deity of innumerability.

3. This tearing down the Temple is the allegorical representation of Self reconstructive development that comprises the three aspects of one's Mind, Heart, and Soul.

4. This term explains the conditions of a Soul having reached a particular state of illumination or conscious harmoniousness with God. It is descriptive of that nature in which the name Christ embodies. The name Christ in Greek is transliterated as Christos, an epithet of Jesus Christ which means anointed. It derives its meaning from the Greek word Crio, whose meaning conveys the understanding of smearing or rubbing on with oil, as when applying such during the rite of consecration (it being liberally applied in ancient times upon those coming into High Priesthood or such related offices). It was by such ritualistic means that power and authority was symbolically bestowed or transferred to another.

ESSAY XXI

THE SQUARE

The intent of this particular essay is to show more so the esoteric aspects of the Square's design in relationship to its use for Self development. As taught in most monitors, a square is said to be the fourth part of a circle. That is to say that if a circle was divided into four equal parts, each single part would consist of a ratio of 90 in relationship to the whole. Therefore, a one part ratio would be 1/4 or 90, a 2 part ratio, 2/4 or 180, and so on and so forth until 4/4 would be reached. This is also seen in the polygonal square, whose four corners consists of 90 degree right angles (see diagram H). In this respects, the figures of the square and circle both bear a kindred relationship to 360 as four 90 degree right angles equal 360 degrees and the circumference of a circle also equals 360 degrees. To understand exactly how the particular working tool of the square serves as an implement for constructing one's moral development, a couple aspects of its nature must be brought into view, starting with its monitorial explanation. It starts out by stating that the square is a working tool of operative masons used to "...square their work... ." It then goes on to moralize its uses among Free and Accepted Masons by saying that it is for "...squaring our actions by the Square of

Virtue... ." Although this is quite true indeed, it unfortunately provides little to no understanding to a reader who is not familiar at all with the stonemason's trade or the terminology associated with it. The use of the word square to define what a square is, is about as effective as using the word fortitude to describe what fortitude is. Therefore, in an attempt to further elucidate its meaning, this tool's function along with some of its historical significances, will be herein given. Hopefully, it will aid in not only drawing a comparative understanding between stonemasonry and Freemasonry, but provide also some insight into its spiritual points of understanding.

In the most earliest ages of Anunian Theology, which embodies the cosmogony tradition of the Egyptian deity Ra and many other divinities of the city Heliopolis, we find a tool associated with the square's use resembling a pedestal. This pedestal is seen depicted in many hieroglyphics with various Egyptian gods standing upon them, the most frequent being Maat, the goddess who was the personification of constant Order, the first Law that emanated from out of Ra the instant he stepped out onto the cosmic waters onto this pedestal to begin creating. The pedestal was a symbolic expression attributed to her as the representation of constant Order, Truth, and Justice, these serving as the foundation and basis from which all the other deities and their virtues were established and governed by in their operations. The different depictions of these gods and goddesses standing upon their pedestals signified that all their subsequent workings rested upon and was always regulated by Order, Truth, and Justice. In this respects, the nature of Maat resided in all the spiritual and material operations of Life, and was the underlining gauge of veracity when it came to all their works, including the heart of man(1). As all the operations of their works were carried out from upon their respective pedestals, so can such same comparatives be seen in the use of the dais from which the Three Principal Officers stand upon when carrying out their respective duties in the Lodge. In both instances of operations Truth serves as the virtuous foundation from which any and all subsequent actions are to transpire. This same understanding is clearly expressed in the monitorial rendering concerning Truth: "Truth is a divine attribute and the foundation of every virtue...by its dictates, we endeavor to regulate our conduct." This monitorial lesson is to teach that Truth is the foundation upon which we are to erect our spiritual and moral temples, that every virtue we work to develop and incorporate in our lives is to be gauged by Truth.

The moral congruences of the Pedestal with that of the Square are not only that of a speculative nature, but also one of an operative and geometrical nature. The appearance of the pedestal was not shaped as an alphabet capital L (as in the appearance of the square as seen today), but rather resembled a ruler whose end was cut at a 45 degree angle. Robert Brown mentions in his work titled Stellar Theology and Masonic Astronomy that this was regarded as the Cubit of Justice and was carried by the Stolistes in their ceremonial processions "...by which perpendiculars and right angles and squares might be laid out." To lay out a right angle or to square a corner is a term used to describe a process of bringing a perpendicular line in exact conjunction with that of a horizontal line by removing all surrounding shapes of irregularities upon a specimen. When pertaining to a stone's surface and its edged lines, the process of removing irregularities that prevents this is called the work of hewing and is to be performed until such standard has been achieved. When this condition appears to have been reached it is then said to be squared, but in determining whether this is actually so, it is tested by an implement which bears the same name called a Try Square or a Square for short. This is the operative aspect of its meaning and use. Now, when comparing the square's moralistic view with that of its geometrical operations just described, we see their connective understanding in the effects they both bring about. For whatever that has been made just, exact, upright, level and true, is symbolically conveyed in the word square by relation of the working tool. This word expresses not only such governing law of condition that reflects in creation as well as in the rules of architecture, but also in that which concerns ourselves in forms of Self building. So when this word is used in various euphemisms such as, "Square yourself away," or "...a man of square dealings," or, as rendered in Masonic monitors, "...squaring our actions," it means, by emblematical comparison to the actual tool, to shape and mold oneself into a state of character that is to be morally upright and level as the horizontal and perpendicular lines depict when intersected. When done, it brings about right motives, right thought, and right actions, as the right angle has come to symbolize. In Freemasonry this stonemason's tool is called the Square of Virtue and serves as an emblem of morality whose Truths make up the foundation and requisite standard by which we measure the veracity of our actions.

These virtues of the Square are the spiritual principles of Truth that are expressed in the written Laws of the furniture of the Lodge which has been "...dedicated to the service of God, because it is an inestimable gift of God to man"(2).

In further esoterics, it is to be understood that the nature of the term square also geometrically represents a right angle of 90 degrees. Now, when a 90 degree right angle is evenly divided in half from the open end of its hypotenuse diagonally down towards the point of its connecting apex, it leaves such respective arms with ends cut at a 45 degree angle, which gives the appearance of the hieroglyphic pedestal before mentioned (see diagram J). In respects to these 45 degree angles, they are what's termed as oblique in comparison to the position of a 90 degree right angle (see diagram I). As these angles are assigned to each respective arm when separated, it is in these two distinct limbs that both the Level and Plumb can better be seen in service to the Square. For as the Level establishes horizontals (which can be seen depicted in the position of the lower arm), and the Plumb serves to establish perpendiculars (indicated in the position of the other arm), it is only by the conjoining of the two in relationship to each other that serves to prove whether their positions are actually true to plumb and level (see diagram K). For if either are moved in the slightest degree away from each other, an oblique nature will occur, whether that be an acute or obtuse angle. In either case, a slant position will nonetheless be present. (see diagram L and M). Only when these are united can it be said that the relationship of the two are just and made perfect, both then proving to be harmoniously congruent in relationship to each other. Therefore, in respects to the steps of one's temple development, it has been suggested that the 1st Degree stands oblique at an 45 degree nature "...forming the angle of an oblong square." The 2nd Degree has also been suggested to stand at this same 45 degree oblique nature, forming also the angle of an oblong square (but in respects to a different temple part). But when the consummation of these these two angles (like the two appendages of the Level and Plumb) harmoniously conjoin by means of proportionate and developed equanimity, then does that which was formerly termed oblong comes to form "...the angle of a perfect square," (90 degrees). This is not only embodied in certain aspects of degree conferral, but is alluded to in the Three Principal Officers and their respective jewels. Let us further consider.

As the jewel of the S.W. (the Level), and the Hour Glass symbolically represents the operations of time and death that's indiscriminately imposed upon every man, we see that every human enters on this Earth in an horizontal position upon birth (unable to stand upright), and by the workings of Time (his lifespan), he will be made subject to this same position in the grave by the Leveling effects of Death. This position could be symbolically attributed to the horizontal line that this tool depicts. In respects to the J.W.'s jewel (the Plumb), one can see the symbolic depictions of the rectitude of Life being expressed in its perpendicularity. For as a seed is sown in the bowels of the earth in a cloaked and darkened state to rise forth by the Sun's Light and ascend thenceforth to its point of maturation, so does such attests to the Divinity within man becoming awakened from its earthly tomb of Darkness to thenceforth ascend to its state of maturation upon death. This ascent could be symbolized in the perpendicular line in which this tool effects. Now, as the rectitude of Spiritual Life hinges upon the requisites of Material Death, so does a perpendicular line hinges upon a horizontal line in forming an upright 90 degree angle of a Square. This is to say that the Just and Square posture of Life can only be formed by death having occurred along some point of one's earthly life. This is where the aspects of material consciousness ends (that point where the horizontal line stops) and simultaneously where the awakening of one's spiritual consciousness begins with the Plumb. That precise point where the Plumb and Square converge constitutes the awakening of the Mind and is where the jewel of the East begins to take developing form by the gradual upright ascent of the Plumb. It is for this reason that the jewel of the Square is found in the East with both arms suspended downward and its point of convergence facing upward (all things stemming from a spiritual point of the Mind). This is also equally true in respects to the candidate's approach from the West, wherein the square's point of convergence (in relationship to its position upon the altar) is facing West, such being esoterically indicative of one's Mind having entered the temple from a material point of consciousness. In a geometrical sense, if these two respective squares or 90 degree angles of the East and West were to come together at the altar, surprisingly it would form a polygonal squared box with four right angles (as two more 90 degree angles would come to form on the ends of the North and South). As a result of this union, there would be four 90 degree right angles in all, hence 360 degrees of a whole having been established by two halves. This reconstruction does not automatically happen; however, it's the result of hewing each face of a stone (working on each aspect of one's temple Self in relationship to those particular Truths extracted). Therefore, as it pertains to the East, he who wears such emblem with the square's point of convergence facing upward and its two arms extending down, as the W.M. also wears, further signifies that he stands not only in an equal and just relationship to the Level and the Plumb by means of spiritual Reasoning and Truth, but is able to cast such Light that draws the body together as a whole. It is for such reasons that he rightfully wields the Gavel. As it is the primary responsibility of the W.M., who bears this jewel to dispense Masonic Light, govern the Lodge, set the craft body to work, and give them proper instructions for their labors (all which attests to the duties of just rule and governing order), so is it the Mind's commissioned responsibility to carry out and perform such same duties in respects to the anatomical temple and operations of his Body.

In one's attempt to raise forth their Being from a horizontal flat to that of an upright perpendicular (one that is to be regarded square and just), the requisites of how to do so are alluded to in the monitorial comments concerning the ashlar. As an ashlar represents both a stone and a practitioner of the Craft, the hewing works upon both requires the use of a square for trying (testing). Where stonemason's use operative working tools in accordance to the rules and designs of architectural building, Speculative Masons utilize speculative tools in accordance to the rules of spiritual building and designs of morality. Therefore, in the sense of hewing, the works of a Speculative Mason consists of developing oneself from a rough moral character to a perfect moral character by means of 1, "...a virtuous education..." (cultivation of the Mind). 2, "...our own endeavors..." (one's Will expressed in the operations of their applications and works of Love), and 3, "...the blessings of deity..." (all the provisional graces afforded to the Soul accompanying the Laws in His World Temple of Creation). In the outlining of these requisites, a virtuous education is listed first in the process, which once again directs the focus on the initial works of the Mind to be had in the perfecting of Self. As the dictates of the Volume of the sacred Law serves as the guide to our faith (sacred religious texts), it incorporates the basis of both the Cardinal and Theological Virtues that makes up this virtuous education (Truths). It is by these and their applications that an ashlar is to be made perfect (hew himself into a square position). In this respects, it can be seen how the

Earthly requisites of moral conduct, denoted in the Cardinal Virtues, and how the the spiritual requisites of conduct, denoted in the Theological Virtues, when combined, establishes the fellowship of a Divine God with that of material man. To have such fellowship is an expression of the Soul that has became Centered and Just between two aspects of himself and has obtained that Perfect state of Divine Providence alluded to in the number 7 that's associated with these virtues (4 Cardinal, plus 3 Theological, totaling 7).

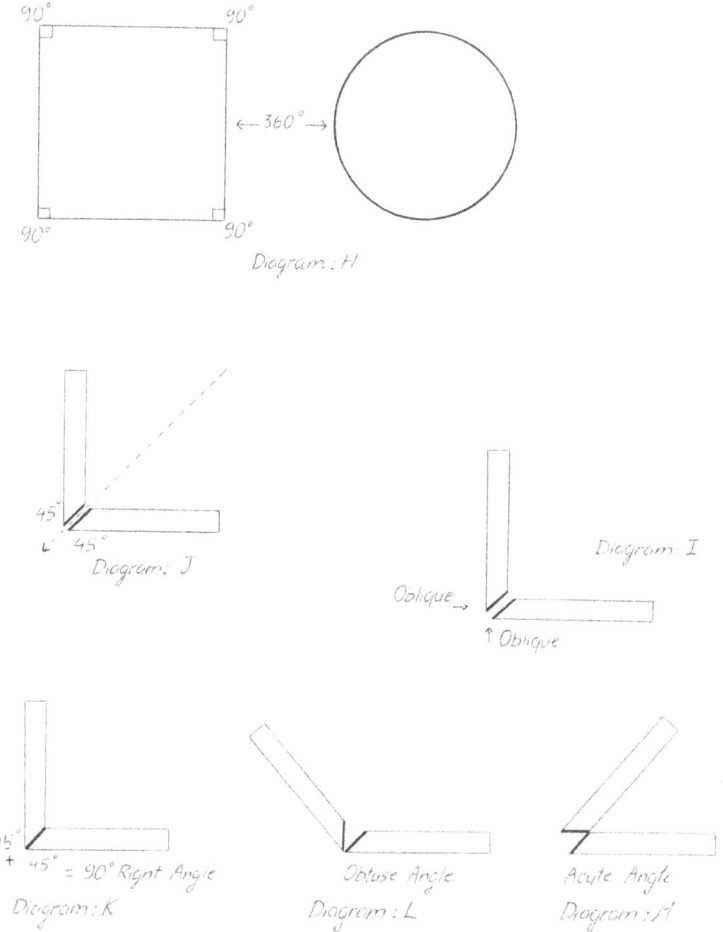

Universal Craftsmen

ESSAY XXI ENDNOTES

1. In the teachings of Anunian Theology, the religion of the early inhabitants of Anu (more commonly known as Heliopolis), the goddess Maat uses the scales of justice in presiding over the judgement of Souls by use of a feather in the weighing of man's heart.

2. This is what's also termed as the V.S.L. (Volume of the Sacred Law), whose instructive Truths can be found embodied in material creation as God's Trestleboard designs (the living Law on display). It has been moralized and written in various allegories, maxims, and enigmatic veils of sacred religious texts. Both of these embodies the aspects of the Divine Law intended to instruct the Mind in the Architectural designs necessary for building oneself.

ESSAY XXII

JEWELS

The Three Immovable Jewels are the Square, Plumb and the Level and are termed immovable because of their assigned locations to the Masonic stations and officers associated with them. Another reason for why they're considered immovable is due in part to their corresponding relationship to the three virtuous aspects of God that are also immovable, or in other terms, immutable (these being Wisdom, Strength and Beauty). The virtuous aspects associated with these jewels attests to the nature of a Divine Creator who has imparted (in measure), these same Divine qualities unto man. As these jewels are also classified as working tools, its not hard to distinguish why they would be called immovable or immutable. For as the Square in the East symbolically depicts that moral standard which should characterize every real Mason, it also depicts that fixed and just standard in which the Law operates. Just as the working tools of God's Truths are constants in the regulation of His Temple, so should this be the case concerning the Mind's regulation of the Body. Now, when looking at the Plumb, it being associated with the South, it symbolizes that which must be erected upright, leaning to neither the prejudices or passions of one's personal self interest. It is that fixed criterion line of Law and one's Duty to it that facilitates progression along the path towards completion. It is written in the book of Acts, Chapter 10, verse 34, that God is not a respecter of persons. This is to say that His Truths and virtuous nature are impartial and pertains equally to every man, that he doesn't play favoritism. Just as the workings of God's laws are unbiasedly upright, so should we execute the practices of our virtues and carry out our Obligations in this same unprejudiced manner, being not swayed or lured away by the enticements of money, power, prestige, or fear. The Level, being associated with the West, depicts the Strength and Power of the Creator, in not only all of Life, but also over Death. The essence of His Power stands witness in all things material, while yet being an ever present force of Spirituality that circumferences all. Just as the Level establishes balance, stability and equilibrium, we also see upon this horizontal plane of existence all being equally subjected to Life and Death. We all live, and we all must die. And just as we see Death in nature occurring in all things, which mysteriously gives way to Life again, so should we die daily to our immoralities, so that we can live once again as well. These immovable jewels are constants because they are the nature of God being a Law unto Himself in which he could not change and still be God. In Him we have our Being and by these laws everything exist and are ever working to maintain perpetual order as alluded to in the officers of the Lodge. For even when the officers of these stations have moved on towards other Masonic offices, these jewels remain fixed to the stations in which their virtuous attributes have been assigned to, these having first been instituted at the Dedicating of the Lodge like they were lawfully instituted at the creating of the World(1).

In regards to the Movable Jewels, which are the Rough Ashlar, Perfect Ashlar, and Trestleboard, these are termed Movable, because of their no particular designation of placement within the Lodge (different jurisdictions having their own governing standards for such, although upon the steps of the East to the North and South is generally more common). Another reason for why these may have been termed movable, especially when pertaining to ashlars, is the transformational states in which they appear to undergo (one reflecting a rough unrefined state of condition at its initial extraction from out of the quarries, and the other, a worked form of geometrical symmetry upon its completion). We find that the Trestleboard also appears to undergo these same transformational changes as we see its architectural designs undergoing developing stages since its conception. Even though we see the evidences of these transformational changes all around us, it is my personal belief that although these class of jewels may be termed Movable, perhaps because of their working developments from an operative standpoint, this; however, may not be so much the case from a speculative standpoint of view. Before explaining such basis of reasoning, an understanding of what a Trestleboard actually is will be afforded. Aside from its typical Lodge uses pertaining to the posting of events, a Trestleboard, as written by Albert G. Mackey in his Lexicon of Freemasonry is a "...board placed on a wooden frame of three legs. Masonically, it means the board on which the master workman lays his designs to direct the craft in their labors. In speculative Freemasonry it is symbolical of the books of nature and revelation, in which the Supreme Architect of the Universe has developed his will for the guidance and direction of his creatures in the great labor of their lives, the erection of a temple of holiness in the heart." Therefore, in light of his definition, it is to be understood that just as an operative stonemason utilizes the pattern of designs delineated upon boards and canvasses as their guiding instructions for building material temples (what could be termed today as blueprints), so do speculative craftsmen use the designs and patterns of the moral and Spiritual Law delineated upon the canvas of Creation and the parchments of sacred and religious texts for building spiritual temples. These designs are being ever revealed and increasingly understood by man's discovery and desire to come into relationship with the Law's purpose of bringing about the maturation of Life. As these Trestleboard designs are the workings of God's Will (they having had their initial emanations from out of his Omniscient Mind), the transformative changes they appear to undergo from a state of spirituality to a state of materialization (creation), would certainly lead one to believe that these are movable as evolution seems to bear witness to. However, this evidence comes only as a result of post consciousness (after one's awareness). This is to say that man can only discover what's been made affordable for discovery. What he comes to unveil has long been a part of creation already (all the Trestleboard designs of Life having already been delineated and established as a result of the Law). He's just now coming into discovery of it. The thing itself wasn't lost or hidden. It's been long present and made operational ever before anyone's revelation of it. Therefore, whatever a man now becomes to be cognizant of constitutes not only Light (increased Consciousness), but also proof that he was ignorant of its existence all along, and therefore it wasn't the object that was in Darkness, but rather he himself. This is equally true of what lies within man and further points to a hoodwinked state that all of mankind is in (to a certain degree or another). That there is another state of consciousness that lies beyond our ability to always be immediately cognitive of is self evident. This goes beyond just seeing the material designs of what's presented upon the Trestleboard of Creation, but seeing also the Spiritual lesson it affords (as all that's been created is of a dualistic nature). This is of great importance pertaining to one's level of ability to see what is present and what one believes not to be, but really is. Many see the Letter of the Law, but very few see the Spirit of it(2). The material and spiritual are ever present around us, but when one looks from out of the windows of material consciousness, they see through a lens of materialization and therefore can only perceive materialities. This gives one the belief that the other existing state is distinctively separate and apart from the other; however, these two existing states are one existing whole which are not being created as a new temple (the temple already existing of both Creation and of Self), but rather it is the unveiling of our own consciousness by means of search, discovery, and developed understanding that is moving (progressively developing), not the Trestleboard designs of the Law. This is the same case concerning the nature of ourselves whose perfect state of Divinity resides WITHIN, (although many are looking for it to be a material heaven somewhere in the far off). Here's a reminding jewel to all Masons: The ashlar that is made perfect is hewn from out of the same ashlar that is rough, it being the embodiment of one singular created stone, (one being visibly apparent, the other hidden, but both nonetheless of one mass). It is by the gradual unfoldings of the Soul's Consciousness that man comes to see and understand the unchangeable Universal Principal that all is One as a Grand Design, and that it is only our state of unconsciousness that facilitates the appearances of two temples of separation (Movable and Immovable). It must be kept in mind that the Lodge and all within it is a symbol of the World, and that the designs delineated upon the Trestleboard are symbolizations of real spiritual Truths having been made visibly evident for man's works to unveil within himself(3). Therefore, when man begins to orientate his consciousness towards God to become One by the instructions of the Divine Law, he no longer sees the illusion of separation, but instead just One Truth. This is where the uniting of the Three Immovable Jewels (the Spiritual aspects of God's workings as the principles of Divine Law), and the Three Movable Jewels, (the consciousness of our own material existences), comes together as One to establish Harmony as the Six Points of the Star of David alludes to.

Now, all of this sounds good, but how does any of this pertains to moral development? Well, many of us usually think, act and feel from only a material perspective of consciousness (the Movable Jewels of our material consciousness, our material faculties and senses). We become cognitive of our choices mistakes, feelings, and how they came to effect the lives of others AFTER the fact, but by this time the damage in many cases is done, and we are left having to experience the unpleasant effects of the Law's just recalibration (Karma). It is only hoped that a lesson has came to be learned that will afford us Wisdom in future times. This is something that many of the incarcerated can well relate to. Now, on the other hand, when man becomes one with God through the workings of his Laws (His Divine Will), he thinks before he acts. He contemplates the circumstances and conditions of his choices and considers the ramifications of their effects upon all Life (not just simply his). He realizes that what he does effects the world all around him, and that each man is not just a material individual, but Spiritually One, all having derived from the same source of Divine Life. This understanding comes by mental awakening and developed understanding had ironically by the wisdom of previous experiences. How many can look back in their lives with more enlightened eyes, wishing they had made better decisions in life (especially morally in some instances)? Although many of us didn't do so then, the experiences we encountered has certainly made us a great deal wiser today. To conscientiously exercise with deliberate effort to travel the high road automatically draws and transforms the aspects of our lower beings upward towards the Spiritual nature of God. When this occurs we are becoming harmonious with God as we begin to exemplify that perfect and just state between our mortal created nature and our Divine Immortal Beings.

Universal Craftsmen

ESSAY XXII ENDNOTES

1. A Masonic ceremony that establishes the use of a building as a newly formed Lodge for purposes that are to be thereafter, sacred and holy. It's consecrated by purification rites using certain and well known instruments of Freemasonry.

2. The letter of the word is one who see the signs, symbols and sacred writings of Truth only from a material or literal point of understanding. This is one of the most common veils found to exist among many religious practitioners.

3. The Trestleboard is not always presented as an actual distinct object such as a board or canvas with drawings upon them, but is also understood as the collective symbolisms that represent the moral Truths to be conveyed to the candidate found all about the Lodge.

ESSAY XXIII

OPERATIVE AND SPECULATIVE

Masonry is denominated under two classes of practice, one Operative, the other Speculative(1). Their provisional uses, outlined in the Fellow Craft Degree, incites the Mind's contemplation of some of the wondrous beauties of nature and mysteries of man. In further exposition of these, a brief description of each will be given before rendering their symbolic overviews. Operative Masonry is the actual stonemason's trade, whereby one's knowledge and skill use of stone, mortar, working tools, and various other implements, are all employed for the constructing of a material edifice. Whether that edifice becomes to be a house, cathedral, or a simple shed of some sort, the elements of its composition all still derives from the natural resources due to Earth's creation. All materials, even the men employed in its construction, have undergone developing changes in order to be made employable for uses. In this respect, we see Operative Masonry employing both the elements of science and labor. In ancient times the knowledge of this science and its trade secrets were shared only among those who were actual stonemasons in which they freely traveled to various kingdoms being employed to erect many of the famous edifices we now come to know. Although they were denominated as Operative Masons, they also practiced Speculatively as far as it pertained to their obligations concerning God, morality, and Self. They organized themselves under various stonemason's guilds, in which many of their regulations later became incorporated in the draftings of the Freemason's Constitution. As the spread of Freemasonry increased in membership, its speculative nature became to be the dominant practice (as men of nobility, and various learned professionals came to be among its standing members). This became so much the case that the organization eventually emerged to only exist as a Speculative practice. So with Speculative Masonry, "...we learn to subdue the passions, act upon the square, keep a tongue of good report, maintain secrecy, and practice charity... ." Its application of building pertains to the temple of Self, in which its stones, working tools, architectural designs, and various other implements of practice are wholly of a symbolic nature altogether. It employs the basis of its symbolisms from that of the Operative stonemason's trade for purposes of conveying lessons of morality and spiritual Truths. These are designed to bring about developing changes of Self betterment by invoking inner contemplation that raises one's Consciousness. This is what was alluded to in the 24th Landmark as offered by Albert Mackey in his book titled Mackey's Jurisprudence of Freemasonry which reads: "The Foundation of a Speculative Science Upon an Operative Art and the symbolic use, and the explanation of the terms of that art for purposes of moral or religious teaching, constitutes another Landmark of the order(2). This Landmark suggests that the practice of Speculative Freemasonry derives from the stonemason's trade, and is therefore, inseparably hinged upon its material workings for its spiritual understanding. This is not hard to see as we find their compatibilities expressed in the laws of architectural building, especially when considering the comparative aspects of an inner temple requiring a material or external body. For what other purposes would a body serve without the viscera of its internal(3)? Even though both have their own independent establishments of form and designs under their governing operations of the Law, they're both still dependent upon each other in order to fulfill the purposes of one common goal. It is in this manner that one can come to see the purposes for which creation serves as a material foundation in raising up one's consciousness unto spirituality.

Now, as Operative Masonry could be symbolically attributed to matter and all its external aspects of form (creation attesting to this as a

Divine work having been operatively crafted unto visibility), so could Speculative Masonry be symbolically attributed to the internal working of this same matter. Although creation is materially visible all around us, our understanding of its inner workings is still veiled to a great extent. It has been by sought study, and unfortunately trial and error, that man has come to be provided with some of its spiritually instructive Truths(4).

In this manner, all creation entails two aspects, the material form, and its spiritual function (the Operatively external, and the Speculatively internal). Such is the same case concerning man where we find the material body serving as the external form that embodies his Life Force. The aspects of these two natures pertains to all of creation, and serves to instruct the Mind. This is even seen alluded to in the words Operative and Speculative, whose states of conditions are implicated in their root words themselves, one being operate, the other being speculate. Here it is seen that one necessitates the employment of the Will and the uses of its bodily members, while the other concerns itself with abstract thought and reasoning (the use of the intellectual faculties of the Mind). Although these consist of two different aspects, they must still come together as one in order to manifest whatever that has been envisioned. The resulting manifestation of whatever that was initially conceived bears witness within itself that these at some point were one, and are are still one. This is one of three great principles that serve to facilitate Life and its consciousness as we now know it. For without materialization of the created Temple there would be no symbols from which a Speculative practice could draw from in conveying Truths to the Mind. This is where creation becomes most relevant as it is the evidence of an operative work by a grand Architect whose Trestleboard designs serve as blueprints for man's developing Consciousness.

Having provided some distinctions of these two aspects of Masonry, it's befitting to now show how they impact one's development.

Operative Masonry has gifted man with its architectural rules of building, and by it, he has came to erect institutions of learning, temples of worship, and centers of research. It has enabled him to construct habitable and lasting structures for the best benefits of his well being and protection. It displays those forces of Wisdom, Strength, and Beauty that's been divinely imparted to him by his Creator and appeals to that nature inherited in the aspect of man's very Soul: a desire to Create. Although Freemasonry today is solely a Speculative practice in comparison to that of Operative Stonemasonry, there are those, perhaps unknowingly, who are still Operative Masons (the word Operative being used here, not in the sense of an actual stonemason, but of one who builds only as a materialist). These are those who've became enamored by the shiny jewelry and beautiful regalia while the luster of their Soul has became a dull tint and the whiteness of their aprons dingy and sullied. It is that person whose able to recite their Masonic monitors in their sleep backwards, but possess none of the spiritual depths and understanding of what he speaks. He has more jewels around his neck than Mr. T., but no Jewels of his office found about him. Seeing only the material benefits (numbers, dues, and annual returns), he trades quality for quantity, experience for expedience, and morality for membership. These are those who erect edifices of materiality unto themselves and not spiritual temples unto God. Now, this is not to say that the outer works of beautification and the administrative affairs of the Lodge serves no purposes, for the external form is essential to the internal aspects of a temple just as the exo skeletal form of a body is to the organs. However, it should never be had at the expense and neglect of the internal. Christ described it best when he referred to such as white washed tombs. The exterior is brilliantly white (the material works which can be seen by the eyes), while that which is hidden within is decayed and spiritually dead. Freemasonry is a Speculative practice and is taught to be "...a beautiful system of morality veiled in allegory and illustrated symbols." That which lays visibly seen upon its surface as the material rites, symbols, legends, and monitorial lessons are all external forms or operative designs of that "beautiful system." That which comes to be unveiled from these designs are really what constitutes the deeper aspects of its practice and should be regarded as the more substantial.

Now, in equal and opposite respect, there are those on the other hand who attempt to discard the operative altogether for the speculative, and for a lack of better term, have became ascetic, or in terms of less severity, spiritualist. They would evangelize to a homeless man about the goodness of God, departing with "May God Bless You," all the while never having given thought to his destitute condition. They negate all things relevant to the material world in their practice (T.V. music, phone, motor operated tools and even motorized transportation in some cases), failing to see the purposes for which materiality serves in its appointed times and seasons, and that the foundation of one serves as an launchpad for the other. This lesson was conveyed to me by one of my mentors in an allegorical story that had been told to him about a man who had gotten caught in a torrential downpour. Newscasters had reported on several weather channels that evacuation should be immediately sought, in which his response was "I will be alright, my faith rests in the Lord." After some hours had passed, the waters having risen to the roof, one of his neighbors passed by with a speedboat and beckoned him to climb aboard. To this, his response was, "Thank You, but that's okay, the Lord is my rock and salvation." Shortly thereafter, a helicopter comes to hover over the chimney, which is now about to be submerged, and proceeds to lower a hoister for him to take hold of. To this, he replies "God will save me. He is my buckler, an ever present help in times of trouble." Well sure enough the poor fellow ends up drowning to death, and as he comes to stand before God, he asks, "Lord, did I not keep the faith…did I not seek after those things which were spiritual, keeping my eyes upon you and the kingdom of heaven?" God's response was, "Indeed you did my son." Well why didn't you come down to save me when I proclaimed your name," the man asked. God looked at the man and said "You gotta' be kidding me, right?" This story teaches that having only one view of developed perspective retards consciousness, and as a result, causes one often times to miss the boat. Let the following be seared into the Minds of every Aspirant of Truth and Builder of Self, and that is this: Spiritual Faith Concealed Induces Material Works Revealed. They are one and the same aspects of Law working to bring about maturation, So in order to ascend to the Spiritual heights of Divinity (Speculatively), we must first begin to build together here as One (Operatively). This is what 133rd Psalm also beautifully conveys to its students.

Universal Craftsmen

ESSAY XXIII ENDNOTES

1. These two classes of practices in their deeper understandings are the institutions of corporeal matter and the energy or light that vitalizes that corporeal form, hence Material Darkness and Spiritual Light.

2. The enumerations of these Landmarks are definitive and varies among Grand Jurisdictions, some listing only a few, others believing them to be inherited in many of the rituals themselves, while others having chosen not to employ or officially list any of them at all.

3. Although this term anatomically pertains to the vital organs of one's body, one should equally consider that all material form entails an inner aspect of energy force that constitutes its vitality.

4. By man's encountering of the material, he's afforded the opportunity to unveil the inner nature of its Truth for spiritual uses of obtaining greater harmony of his own existence and further development under the Law.

ESSAY XXIV

WINDING STAIRCASE

With continued progression one inevitably comes to encounter the Winding Staircase and the story surrounding it. As this story has no historical or evidential basis of actual occurrence, it is only intended to serve as an allegorical means for conveying certain philosophical ideas and Truths. It was for this purpose that stories, legends, and traditions were first crafted into Freemasonry's Speculative design. It has been said that the ritualistic practice of using stairs for instructive purposes are of uncertain origins, but that it may have derived from the ancient religions and their temple designs. Despite this uncertainty, we find its use in Freemasonry today being employed as a means for craftsmen to further submerge their minds into greater depths of wisdom and abstract thought. As these are copious with various esoteric ideas, only a few herein will be expounded upon.

When viewing the compositional designs of these stairs, we see it being comprised of 15 steps whose ascent is said to begin after one crosses the Porch Pillars to enter up towards the Middle Chamber. These stairs wind from left to right in allusion to the Sun's course of travel and is symbolically depictive of our pathway of life's development. It is also to impress upon the candidate both the arduous and unexpected turns in his own life course. This symbolically emphasizes the necessity of employing both his Mind and Body in Self development. In doing so, he learns that each step becomes more and more difficult in its ascent whereby his understanding and development of one is predicated upon the former. It is in this manner that Freemasonry is a progressive science, it employing a systematic approach for obtaining higher levels of moral being by means of contemplative studies, moral instructions, and applicative lessons of spirituality. By use of these constants (scientifically speaking), results come to reflect in one's own nature which gives way to advancements. It is therefore in this aspect that when looking at the natural design of any stairs, do we come to see their facilitating purposes (their means for transporting something from one point to another, whether that be of ascent or descent). It is in this sense that the Winding Staircase philosophically displays both its symbolic and utilitarian services for the Mind. Now, as progression entails transition from one state of condition to another, whether by growth or development, so does the Winding Staircase depicts the means by which one can elevate their Minds from one particular state of condition to another. Now, as there are two fixed points that are bridged together by graduated steps, the law demands that more and more Will power be employed in order to ascend. This is because these points are located on uneven planes of separation (top and bottom). The gravitational pull of the spinning Earth that makes it difficult to ascend does so, not to keep keep one from ascending, but rather to teach that there must be an exertion of both one's mental and physical energies in order to do so. This natural resistance is the counterforce that facilitates growth and development and is no different in how we as infants had to employ both our Minds and Bodies in going forth from laying on our backs to eventually learning how to crawl and then walk. One's progression up these stairs are a symbolization of the Mind's efforts to obtain and apply both the education and Truths intended to aid in maturating the Soul. This is why at various points along the candidate's ascent he is afforded various esoteric instructions pertaining, not only to his steps, but to also certain wisdoms and instructive lessons associated with these. These are afforded to him by a series of progressive advancements that ultimately serves to bridge together two separated points on uneven planes, these symbolizing the beginning and ending points of separated consciousness. This is why these series consists of three divisions of steps (3, 5, and 7) as man is considered to be of three main divisions himself. In showing this, these particular numbers and their symbolic understandings will be briefly touched on.

When looking in the remote past, it was held among various schools of mystic teaching that the nature of numbers entailed both good and bad omens. This was especially noted among the teachings of Pythagoras who propounded that odd numbers were sacred to the gods, and therefore, holy, and that even numbers were of opposition, and therefore evil. It has been commented by some writers that this belief, having stemmed well before Pythagoras's time, may have been deliberately incorporated into Freemasonry as we see only odd numbers employed in the staircase's design. The reasons, although conjectural to some, stems from the idea that the earliest composers of the Masonic monitors (all later monitors having derived from these), were practitioners of various occult schools of ancient thought, and that they possibly (having been influenced by these) may have veiled some of these ideas into the monitors in which they later constructed for Freemasonry's use. In early observance of these three series of odd numbers, it will be noticed that the number 1 is not shown as it bears an unique relationship to both itself, as well as to all other numbers. Although in numerical value it certainly is a precursor to the number 3, it is the only number; however, that's not predicated nor dependent upon any other for its own existence, but yet and still, can be found to comprise all other numbers for theirs. In this aspect, it is distinct and finite within itself; however, when employed in the operations of development and progression, it shows itself also to be pluralistic and infinite. When considering this finite point from both a philosophical and religious aspect, it conveys the idea of unity, that state of Oneness from which all things have their origin of being (the First Great Cause attributed to God). Therefore this same point, numerically expressed as 1, is a representation of both God and the candidate's Soul. It is this same spiritual force of Life that stands at the bottom of the staircase in its embryonic stages of unconsciousness. It is from this point of numerical symbolization that when he takes his first step he immediately goes from a state of repose to a state of motion. When faith (one), duplicates itself to become the expression of one's Will (two), the numerical expression of growth and development comes to then be symbolized in the number three. It is of considerable interest that many of the ancient schools of thought held the number three to be equal and even sometimes of greater importance than the number one (believing it to serve as an all inclusive representation of one and the same deity operating in three different aspects). The Pythagoreans regarded it so much so that it was said that they disregarded the number one altogether and began their numerical enumerations with the number three. The high regards for this number is certainly not without merit, for even in the operation of Life we can see the triune workings of a force seemingly pervading everything existing. When considering all the evidences in which this number tends to reveal itself, it becomes quite suggestive that its harmonious workings witnesses, not only to the nature of One Grand Designer, but one whose numerical aspect undeniably exists even within our own temples. This is witnessed to in the three aspects of our mental or intellectual nature, the power and volition of our Will, and the unfolding awakening of our Soul's Consciousness (Mind, Body, and Soul). This expression of governing Law is so intimately interwoven in the operations of creation's design that to remove or even attempt to circumvent one of these in use, would result in a breakdown of harmony and orderly operations. This speaks volumes concerning what may be lacking internally within mankind (seeing that more than ever we have became divided and seemingly without order). It is for such purposes of building the temple that the three Working Tools of the Principal Officers are afforded to the candidate upon these first three steps. By these, one is to understand that the three operations of the Principal Officers are of One harmonious nature which serves to govern and build the entire temple. By the operation of these he learns to think, act, and live in harmony with the Laws of God.

With the craftsman's continued progression, the next series of steps he comes to encounter is five. In numerology the number five has its symbolical association to the consummation of inequalities, it being the sum of the first even and odd numbers 2 and 3 (excluding 1); and because of the symbolical marriage that is said to transpire between the two, it was regarded as a nuptial sign in which Pythagoras further symbolized in the Pentalpha (the five pointed star commonly referred to as a Pentagram). Its five points are held to be symbolically expressive of health and prosperity, as well as the five extremities of man's limbs (2 legs, 2 arms, and 1 head), which, when all are outstretched and all exterior points are connected together by their lines, forms the shape of a Pentagon, thus alluding to the idea of separated parts being brought together to make a unified whole. These tidbits should provide some further illumination pertaining to the Blazing Star, not because of its appearance (as this varies with Lodges), but because of its symbolic implications of every Master Mason's Raising. For as the Sun dispenses its rays of vitality, health, and essence of prosperity (all things relative to one's physical being of Life), so should every Mason dispense those illustrious Five Points of Fellowship that cultivates each brother's spiritual well being of Life. It will only be by the cultivation of Love that man, with all our material differences, will be brought together for the greater benefit of advancing our civilization as One. In more of a metaphysical viewpoint, the number five also has its symbolic associations to the Elements of Earth, Water, Fire and Air, with the fifth being Ether (a symbolization of them all having became One in a stable and perfect state of equilibrium). That all these different propensities still work under the Law for the greater benefit of development is a testament to the spiritual design that this number reflects in Life. This evidence lies also in the Five Senses and Five Orders of Architecture whose symbolizations are both found upon these steps. For with the five senses, life's experiences are made cognitive to the Mind for processing, disseminating, and regulating temple operations. These work together to effect harmony and continuity. This same understanding lies in the Five Orders of Architecture, each attesting to a period of civilization where a country's architectural and scientific advancements added greater worth to their quality of life. These proved to have been beneficial in not only their times, but also ours. For by the architectural knowledge extracted from among their ruins (coliseums, aqueduct systems, and temple excavations), we've come to build and further advance our own civilization for some of the most beneficial purposes of our existence (factories, military bases, hospitals, and space stations, just to name a few). It therefore serves as no surprise that allusions of evolution can be seen in the orderly designs of these pillar's construction. For just as the base of these pillars are located at the bottom and their capitals at the top, with all their other particulars found in between (their toros, flutes, volutes, abacuses, etc.), so is the Universe ever expanding from the foundations of its Creation to the Eastern summits of Divine Providence.

In the candidate's last and most arduous ascent, he approaches the last series of steps consisting of 7. The nature of this particular number is shrouded in much speculative thought and is profusely found in both secular and religious writings. For we read where God created the world in six days, consecrating the seventh as a sabbatical rest. It took seven years for the building of King Solomon's Temple. There are seven degrees of what some constitute Ancient Craft Masonry, the Royal Arch being considered the summit. There are seven planets by which the ancients formulated the basis of their metaphysical studies. The Jewish Menorah is composed of seven branches, and we find the Koran speaking of seven hells and seven heavens. These are just only a few witnessing aspects of this number's profuse use. Now, as we can see an union of odd and even numbers in the sum of the number 3 (1 plus 2), as well as in the number 5, (2 plus 3), so is this found also in the number 7 with 3 plus 4. This is an allusion to the Law of spiritual and material differences becoming harmoniously united to bring about progression and increase. Having been told in numerology that the number 7 symbolizes the state of completion, perfection and Divinity attributed to God, we see how mathematics works to bring about progressive development. For in order for perfection to be had, all prior states of even and odd values must harmoniously come together in order to facilitate progression towards an intended goal. As it stands there can be no number 7 without having the numerical values of 6, 5, 4, 3, 2, and 1. Neither can there be a number 6 without having 5, 4, 3, 2, and 1. This goes without saying for the rest of the numbers. This aspect of mathematical law is embodied in Creation as a divine testament to the Great Builder's Wisdom. This same Truth concerning even and odd consummates is veiled in the geometrical figures of the Square and Triangle which is vividly seen in the structure of the Pyramid, it's base being composed of 4 lines, while its adjoining sides that make up its apex is composed of 3. Here again we find allusions to the architectural law of proper building seen in the material foundation (represented in the Square and the number 4) that gradually progresses upward in spiritual ascent (represented by the Triangle and the number 3). When adding these together they equal 7, the material and spiritual having came together to depict the just and perfect nature of God expressed in the Laws of Heaven and Earth.

Now, as it pertains to Freemasonry, we find this same symbolic understanding depicted also in the wisdoms delineated upon the 7 steps. For it is in the first 3 wisdoms, classified as trivium, that constitutes the lower division of the Liberal Arts, whereas the remaining 4 are what's termed quadrivium and are considered to be the more advanced studies of Liberal Science. These serve to aid and educate the Mind in the workings of the natural Law and are sufficient means for one seeking general employment, or for one seeking to advance themselves further in other curriculums. Upon these, all of today's agricultural, medical, and technological advances have derived. When looking at the numerical design of this staircase's division, what can be seen upon closer investigation is a systematic progression of ascent by two's, which is brought about by the consummating works of differential polarities (the adding of even and odd numbers to establish the next sequential increase of progression, hence 3, 5, 7). In an esoteric understanding of building Self, each one of these series could be symbolically ascribed to the specific works that is to transpire in one's temple development. When considering this, the number three would then be ascribed to the works of the Mind, it serving as the basis by which all other progression is facilitated. The number five would be ascribed to the Body along with all those temple components that facilitate the operations of developing manifestation (such extenuation of the Heart's Will). And the number seven would then be ascribed to the Soul having became endowed with full Spiritual Consciousness (God Consciousness). This state of condition is alluded to in the 5th Chapter of Matthew, verse 48: Be ye therefore perfect even as your Father which is in heaven is perfect." Only by the workings of Love can man's Soul come to possess that state of perfected consciousness that renders its understanding of who, by what, and from whence it came, and even more, whither it travels. The wisdoms afforded upon these steps gradually aids Masons in becoming more and more conscious of the Divine Essence of God embodied in and throughout all aspects of creation (both terrestrial and celestial). Symbolically speaking, if we hold God in the numerical aspects of 1, then all subsequent numbers are nothing more than the nature of God revealing himself to our consciousness through duplicate, triplicate, and quadruplicate forms of materialization, 2, 3, 4,... all the evidences of creation whose wisdoms comprises this staircase. In a macrocosmic sense, this means that the entire design of the staircase is the embodiment of the World having been created by the workings of God's Law? Therefore, ascending such Temple staircase enables the candidate's Soul to gradually become more conscious of God by means of enlightenment and Truth's discovery. The Light in which all Masons are in search of is the Light of Truth which is found all about us in creation. Therefore, to obtain and rightfully apply wisdom in both their material and spiritual aspects, constitutes the same consummations of odd and even numbers in one's staircase ascent towards God consciousness that's embodied in all Life. When considering that the sum of all these stairs amounts to 15, which is the same numerical value for the name Jah (Jah being a shortened appellation for Jehovah in Greek, and Yahweh in Hebrew), it can be understood why the staircase may have been first employed in these ancient temples for instructive purposes. Whether this particular number was later incorporated with this idea deliberately in mind is questionable. Some say its purely coincidental as proof show in earlier times the Masonic staircase having 1, 3, 5, 7 and even 11 steps before becoming to be 15 as it is now. However, irrespective of the number, the reward of its summit still no less harmonizes with every man's hoped expectancy to Consciously behold His Glory and be immersed as One in Divine and Eternal fellowship.

Universal Craftsmen

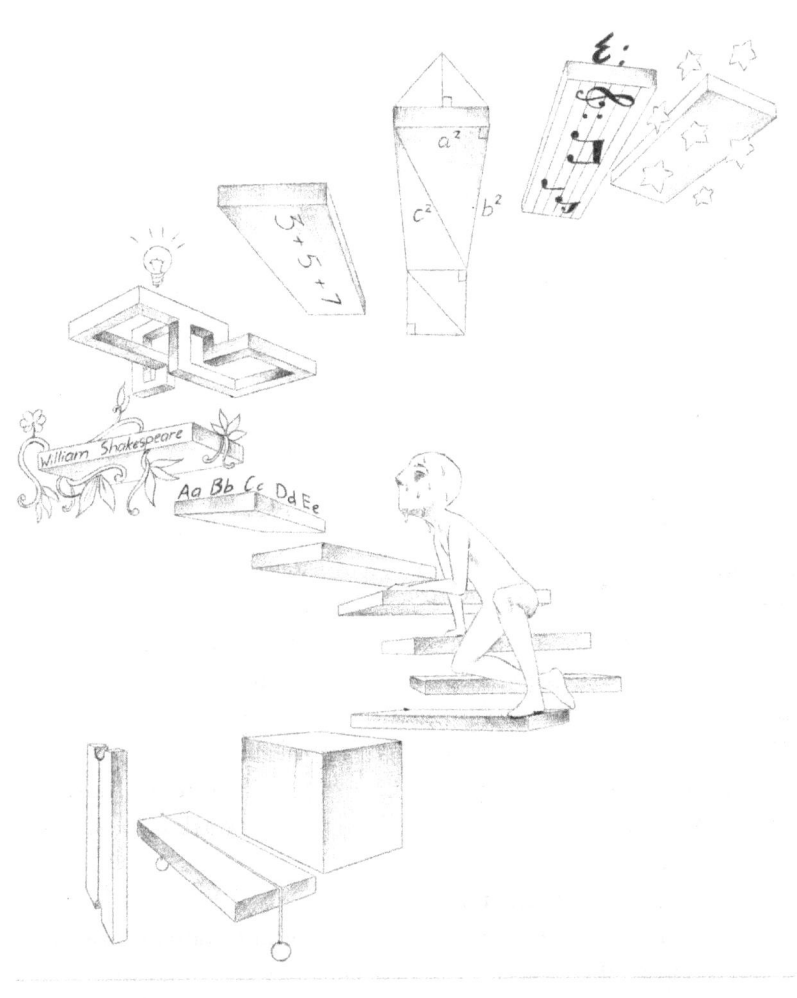

ESSAY XXV

THE LETTER G

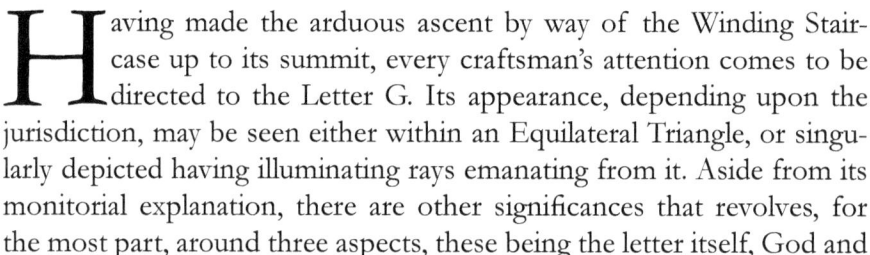

Having made the arduous ascent by way of the Winding Staircase up to its summit, every craftsman's attention comes to be directed to the Letter G. Its appearance, depending upon the jurisdiction, may be seen either within an Equilateral Triangle, or singularly depicted having illuminating rays emanating from it. Aside from its monitorial explanation, there are other significances that revolves, for the most part, around three aspects, these being the letter itself, God and Geometry. As each are esoterically related, an individual synopsis of their understanding will be offered.

When viewing this character from strictly a letter standpoint, it can be found at not only the summit of the Winding Staircase, but also in the East of the Lodge where it is then usually suspended in a relatively high position past the Master's chair, thus making it visibly noticeable from all locations within the Lodge. This particular placement is by no means chance as it alludes to the Life giving principles concerning Light and God that both emanates from out of the unfathomable distances of Darkness to facilitate consciousness. When displayed in more public view, this letter forms part of the emblem that distinguishes Freemasonry as a fraternal society whose placement can then be suspended between the Square and Compasses. When considering this letter's monitorial definition, along with this particular manner of depiction, it suggestively conveys the idea that God and Geometry are the central principles found amidst the operations of these two working tools. As this is the initial that makes up the word God and Geometry, some have postulated that the English language constitutes the origin of this letter's symbolic use in Freemasonry. However, with America being a fairly young country in comparison to others, it stands by reason that such claims cannot hold up against Freemasonry's antiquity of practice in other countries where their languages are of much older origins, but yet and still the G is used to denote the words Geometry and Deity (the initial for these words in other languages being of a different alphabetical character altogether). Such case in points are found in the French, Spanish, and Slavic languages, where the initials for the word God are D and B. This naturally raises the question as to why a letter that bears no direct relationship to the word God in one's language would still be given prominence in their monitors and Lodges. The answer lays in part with the developing changes of script that transpired over the years, as well as with the gradual introduction of Speculative Freemasonry into other parts of the world. The spread of Freemasonry, especially in the Western part of the world, is largely indebted to the English speaking composers of the early Masonic ritualists, who in their attempts to convey the idea of a Supreme Being (yet without veiling the deeper aspects of its Truths that was to be individually sought and unveiled), naturally used the English G of their language. Even though this letter was used, it was still well known among them that this character was only a symbol serving to express another symbol (which unfortunately had already undergone changes). In understanding this, we must remember that letters are only characters, and that characters are only symbols used for expressing ideas and Truths that came to be first understood by man. In an attempt to arrive at this letter's earliest character and its symbolized meaning, the retracing of some of its script developments must be had. Now, as the English language and the appearance of its alphabets are outgrowths of the Roman Latin script, this letter can be seen depicted in early history as not having a lower horizontal bar (a later developed feature by which the letter G later came to have its distinctive familiarity). During this time the letter G looked like a letter C. This is because, as quoted by Webster's

Encyclopedic Unabridged Dictionary of the English Language. "The Etruscans, having no meaningful distinction between the g sound and k sound in their language, used the symbol for both. When the distinction again had to be made in Latin, the small stroke was added to the lower curve of the C." In further retracing, we encounter the Phoenician-Greek script of this letter called the Gamma. In view of this character's historical appearance what becomes noticeably obvious is its angular shape design that faces right, it first having faced left in the Estruscan script and also in some of the earliest Greek. This left face positioning dates back also to the Hebrew script of this character which is called Gheemil. It is here in these two alphabetical systems of Greek and Hebrew, but certainly not confined to these two languages as the Egyptian and Hindu languages attests to, that historical evidences provides considerable links to not only the use of alphabetical characters and symbols to express the idea of deity, but also to some of their philosophical ideas and Truths in which they were attempting to convey.

    When viewing the Greek language, it has been told by various historical writers such as Plutarch, Iamblichus, and Thomas Taylor of the high regards that Pythagoras had for the letter Gamma, and even higher regards for his esoteric employment of numbers and use of Geometry for teaching his wisdoms. For in the gamma character, he saw not only the visual depictions of a square (the chief and indispensable working tool of operative stonemasons which enables one to build by its geometrical applications), but also the symbolical representation of the 4 lettered name of God. This is not to say that he employed the letter gamma as an exact acronym initial for the 4 lettered incommunicable name of the Hebrew deity YHVH (as such can be seen beginning with the Hebrew letter Yod), but what he did see and understand when using this letter was the symbolic correlation of equity and justness, in which the square as a working tool and the operations of a Supreme Being both exemplified through law. As this character was used in his school as an esoteric means for instructing his students, further evidence tends to show that he also saw a correlative understanding between Geometry and God. This is especially alluded to in the symbol of the Tetracty where we see the use of points, and in other depictions, yods, to convey the idea of a Divine Builder operating upon different planes of manifestation. These characters were placed in rows of graduated lines so as to create the appearance of an equilateral triangle. In creating this triangle, four points or Yods were placed in a horizontal line that served as its base. From there, there were three that was slightly offset and placed in a row right above the four. Two were then placed above the three, and finally one above them all. Now, as the Hebrew Yod is the alphabetical initial for the name Yahweh in which the Cabalist used to designate the name of their God, and as the point or open circle was a symbol of deity among many of the ancient practices of the East, as well as the triangle, then what comes to be symbolically depicted are the geometrical expressions of the workings of a Supreme Being stemming from a single point of origin at the top, and then manifesting himself down in gradual descent to the number four. When regarding the number 4 as the symbolic foundation of one's beginning ascent towards an apex (the number 4 in numerology serving as a symbol of materialization), what we then find being symbolically conveyed, is the soul of man rising from his material state of consciousness towards the apex of his Divine origin when building. At its summit lies the single and full state of God consciousness symbolized in the Point or Yod. The works of establishing God consciousnesses numerically culminates in this design when the values of each line are then added up to reach 10 (4+3+2+1), 10 symbolizing both the beginning and ending operations of a thing in one perfect value. Now, as the number five is the midway juncture between the numbers 1 and 10, which also symbolizes marital union between two states of material and spiritual developments of work, it is in this same juxtaposition that the G in Geometry and the G in God stands in relationship between the two working tools of the Compass and Square to indicate the just and perfect balance of the material and spiritual laws. This esoterically symbolizes that both are required for proper temple development. For in one aspect, speculative Masons build their Divine Inner Beings by Spiritual Laws of Truth and Morality, while at the same time utilizing the aspects of an operative vessel to measure and properly execute the designs of Love's labor (Geometry). Just think about it. We exemplify the evidences of our spiritual Love through expressions of our material and physical beings, and as a result, the Soul becomes the beneficiary of this consummation, thus leaving upon it, the imprints that serves to identify its character.

    Now, when taking a closer look at the Hebrew language, we find letters and words that also expresses this same contrasting aspect of work between God and Geometry. This is seen in the letter Gheemil, which was said by Mackey in his Freemason's Encyclopedia, to be "...associated with the 3rd sacred name of God... ,'' In this letter, we find the appellative names of Ghadol and Gibbor. For in these names they convey both the operations of a Spiritual Being reflecting himself in the material laws of building. For in the name Ghadol, which means to make large or great, we have magnitude (whether in body, mind, estate, or honor), and in the name Gibbor, which means powerful, we still see the the laws of mathematical and geometrical applications serving to bring about increase and development. It has been further said by various Masonic writers such as John Cockburn and John T. Thorpe, that the earliest Hebrew and Samaritan script of the letter Gheemil had the distinct appearances of a square, which once again suggests the same idea of geometrical operations as a working tool for building and development. Other evidences of script characterizations and symbols to denote God and his attributes of Divine Law are seen in the Hebrew letter Shiny, which is a symbolization for Shaddai, meaning Almighty. Another is found also in the 3 Yods within a circle and the vowel points Qamets, which is believed to have stood for the 12 divine principles of life harmoniously existing in all three aspects of God. These, among others, are mentioned in the works of Albert Mackey's Lexicon of Freemasonry, and even more in Albert Pike's Lectures on Masonic Symbolism, the Omkara and Other Ineffable Words.

It is by the operations of a material science (symbolically depicted in the working tools of the square), and the spiritual operations of a Supreme Being (depicted in the symbolization of the letter), that craftsman are to build their spiritual and moral Temples. Even though their respective instructions are openly found upon the Trestleboard designs of Creation and upon the open pages of the V.S.L., the Mind has to be awakened to learn and understand these principles of Law that it may instructively consummate together all the parts of the temple necessary for erecting up the Soul. It is my opinion that Dr. Mackey alluded to this by using another means of symbolic thought to convey such understanding. In his work titled Symbolism of Freemasonry, he attributed one of his learned discoveries to a man named George R. Glidden, a pupil of Michael Angelo Lanci, who had employed a cabalistic technique of reversing the 4 letters of the Tetragrammaton from YHVH to HVHY, which in return unveiled an interesting revelation. When this was done, he found that the letters then read as HO-HI, which "...in Hebrew ho is the masculine pronoun equivalent to the English he, and hi is the feminine pronoun equivalent to she, and therefore the word HO-HI literally translated is equivalent to the English compound He She; that is to say the Ineffable name of God in Hebrew... ." I believe this reveals a more elucidated understanding of the meanings I AM, and I AM THAT I AM, or I BE THAT WHAT I BE OR SHALL BE, which are the expressed states of condition that are said to be the meaning of the 4 lettered consonant name YHVH(1). For as the Hebrew word Havah means, not only to Be, but also to exist, we come to see a deeper implication of life symbolized in the meaning of I AM THAT I AM, or I BE THAT WHAT I BE OR SHALL BE. For in order for life to take on any form of inanimate or animate Be-ing, it must come by way of the Spirit (the vital principle within all Creation), and as the genderfication of the Spirit has always been feminine, this would then represent God as being the male. That, which results from their harmonious operations, would therefore be the representation of Light (the Soul that would go forth TO BE in all its various aspects of creation). As these aspects are all actually One, God is all THAT BE in every aspect of the seen and unseen form (past, present, and future). This would then convey the symbolic idea that God's nature is androgynously One in Spirit, but materially separated in polarizations. (as with the case with male and female). Now, in saying this, we must keep in mind that God is neither male nor female, but that these are only anthropomorphic expressions that helps to formulate comparative understandings of the polarizations of the Law's workings. When such is properly understood, it reveals not only the esoteric means of one's reconstruction of spiritual consciousness, but the means of becoming harmoniously One with God. For in the tetragrammaton YHVH, we see the Law's quaternary aspects being symbolized in the 4 separate letters that makes up the whole of a Divine Being, the case also being with man (we having been created in his image). In this symbolic view, the Y would correspond to the Mind, the H to the Heart or Spirit (Will), the V to the Soul, and the H to the materialized Body (the duplication of the Spirit having became visible). It is of considerable interest that there are vowel points missing in the Tetragrammaton that serves to establish its correct pronunciation. Is this a symbolic allusion to what's been lost within man's temple that requires finding in order for wholeness and perfection to occur? If so, this should incite us to view closer the history of why and how the Ist Temple became destroyed, and even further how the 2nd one was rebuilt.

Even though the exact time as to when this symbol was first used may never come to be definitely known, it is my opinion; however, that irrespective of the character, whether that be a G for God or Geometry, a Gheemil in Hebrew, a Gamma in Greek, or even a Yod, Point or Equilateral Triangle, all such representations of a Supreme Deity and its attributes still serve to convey one universal Truth of importance, and that is that the Truths of a Divine Being reflects in both aspects of spiritual and material existences to aid in the development of our Souls. It is these evidences that anchors one's hope and keeps them traveling ever Eastward.

Universal Craftsmen

ESSAY XXV ENDNOTES

1. Although it has been cited by some that Albert Mackey's suppositions concerning this has no basis of Masonic merit (as many of his claims have been said to have derived from erroneous views), the idea of one's attempt to reconstruct their God consciousness by consummation of perceived differences is a work that was taught in different ways by various different schools throughout the ages. This is where the Truth, whose Universal Oneness in spirit, is found in the results of its application and not so much in the material modems and means to get there. Even though the material vehicle may differ in form, the Spirituality of Truth doesn't. Examples of this are found in the symbolic conveyances of the phallus and cteis, the Mind and the Heart, the Sun and the Moon, and God and the Holy Spirit. Although all these are different modems used in different wisdom schools to teach and convey a Truth, their results from proper understanding and application are Spiritually One. This is what I believe Mackey saw and was attempting to convey as a Truth in this comment.

ESSAY XXVI

PASS/PASSOVER

In the 12th Chapter of the book of Judges, there occurs an incident where the contentious and greedy spirit of the Ephraimites caused them to war against the Gileadites. This was because they had not been solicited by the Gileadites to help fight a war against the Ammonites which prevented them rights to share in the bountiful spoils of war. Unable to reach a peaceful resolve, Jephthah, the Gileadites leader, engaged in war with them in which he utterly defeated them. Upon doing so, he also set up checkpoints along the banks of the Jordan River to prevent the fleeing Ephraimites from being able to pass back over. Whenever an Ephraimite would reach the banks, he would be stopped and interrogated as to what it was he sought to pass over, in which naturally his response would be indicative of a river stream, but because his dialect was notably different (due to his part Egyptian heritage), it would reveal his true ethnicity and cost him his life. It is written that 42,000 were slain that day along the banks of the Jordan River. Although these biblical events entail esoteric particulars made known to every Fellow Craftsman, it also entails significances particular to the regenerative works of Self development. In bringing these to light, various aspects of the Jewish

Passover will be brought into view as these are significantly relevant in understanding this esaay.

Although the Passover was instituted with the Israelite's Exodus from out of Egypt, its first commemorative observances (aside from the initial event itself), took place in the wilderness of Mt. Sinai according to the 9th Chapter of Numbers. It was decreed to be perpetually observed every year, and was written in the 12th Chapter of the Book of Exodus that if one was to ask its meaning, it should be given in response "...it is the sacrifice of the passover to Jehovah, who passed over the houses of the sons of Israel in Egypt when he plagued the Egyptians, but he delivered our houses." This significant event is said to have taken place on the 14th day of the month of Abib in the year 1513 B.C.E., the calendar month in which the Hebrews called Nisan. It is said to have taken place around about midnight on a full moon. Now, when viewing this word's meaning which is pretermission or exemption (pretermission meaning to let go or let pass), one can see how befitting this appellation is. For it is written that the "...Lord smote all the firstborn in the land of Egypt, from the firstborn of Pharaoh, that sat on his throne, unto the firstborn cattle...." but passed over all the doors that had adhered to the specific instructions given to them by Moses. Those who followed these instructions were not stricken with death and subsequently were led out of Egypt. Keeping in mind that the Hebrews had two calendars, one sacred and the other civil, we find the civil calendar beginning its year with the month of Tisri (mid September to mid October), while the sacred calendar began its year with Nisan (mid March to mid April). This serves of particular significance, for it is in this same sacred calendar month of Nisan that not only the Israelites entered into the Promised lands, but is also when one begins to see the laws of nature starting to bear witness to the Divine principles of Temple Regeneration. For as the Hebrew month of Nisan corresponds to the Gregorian month of mid March to mid April (mid March beginning the vernal equinox and Spring season), what comes to be then seen are the early signs of vegetative life, along with plush and fertile landscapes, all attesting to the fecundity and strength of Mother Nature's provisional abilities. Aside from this month's Easter celebration(1), this particular month also marked the beginning of barley harvest whose seeds had been previously sown in the month of Bul (known more as Heshvan (mid October to mid November). It was in this month (Heshavan) that the early rains of autumn served as a veritable sign for planting barley and wheat, in which the increasing rains would continue into the months of Tevet/Tabeth through Adar (the calendar months that corresponds to our Winter seasons of mid December to mid March). Wheat, taking only slightly longer to mature, was harvested right after the harvesting of the barley crop. It was these two crop grains that were the major commodity of agricultural during those times. It was also used as a form of currency, it being one of the wages given to the Temple workers. As a religious ordinance it was used as a wave offering by the High Priest in the first fruit offerings unto God in the 23rd Chapter of Leviticus, 10th verse. It is of no coincidence that this is the same crop that Ruth diligently gleaned the fields of Boaz's for and was given additional measures of to carry home to her mother in law, Naomi. Now, as this crop comprises 1 of 3 wages outlined in the Fellow Craft Degree, it is also in this same degree we find allusions of it at the scene of events transpiring between the Ephraimites and Gileadites. Different illustrations depict it as a sheaf of wheat being suspended on one side of a riverbank. Others show it as being suspended near a waterfall, while still there are others that show it as an open field teeming with its abundance. Regardless of its different depictions, what's commonly seen among them all is the presence of water standing as a precursor to passage, which when considered strictly from an agricultural standpoint, conveys the idea that a plentiful yield is predicated upon adequate irrigation of the ground in order to reap a bountiful harvest. From a philosophical standpoint, it conveys the idea that generative and regenerative development is necessary for growth and maturation. This is witnessed to throughout the bible where we come to see this same reoccurring element of water presented before a particular state of increase occurs. This is particularly notable in the crossings of the Red Sea and the Jordan River. It is in this esoteric understanding that water serves as a symbolic expression of Life and Death, and when properly understood and employed in accordance to the Divine Laws governing such, it facilitates the Mind's awakening and the Soul's development unto full maturation. It is by such waters of Truth that a degenerate Mind comes to be healed and a temple edifice reconstructed. This was symbolized both by water and also nature's annual reemergence of life after Winter's passing, and was the underlining Truth symbolized in Christ's statement: "...except a corn of wheat fall into the ground and die, it abided alone, but if it die, it bringeth forth much fruit"(2). In this understanding lies the conditions of prosperity and abundance, these indicative of the idea of "plenty." As the promised land that laid before the Jordan River was described as a land to be "...flowing with milk and honey," this wasn't just a depiction of the material abundances that awaited the Israelites in their crossing, but more so a symbolization of that rich state of spiritual wholeness pertaining to the Soul. This is what the word shalem/salem signified as a city in the name Jerusalem (the same promised land that the Israelites crossed over the Jordan River to obtain). For the word salem just doesn't mean peace alone, but in its fullest sense, complete, whole, just and perfect, a condition that comes about by gradual development. For the Israelites, this came by way of many hard fought battles, spiritual lessons and underwent disciplines. They were even prevented passage over into this land and had to remain in the desert of Sinai for 40 years as their own disbelief and disobedience was evidence of their underdevelopment(3). This symbolically suggests that a desolate and dry Heart cannot generate increase unto the Body, and certainly not unto the Soul, especially when the Mind hasn't been irrigated with the regenerative waters of Truth. Without this there can be no growth.

Now, as there are two sides to one coin, so are there dualities to understanding this one element. For upon one side of the waters and its banks lay all the provisional substances that promotes growth and increase, while on the other side lay all the degradations of life that stifles it. Although these are of two distinct natures, they operate for one harmonious purpose to bring about birth, growth, and maturation in due season. One suspends as it induces development, the other facilitates as it supports progression. This understanding is symbolically depicted in the Israelites' passover crossings but the Egyptian's prevention, and in the events that occurred also between the Ephraimites and Gileadites. For as death fell upon the Egyptians when they tried to pass over the same Red Sea in pursuit of the Israelites, so did the Ephraimites meet with this same terrible fate in their attempts to pass over the Jordan. In both of these instances, further development was required as disbelief, disobedience and deliberate despondency to the instructions of Truth are what brought about their demise (despite the pleadings and urgings of both Moses and Jephthah to their oppressors). On the other hand; however, we see where both the Gileadite's and Israelite's compliance and positive responsiveness to the law procured for them passages unto greater Life. As far as the Ephraimites' different pronunciation of this word from the Gileadites, it introduces the nature of not so much their linguistical or ethnic differences, but the contrasting differences of their inner natures (one being inclined to seek only the passions of material gain; the other seeking the higher aspects of spirituality). One is depictive of an unregenerated man as an unborn. The other is depictive of a regenerated man having been born again. Further evidence that supports this is found upon the basis of the word Jordan, whose primitive root means to fall, to descend, or descender, and is the waters they attempted to pass over to the other side on. Now, as we are already acquainted with waters being symbolical of the Mind and of life sustaining Truths, the principles of temple regeneration becomes even more apparent when considering the words' meaning in connection to the many baptisms conducted there. For then, the understanding of one's baptismal immersion and reascent from these waters, would constitute the symbolical descent into death from one mental state of consciousness to the awakening of another, in which the water serves as a veil that divides the two. This would then ritually depict the descent or fall that brought about the Soul's lost consciousness of God and its reborn ascent in recovery. These further find their veils in the Soul types of Adam and Christ (one being birth into materiality, and the other rebirth unto spirituality, even forth unto the fullness of God). It is in these two transitional states that the symbolical significance pertaining to the Lamb can be seen to have an universal understanding rather than one that only applies to a certain religion. For the Lamb would then serve to signify every Soul's circumambulating course of earthly descent and cosmic ascent, whose immersive initiation into those greater degrees of conscious Truths becomes to be celestially signified by the zodiacal Ram of Aries (Lamb), one of the heralding signs of spiritual rebirth under its particular age of evolution. As the Passover is 1 among 3 major observances among the Hebrews, we find that it coincides, not only with the sacred calendar of nature's harvest cycles of crops, but also with the triune design of the cosmic universe as well (these additionally having their alluding to the various aspects of man's temple). Man is a microcosmic world that's keyed to the grand designs of God's Temple and its governing laws; therefore, each aspect that's sought, learned and mastered in the nature of Self, is a particular veil being pierced or passed over towards establishing a macrocosmic consciousness of God himself. Such is the greater understanding veiled in the ripping of the veils of the Temple, which is reported to have occurred at Christ's death in the 27th Chapter of Matthew. Among Christian believers, Christ serves to be their

Passover that atones for their sins and grants them access past these veils. In understanding that Love bridges the gap between material weakness and spiritual aspirations, in which Christ stands par excellence, we should not relinquish our commitment to effort altogether, which would only cause impotency rather than growth, but instead, we should use this as the basis and motive for why we labor.

    Now, as the Passover may be considered to be confined only to the events surrounding the Israelite's exodus from out of Egypt, its occurrence (in the strictest sense of its definition), can be found depicted in other events where death was pretermitted for the greater development of Life. Such examples are seen in the events of Noah's Flood, where he was saved from the perishings of an old Earth for the beginnings of a new; the story of Jonah and the whale, where he was saved and transitioned over onto the banks of Nineveh to carry out a work; the various baptismal occurrences that took place in the Jordan river, where the Souls of many became awakened to new Life; not to mention the events in the 3rd Chapter of Joshua, where the Jordan was parted like the Red Sea and the Israelites once again passed over onto the other side to dry land. I believe also Abraham is a representation of this same passover. For he was called from the land of the Chaldeans (known also as Shinar, and later as Babylonia) onto the other side of the Euphrates River. It is written in some of the older manuscripts of Freemasonry that it was here at "...Babel where language was confounded and Masonry was lost." As a result of this passing over, Abraham procured by means of faithful obedience, a covenant promise of Life that would be perpetuated through his seed unto all subsequent nations and their religions, for he was not only regarded as the father of many nations, but he came also to be called the Father of Faith. It is upon such evidences outlined in the 4th-6th Chapters of Romans that suggests the term Hebrew doesn't merely symbolizes an appellation of one who came from Abraham's loins in terms of lineage alone, or of that pertaining to Abraham's change in geographical location, but more so to that transition that expresses one having left from a lower aspect of material consciousness to seek out the greater promises of spiritual Life and its Truths. This transition constitutes the same obligating covenant taken by every Mason which imposes upon him the works of Spiritual Regeneration (Temple Building). Therefore, anytime one begins to render forth Truths from a state of mental acquisition to an employed state of application, it constitutes a passover. To slaughter and sacrifice the lower passions of materiality that fetters the works of spiritual progression, constitutes a passover. To descend within one's own temple of Darkness where lies undiscovered Truths to resurface the wiser as a result, constitutes a passover. And when we ultimately come to be placed in the bowels of the Earth to be raised up beyond this mortal veil having to stand upon the banks of the cosmic waters of Life seeking entry to the beyond, may every faithful and true craftsman be able to render the pass that allows such passage, because this too will also constitute a passover.

Universal Craftsmen

ESSAY XXVI ENDNOTES

1. It taking 28 days for the moon to undergo all its phases, a full moon occurs 14 days of the 28, wherein Easter is celebrated the 1st Sunday after the full moon on the 21st day of March, or whenever the full moon occurs after this day. If the full moon happens to occur on a Sunday, Easter is then celebrated on the following Sunday. It is of contemplative interest that the event of Easter, Spring, the increase of greater life depicted in the Israelite's Passover, certain crops, Christ's resurrection, and many other events, all points to the idea of abundance and increase.

2. St. John 12th Chapter, 24th Verse.

3. Numbers, 14th Chapter, 1-35th Verse. Also the number 40 has its esoteric connection to preparation and development, hence the Israelite's 40 years in the desert, the Flood rains of 40 days and 40 nights, Christ's 40 days of being tempted upon the mountain, and 40 weeks (9 months) of pregnancy in child birth.

ESSAY XXVII

COMPASSES

In the early candidacy of the Craft Degrees, an Entered Apprentice is taught that the Compasses are used to circumscribe his desires and keep them in due bounds. He learns this same instrument also constitutes 1 of 3 Great Lights in Freemasonry. He later comes to discover as a Master Mason that the most valuable tenets of Masonry, those being Friendship, Morality and Brotherly Love, are found between the two extended points of this instrument and are as vital to the institution of Freemasonry as the organs are to the human body. Even though the Compasses are found throughout the Craft Degrees, it is the Third Degree; however, that a plethora of esoteric thought begins to open up (this being the primary working tool of that degree that marks the candidate's travels on towards the greater aspects of temple building). Therefore, as one "travels to foreign lands" to work, he comes to develop more proficiency and understanding of not only this instrument's use, but of also the other working tools and their spiritual applications for building. Even though these discoveries cover a broad range of ideas, they all nonetheless revolve around the conceptualization of one's Soul awakening and its several degrees of development. If an inquisition was to be had regarding the point when such awakening is believed to occur, one would need no further than to look at the compasses and their particular manner of operations for the answer. For when looking at its construction, we see it being equipped with two extendable legs, one which establishes a fixed point, and the other that circumscribes a 360 degree line around it. When executing such, one can't help but see that familiar symbol known as the Point in the Circle. When reflecting upon this symbol's monitorial rendering, candidates are informed that the point in the center is a representation of the individual himself, and that the circle is the boundary line of conduct in which they are never to allow their passions, prejudices, and interest to betray them. Therefore, the circle is a symbol of the law and the dot is a symbol of our being, which when compared to the operations of the two compass legs, entails both our post consciousness and Soul seed consciousness. In addition, this same point that one of the legs make is also the microcosmic egg of primordial unity from which all Life is believed to have emanated from. Now, when considering all having derived from this point, the void and formless state depicted in the first 3 verses of Genesis in Chapter 1, harmonizes with the idea of limitless expanse having been circumscribed by the Laws of Divine Order (symbolized in the operations of the Compasses). The center of this would be where the conception of Light and its subsequent development of creation would occur to then fill up the void of unconsciousness. In a macrocosmic sense, Light is the beginning of Life, and Life is the beginning of Consciousness. This is what the point alludes to in both Creation and Man., and is for such reasons why this instrument is regarded as a Great Light (it serving as a provisional womb for the consciousness of Life and its subsequent development unto maturation). These stages depict the range between the point and the circle that has resulted from the Soul's descent through the celestial spheres to its now material abode of the terrestrial body. The Soul's conscious knowledge from whence it came remains cloaked (hoodwinked) within its lower nature until rebirth. This unveiling revelation is symbolically depicted in the expansion from a closed dot to an open circle, in which the circumference line of the circle represents the Divine Law that circumscribes and governs the works of man's development. When this awakening takes place, birth from out of the womb occurs and the consummating and developing process of another begins, hence progression. As one's enlightenment and understanding increases so will their awareness of the Law's working presence also increase. As the universe and man are of a ternary aspect, both being born out of evolutionary degrees, it is in this same respects that the compasses bear a ternary relationship to the development of creation. This esoterically stands to be the reason why no Lodge of any Degree can be opened without it, for everything under the laws of creation is predicated upon a beginning point of conception and a process of development, which is symbolized by one leg of the compass that establishes the dot and the other that establishes the line of eternal perfection. The binary workings of these two serves to create one symbol, which in return allows for the 3rd aspect to emerge (Life within the provisional conditions of a womb). This process must continue forth in every part of the temple until a whole and complete edifice has come to be brought about. It is then that all the works comes to be circumscribed within the womb at the final stage of completion that results in a perfect Temple of God Consciousness. Therefore, it is to be understood that the ternary process is not limited to just one temple part and its reconstruction, but rather is a process that occurs in every part that serves to make a whole. This is Masonically comparative to every stone having been made whole and perfect before being brought to Jerusalem to be set as a permanent part of the Temple structure. Bearing in mind that the compasses constitutes one of the Three Great Lights, and Light (whether material or spiritual), facilitates conscious awareness, it then stands by evidence of creation alone that any particular Lodge opened for Degree work must naturally possess a representation of this as a principle of law (if it is to be held true that a Lodge is a symbol of the World), for if there was no Light in the World, how could we be cognitive of the evidences of Life, Morality and our Souls. Other evidences that witnesses to the works of progressive development is found veiled in the geometrical figures in which this and another Great Light forms. Let's consider.

    In the Craft Degrees, the geometrical design of primary interest is the 90 degree right angle, it being also an allusion to the right angle Square, and further to a four cornered square when developed. When 4 of these right angled squares are inverted and conjoined together, it forms a cross whose point is located in the center and is 360 degrees. When a four cornered square is fully established, its outer angle of degrees totals also to 360 degrees. All these are created by the working tool of the Square whose operations pertains strictly to angles and constitutes also a Great Light. Now, in respects to a circle, the same number of degrees are also found in a single point that establishes the beginning delineation that then goes forth to make a circle. When such circle has been created, its outer circumference comes to also equal 360 degrees. In both cases of the beginning and ending operations of these two Great Lights and their geometrical figures one can see the point being the fixed location from which both their development and completion has derived. This same understanding is ritualistically conveyed in the candidate's reception into the Lodge, in which he is received upon the "point" of a sharp instrument and is then aided forth "around" about the Lodge in perambulation. It is then within this circular space of a womb which comes to be squared off, that the works of development necessary for bringing him to Light occurs. The experiences that transpires while in his hoodwinked state symbolically expresses his forging development from a state of unconsciousness (a form of ignorance) to his state of illumination (his birthing consciousness in the center of the East). This ritualistic expression of birth that transpires in the Lodge is to be one that transpires in the lodge of the candidate as it pertains to him coming into more increased levels of conscious Truths, hence Light. In reality the exact "point" of one's awakening occurs when their desires germinate with the Living Waters of Spiritual Truths that brings about Life. When faith and works meet that's when development begins to form. Although different levels of development comes to be had by the candidate as he progresses in degrees, the building of his temple is still not complete, for he has yet to come conscious of more and even further Light that awaits him in subsequent degrees of the 2nd and 3rd. For as it stands, he has not yet learned of the temple tragedy that is to occur which is a post representation of his own tragedy that has already taken place as a result of his own materialization. It is then that he comes to realize that he must dig and sift through the ruins of his 1st Temple foundation to unearth the necessary Truths to rebuild the 2nd Temple. Therefore, when he is being brought to light in each degree of Craft Masonry to discover the points of the compass legs having been raised in successive elevations above the square, what is being symbolically conveyed in its greater sense, is the womb of Life (symbolized in the circle that these legs make) concentrically expanding forth from a point of Spiritual conception to a point of material consciousness in which more Light is increasingly permitted until full spiritual awakening is had (rebirth). As the candidate is naturally already existing, his new found discoveries of Truth are had in hindsight as the Mind's eye which sees spiritually was formerly hidden under the Square in Darkness. When he comes to be born and develops into maturity, he looks back and sees the triple stages of darkness and the lessons that aided in his development with Spiritual clarity.

Now, as the Compasses are regarded more so for the higher aspects of trigonometrical calculations and measurements pertaining to volume, space, time, and distances, it becomes easy to see how their lofty operations share symbolical correlations to that high state of the Soul's origin Therefore, in transition from the plane of material Truths, to those that lie found upon the planes of further spirituality, the Master must experience a passing over from the Square to the Compasses. This is where, as a Master Mason, his travels to "foreign countries," his pursuit of the Master's Word, and his wages received for work (which are always the obtainments of Truths), leads him to encounter the Capitular Degrees of Freemasonry, in which he discovers the changes in the Square and Compasses appearances altogether. In this aspect of advancement, the right angle of the square in the previous Craft Degrees changes to a circular quadrant (a semi circle). And as these changes are relevant to the esoteric Truths of the higher degrees of the Royal Arch, it suffices to only say that it is upon this plane that one comes to encounter the more sublime Truths pertaining to not only their temple, but to also some of the most abstruse ideas pertaining to God, the development of Man, and the Soul's relationship to the cosmogonies.

In a final view of the Compasses' symbolic uses for progressive development, it can be comparatively seen how energy proceeding from out of the East of one's Mind when dispensing out its instructive works, has this same symbolical process depicted in the operations of the Compasses. For it starts out at a beginning point and goes forth to delineate its circumscribing work and then returns back to itself. In both depictions, a circle is thereby formed in which manifestation becomes to be developed in. This calls to mind the painting by William Blake called the Ancient of Days Measuring Time, which is considered by some to be God stretching forth his hand from heaven with a huge pair of compasses extending towards the Earth, conveying (in the opinion of some) the idea of a Divine Architect circumscribing and crafting creation that will inevitably return back unto its own origins. Now, as the Mind is the 1st emanating principle of material consciousness, whether in descent or ascent, it becomes more clear also in the works of redevelopment why the Compasses constitutes a Great Light that's dedicated to the Craft rather than to any one particular individual. For as the Compass leg returns back to itself, so has the gift of Life and Light been afforded to mankind as a means of facilitating the return of the Sons of God back to their full state of Divine Consciousness. Such is the macrocosmic aspect of Light being drawn in on all sides of the Circle back in unto itself.

Universal Craftsmen

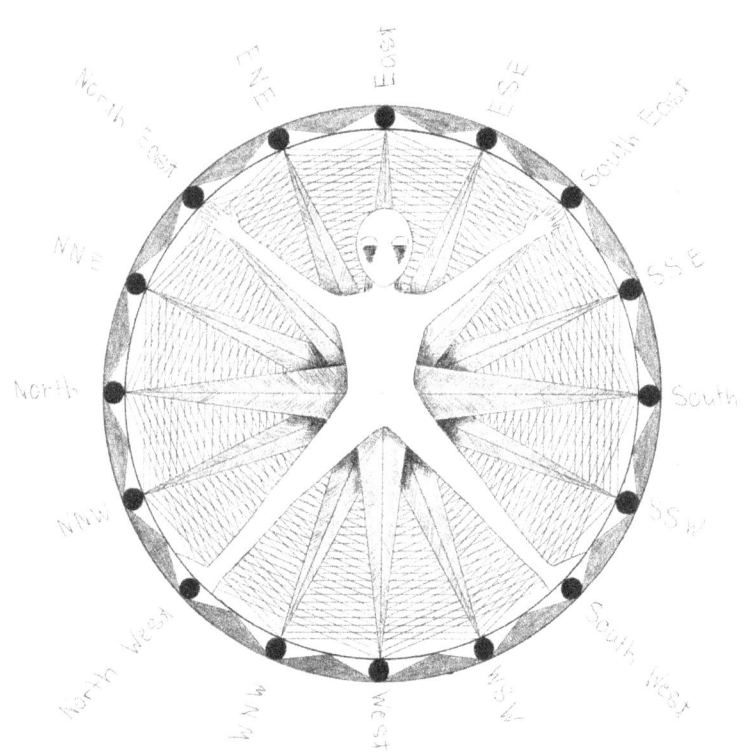

ESSAY XXVIII

HIRAM ABIF

In exposition of this Masonic figure, a brief overview of the words Abif and Hiram will be offered so that further insight into the esoteric nature of this character can be had. When looking at this word in various literary texts, one will notice the different variations of its spelling ranging from abif, abi and abiv. This is due in part to both the various time periods of certain biblical texts and the alphabetical changes of the Aramaic and Hebrew translations of these texts over into the Greek and English versions of the Bible. According to the New Strong's Concise Dictionary of the Words in the Hebrew Bible, the word abif has its Hebraic derivative from the primitive root word ab which is composed of the first two alphabetical characters Aleph and Beyth. These two characters alone render their definition as "father." When the Hebrew letter Yod is added (this having the sound of what a silent I makes in English), it establishes possessiveness, which then renders its meaning as "my father," hence the word abi. When adding the letter Phe, whose alphabetical character entails also the letter Vau (this character creating the sound of what an English F and V makes), it comes to express further possessiveness, which then renders its meaning as "to be of, or to be from my father," hence the word abiv or abif. It was upon the basis of these root word's possessives (of and my), that the text in 2nd Chronicles and 1st Kings came to be understood as "Hiram My Father," or "Hiram Of My Father" in the literal biological sense. However, this word can also be used in a figurative sense of possessiveness to ascribe character traits or prominency to a person, and when used as such, it is often accompanied with rank, honor, or some type of descriptive virtue or title. Some examples of these are chief, overseer, master, excellence, noble, righteousness, etc. It customarily signifies one who is considered to be the first, the inventor, or possessor of something in which they are highly noted for among others in. When pertaining to various occupations, especially the working trades of those times, it served to distinguish a person who was highly skilled in their particular field of service, and was one who was often an indispensable asset to the King in both the aspects of civil and ecclesiastical polities. Sea Merchants, Weavers, Architects, Financial Advisors and Fortune Tellers were just some of the craft occupations in which Kings in those times were vitally dependent upon. So when the word ab was used in this sense, it didn't necessarily mean one who had came by way of biological descent (as in a birth father), but rather one who had came by way of, or was from a particular occupation, status, character trait or virtue, and in return, had been assigned this possessive title and name (father) as a figurative attribute to which their character of being, or nature in work displayed such. Examples of this are found in such names as Abishag, Abraham, and Abida whose meanings are Father of Error, Father of Many, and Father of Knowledge(1). Therefore, the Hebrew word ab in 2nd Chronicles, 2nd Chapter, 13th-15th verse, is not to be understood solely in the paternal sense of father alone, but from its overall context in building as, "a primary head, chief, principal, or master craftsmen," these all being descriptive virtues and titles attributed to his high proficiency and degree of work. An even more expanded interpretation could be rendered as, "one from among my kingdom, a Father of crafting whose a Master in his line of work."

In moving further to consider the word Hiram, we find two different renderings of its spelling found in 2nd Chronicles and 1st Kings (Hiram and Huram), which appears to be the same name of both a Tyrian King and a man who was sent by this King to assist in the building of King Solomon's Temple (one who was praised as being highly skilled in all sorts of craftsmanships). When looking at this word's transliteration in Strong's, we find Chuwram, Chiyram, and Chiyrom, these being the different forms of the words Hiram and Huram. As this is a compound word, the 1st part of their transliterations are Chuw or Chiy, which means white and noble. Its conditions are associated with blanching so as to make white. It has further connotations that conveys the conditions of glowing radiance as made by the cleansing or shining power of fire (that state of illustrious brightness or whiteness that comes about by process of purification). In these meanings we find the same state of conditions symbolically expressed in the color and virtuous character associated with the badge of a Mason in which our moral character ought to exemplify (white). Now, as white and noble are understood to be the general meaning of the first part of this word, it has, in my opinion, even further spiritual meaning. When referencing this word in Strong's (Chiy), we find that it derives from the primitive root word chayah, which means to live or to revive. Its overall meaning is to nourish and preserve life, to keep alive, to quicken, to recover, to repair, or to restore to life. This is quite befitting as the immortality of the Soul is one of the basis of Freemasonry's beliefs which is made esoterically evident in the ceremonies of the 3rd Degree's Raising. This preservation and quickening pertains to the Soul which is alluded to in Hiram Abif, and is for such reasons why he is not only been attributed such high honors (in which his virtuous moral character in the Third Degree attests to), but is also why a Mason is admonished to keep his badge unsullied (a symbolical condition that's also to be maintained of his own Soul). This same understanding of revivification (the restoration of life), lies also in the aspects in which the workings of the Sun, Truth, and God all serve to express in both their material and spiritual operations.

This is one of the many universal threads of Truths that's been commonly sown in the tapestries of religion, ancient mythologies and legends (all their Truths being of spiritual oneness governed by one and the same Divine Law). The fact that this word has its connections to the Greek deity named Horus is even further evidence of the spiritual meaning of Hiram's name proving as an esoteric veil for the resurrected Soul (as Christ, the Sun, Horus and Heru all shows). (2)

In proceeding further to consider the 2nd half of the word Chiyram, we see the word ram. It is an active participle of the primitive root word Ruwm which means to become or make high, or to be risen or raised up (both in a literal or figurative sense). Another variation of this word's transliteration is also Rum, which means elevations. Now, in both regards, the general idea of loftiness and heights are expressed, which in its Masonic correlations, harmonizes with every Mason's traveling advancement towards the East where his consciousness of moral and spiritual Truths are increased. When we combine the meaning of these two words Hiram and Abif, along with their figurative implications, what then presents itself as an overall idea, is one having been raised or exalted to a high state of noble character or purity, and has come to be ascribed such a title that therein embodies all the virtuous attributes that this state of condition entails. This is important, because what it really means is that the character traits in which the name Hiram expresses, cannot be possessed by a person until they come to exercise them within their own life. Traits are attributes of the possessor who expresses them. Only by one's commitment to self-cultivation can such craftsmanship serve to reveal the Hiram Abif underlying in every Mason.

In proceeding to reveal the significances of why such appellative honors have been further attributed to this Masonic figure, various aspects of both the rites and legends associated with him must be looked into. As Hiram has been said to be one of the Three Ancient Grand Masters of the Temple of Jerusalem, every Mason should be well acquainted with the cardinal point in which he is associated with. This particular location, which has its further allusions to the virtue of Temperance (an attribute of Mastership), stands between the two polarities of the East and West in which Hiram Abif serves as an esoteric representation of. In this sense of further symbolism, he sits as a mediator between the two states of conditions, who, by not only his peculiar manner of death, but also his esoteric manner of exhumation, becomes to be raised to an "elevated" or higher state of conscious being. Now, if one attempts to regard his death and the events surrounding it to be literal, then a conflict of understanding would arise as to how I suggest Hiram was able to experience further consciousness after death, especially, when according to the events, he was murdered, hastily buried, exhumed, and then properly reburied.

Even further conflict would arise if taking into account that the Bible doesn't even mention anything about his death having occurred at all. However, when understanding that the Masonic account of Hiram is not to be taken in neither a historical or literal sense, but as a "beautiful system…veiled in allegory…", then can one begin to see the deeper Truth in which this legend is intended to illustrate. As it is not this essay's intent to delve into the profuse symbolisms of the Third Degree (it requiring several essays alone in order to give it its due credence), it suffices to only say in brief mentioning that the evidence of his elevated consciousness can be understood in the two symbols of the Grave and the Sprig of Acacia. These two symbols show within themselves that the raising and subsequent interment of Hiram's body was not the ending of his consciousness. For by the Sprig of Acacia, craftsmen are further reminded that there is a part of man within him "which will survive the grave, and which will never, never, never die…" This part referenced to is an allusion to the immortal Soul (symbolized in the evergreen properties of the Acacia). And if such part of man can survive the coffin of immortality to venture past this veil of existence to what lies beyond, but yet and still not be afforded consciousness that it may be cognitively aware of its own Self Being, then this would make the belief of the immortality of the Soul in Freemasonry a moot point altogether, because life without consciousness cannot be perceived, whether that be spiritual or material. When we further consider Hiram from a spiritual standpoint of the Soul, his raising halts the Soul's degradation and sets it forth upon the path to be "…conveyed as near as to the Sanctum Sanctorum as the Hebrew law would allow", (as close as to the Universal Consciousness of God that man builds his own Soul to). It marks its exodus from out of the grave of both mental and material existences on towards new and higher states of Spiritual Consciousness. As one is no longer asleep or unconsciously dead, one's Soul's consciousness no longer forgets and becomes lured unknowingly into the coffin of mental ignorances again. It retains its truths for use. A comparative example of this understanding lies in the way we build upon our previous knowledge when attempting to learn new things. Consider the Winding Staircase whose steps are hinged together to facilitate one's mental acquisitions of Truths. By the introduction and use of grammar (word formulation and its proper application), Rhetoric becomes to be formulated for drawing mental imagery that in return aids in developing one's Logical understanding. In one's next step of ascent sought for (in this case, Logical understanding), each one of the former steps previously encountered (Grammar and Rhetoric) must serve as prior supports for obtaining the next progressive step.

In symbolic terms, that which was formerly unknown before conscious discovery and obtainment, might as well have been said to been dead (as its unveiled Truths laid in the grave of one's unconsciousness before having been raised to experience it). However, when enlightenment does occur (a raised state of consciousness), it entails within its new state of understanding the conditions of two states (the past and the present) which is intended to be used to bring one closer to the summits they are aspiring for (that which lies in the future). Therefore, in this particular manner of symbolism, Logic is not only an example of Hiram being Raised to greater ascents of understanding, but also a witness to his Mastership by the other previous applications of development. This means that in our efforts of redeveloping our temples we must utilize what we've learned in our past when considering our choices today. That way we can bring about the existences of what we desire tomorrow. What is more important is that this first must be done within the spiritual aspects of the Mind ever before any physical exertion becomes to be employed(3). This is what constitutes Wisdom. Another example of the high honors in which Hiram's character merited is veiled in the monitorial catechism concerning the Lesser Lights, which reads "...as the Sun rules the day and the Moon governs the night, so should the Master rule and govern his Lodge with equal regularity... ." In this beautiful symbolism, the Sun allegorically depicts that orb of Light that facilitates one's consciousness of Truths that has been made materially visible. The Moon is depictive of that orb whose Truths lay shrouded in Darkness (the Moon not actually emitting its own light, but reflecting the Sun's light from off its surface). But when the Sun is found at high meridian, the high meridian being the apex between the two points of the Sun's rising and setting, one finds himself right back at the cardinal point and virtue associated with Hiram (this being the South and the virtue of Temperance). In this aspect of symbolism neither the Sun nor the Moon (Wisdom nor Strength) can facilitate the development of maturation independently from each other as all Sun with no Moon destroys life, and all Moon with no Sun equally destroys life. One without the other both retards growth. But when both are made to "...rule and govern with equal regularity...," the consummating results are not only Harmony, but the kind of Harmony that develops Mastership (that just, upright and perfect balance). Now, just as the Sun and the Moon are symbols of light, one that awakens the day, the other night, so could the symbolization of Hiram's raising serve as the Mind's awakening that goes forth to develop the Soul from out of the Body's Darkness. Therefore, that which comes to be reaped forth from out of the Earth as spiritual seeds are a symbolization of one's Soul's Consciousness having been mentally quickened by the Spirit. It is of considerable interest that some of the ancient schools of esoteric thought equated the full awakening of the Mind to be the full awakening of the Soul, and in this respect, the work of one was the building of the other (the Mind imprinting its designs upon the Soul). Therefore, one who works to Master their Mind, inadvertently becomes a builder of their Soul, and for such appellative purposes, could be spiritually called Hiram or a Hiramite.

ESSAY XXVIII ENDNOTES

1. Such expressions used today in such phrases as Father Time, the Father of R&B, Father of Lies, etc.

2. The name Hiram is believed by some to be Khuram or Khurum. but actually it is a corruption of the Egyptian god Heru, whose name means the Supreme One Above. It dates back to the pre-dynasty period of Kemet and Ausarian religion (Kemet being the ancient name of Egypt before the Greeks named it Egypt). Here is where we find some of the first attributes, titles and virtues being symbolized in their pantheon of gods, which were all still representations of one God depicted in many different forms to express and teach the various Truths and operations of both his Spiritual and manifested BEING.

3. This is to say that the manifestation of anything to be had must undergo an exertion of the Will within the psych of one's mental faculties until a defined picture of mental imagery is clearly formed. In this aspect of work, the evidence of a triune force is spiritually at work well before those of even a corporeal nature are.

TRANSFORMATION OF THE MIND

BY TRAER R. TISDALE

When contemplating what Freemasonry has done for me since I began my travels, I am in total agreement with all the principles and morals of this "...system of morality veiled in allegory and illustrated by symbols." The core purpose of the Craft is to "make good men better," and this has indeed been instrument in the time and energy invested in the transforming of my mind. After a life filled with many ups and downs and all kinds of trials and tribulations, I began a journey in search of Truth, not only for a desire to be removed from my past, but to also gain knowledge, wisdom, and understanding for my personal development. As a result, I've become spiritually awakened to certain levels of self awarenesses which led about to the profound purpose of my life and has since further inspired me to continue forth traveling this path of enlightenment. Being confined behind the walls of reform is pretty challenging; however, the studies of the speculative aspect of Freemasonry has made me consciously aware of the existence and inexplorable laws that governs it. Masonry has brought about peace and Truth into my life, something I never quite experienced before. In the course of my travels, I have became very fond of one of the working tools of the Craft, the

Level of the Fellow Craft's Degree. I will attempt to explain the symbolic nature of this tool and the awareness it has brought to my life, and how we as mankind could all stand to further benefit from the moral lesson it provides.

In the operative aspects of Masonry, the level is used so that one may build on an even and flat surface without deficiencies or irregularities in balance. This allows for the edifice to be parallel, all parts being equal, which creates the proper balance for the structure to be deemed sufficient for erecting labors. If we incorporate the operative aspect of this understanding in the contrasting structure of our soul edifice, this will serve as a stark reminder of how we are to build our own moral and spiritual temples before God. When looking at the level in speculative Freemasonry, we see its instructive application for use as a symbol of equality, whose idea reminds us that we are all equally level before the eyes of God and that we must all ultimately suffer the same fate regardless of one's achievements, failures or different transgressions we all sometimes suffer. Realizing that we are all bound by the same divine laws, we should therefore seek to exercise more compassion, love, kindness and forgiveness from our Creator. Regardless of one's social status, rank, achievements in life, titles, etc., we must be sure to labor harmoniously without discrimination towards each other. We must fully come to understand, that as humans in this mundane world, we are all bound by the same irrefutable laws of God as siblings born from one Almighty Parent and that we are inhabitants of the same world who are to aid, support, and protect each other. This is what Jesus Christ exemplified during his reign, he himself showing no partiality in his faith practice and display of love to his fellowman. This divine law is so transparent in Galatians 3: 27-29, wherein it reads: "There is neither Jew or Gentile, neither slave or free, nor is there male or female, For you are all one in Christ Jesus" (this verse serving also as the Proclamation to our Order). In a time where we have became so completely divided with our various walks of life, our opposing social views and multitude of faith practices, is it even possible that we could ever come to agree to disagree? How is it that God, the Almighty, the All Knowing, All Seeing, came down to dwell amongst men, revealing himself in his many forms of glory upon this earthly level of existence, but we in return, as mere humans, refuse to meet each other on this same level. We judge each other's transgressions upon the uncalibrated scales of our own self righteousness. We rather live in hate instead of love, we discriminate because of racial or political views and reasons, or because our belief systems are not in alignment with another's. We stifle the true spirit of brotherhood by consistently denying each other the rights and equalities given to mankind as one family under God. These acts of spiritual fratricide only continues to divide us more and more. There's a saying that "A house that is divided, is a house that won't stand." The earth is symbolic of this house and we are the sole tenants of its establishment. So while we are here for this brief time God allows, we should regard each other as divine beings upon this level of earthly plane, whose duty is to construct the spiritual temple accordingly. No matter how stained our moral character is, was, or has become, we have the ability and choice to improve ourselves through life's experiences. This improvement can only be done according to one's own life experiences underwent, and should not come at the expense of being judged before the eyes of each other. That is solely the duty of God. What we learn in life, whether good or bad, is actually good for us. This is part of the journey we are placed here to endure before we eventually return home from whence we came. While convened here, we should he careful not to dismiss or judge a person as being unworthy or unequal when we must all stand parallel before the God of all Truth to give an account of our own actions. The laws of karma are always at work, and every man will indeed reap what he sows. The reason I sit in prison is because of the ignorance I lived in. In hindsight, I see how unconscious I really was, and how I had no sense of direction in life. It has been said by the working of these karmic laws that I've had to accept the measure of my own dealings in accordance to those things which I've sown. However, it has been through the transformation of my mind that I have come to be removed from that ignorance and have come to find serenity even with my circumstances. This transformation is what now guides my positive steps in being a better thinker, a better man, a better son, a better friend, a better brother. As an incarcerated man, I've been stripped of my social status in the world by being deprived of my own civil liberties, so I am now viewed as someone unequal, unworthy in which many in society see my transgressions as something I can never be redeemed from. However, I have learned that the perfect man is not a man who makes no mistakes, but rather the man who displays the ability to learn, grow, and change from his mistakes. His ability makes him spiritually Divine rather than materially perfect. When a man has taken the necessary tools to correct himself internally, the evidence of this change will eventually come to spring forth. Who are we then to say that one is unequal or unworthy of redemption, when we find that we all have been equally afforded these same abilities by our Creator for the uses of our development. In this respects, as it reads in Roman 3:20, and 23, "Therefore by the deeds of the law there shall no flesh be justified in his sight: for by the law is the knowledge of sin...For all have sinned, and have come short of the glory of God." This means that I , nor any other human being can claim immunity from sin error, mistakes, misfortunes, or any of the various dilemmas of life that we may encounter. The fact that we are all subject to the same effects of life's follies and pitfalls reminds us in the emblem of the level that no sin, or man is greater than the other before the eyes of God, and that no one's worldly possessions or material achievements in life will serve to gain them admittance into the eternal heavens. The only thing that ascends when we perish is the soul of the person, another proof that we are equally created before God.

Even though I reside in a place where the culture has long been established to view those in positions of authority as the enemy, and vice versa, I am now able to see people for who they really are as both human and spiritual beings. By the level I am reminded to be constantly aware of my duty to all mankind in treating them with the same unconditional love and compassion, regardless of their position, civil status, rank, or authority, to consider the internal nature of men instead of their external. It is imperative that we understand that when traveling upon this brief time in our physical existence, that God only considers the spiritual entity that dwells within all of us. We should have this concept close to our minds and hearts in our everyday interactions, not only with our fellow brothers, but with all mankind. This will help us to lay aside any detrimental thoughts of the mind, and plant the seed of love and compassion in our hearts, so that the true nature of our existence and intention God had in mind when he created us may come into fruition. In truth everybody and everything in the universe is connected, and this is a fundamental truth that renders us all equal under the laws established. All short comings in life entails valuable lessons within them, but you must make the conscious effort to extract the corrective understanding from them for their developing use. I have come to discover that my time has become my greatest asset, and it serves me a great purpose as I am now able to put things in proper perspective in my everyday dealings with others. As a man who is paying back his debt to society under the karmic Laws, I take pride in freeing myself mentally from all of the vices and superfluities of life. This gives birth to the true me. Once I am able to bring my mind, body, and soul into Harmony, I will have achieved redemption through God, and this is what my mission in prison has become. I solely believe Masonry has indeed made me a better man in both my thinking and actions. I believe the determination of what makes a man really free is not evident in his incarcerated body, but in the liberation of his mind. Man may lock away the body, but he can never lock away the mind. To me this is the true meaning of being "freeborn," not in a physical aspect, but in a mental. This divine right is a choice equally given to all mankind to exercise. It is up to every individual to ask, seek, and knock, so that he may uncover the hidden mysteries that lies within himself and become aware of his own self essence.

Masonry is a unique fraternal order, bringing men of every rank and walk of life together as men at one altar where they can talk and not fight, discuss and not dispute, and all be able to learn the point of view of his fellow man. We remove any hostility that arises from social, political or religious differences. The only way of Masonry is wise in it's beauty, its speculative lessons being concrete in the proper development of that "... house made not with hands." This is the universality that I have found that Masonry incorporates and it is the reason why I pursue the knowledge that Masonry has to offer, because I believe that if this divine concept can be revived into society, we can create a healthy environment for all human beings to dwell in.

In closing, consider Ecclesiastes 3:19-20: "Surely the fate of human beings is like that of the animal; the same fate awaits them both. As one dies so does the other. All have the same breath: humans have no advantage over animals. Everything is meaningless. All go to the same place, all come from the dust, and to the dust all return."Let this verse serve as a basic reminder of how we are to see both the world and each other at large, remembering that it is God in whom we all serve and are erecting our temples to. No matter our faith, social or political differences, we all come from the same place, and from that same place we shall return. Staying mindful of this verse will humbly redirect the focus of our constructive efforts to its proper source while traveling upon this level of time, so when that ultimate day of judgement comes, and we stand before God, we will all be accordingly judged by the faith and works of the spirit and not by the failings and shortcomings of our material bodies. I am thankful to have come into contact with like minded brothers, who are all on the same path of transforming and redeeming themselves from that rude and imperfect nature we are all subject to.

May God bless all those who've had the opportunity to read this, along with any works of the Universal Order of Craftsmen. May all your travels towards the Light of the East serve to cultivate within your souls the Spirit of Brotherly Love, Relief and Truth.

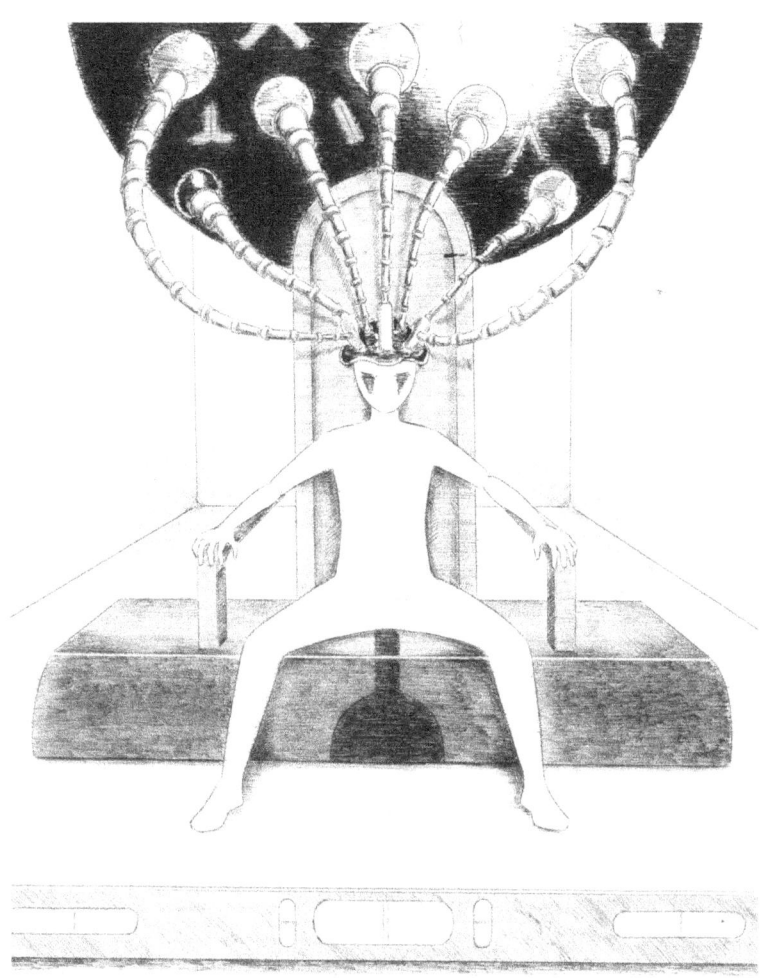

LIFE IS AN ART, LIVING LIFE IS AN ARTIST

(contemplative thoughts of Minh Du)

Mother Nature provides us with every necessity of life, many which we simply take for granted. How many people stop to give thanks for the oxygen they breathe? The delicate softness of air that blankets the earth envelops us like a mother's warming arms genuinely holding her first born. We are living and breathing right now because of that exquisite warmth found in the designs of mother nature's embrace. How and when did we ever become too busy to appreciate its divine presence? I am thankful that God's love is unconditionally good even when we are not. The Blazing Star will never stop to emit its burning heat for the immortal souls of the living just because we fail to give it its due attention, nor does its light ever becomes any less dimmer when veiled behind the murky curtains of the clouded canopy.

Creation varies in colors and designs filled up with the light of divine providence to light up the void within itself. This fabulous and marvelous architect is the fantastic spectrum between black and white from out of nothingness. From the dawn of the soul's awakening, it was realized that the universe could have no light if there was no darkness; therefore, this Magnificent Designer painted into existence the portrait of Creation and gave all things consciousness, and with that, its living purpose. Living that purpose is living life. One gives the other meaning. This truth is revealed to those whose discovered that life's operations of heaven and earth are actually the operations of themselves.

Every living organism in the world, down to its smallest molecular atom are all connected to each other like a strong chain link of a bicycle. If one link becomes missing, the propulsion work of the bike becomes vain. The Grand Architect of the Universe has designed creation perfectly perfect so that each individual entity has its own purpose in playing an equally important role in life as a series of links stably bound to each other. As one chain, they generate the Force of the Almighty to pull the whole universe. The wheel of life slowly turns to uncover the splendid treasures which lay hidden within the nature of ourselves. We need only to open our eyes and truly see them.

Masonry, whose ancient and sacred practice of being "...a system of morality, veiled in allegory and illustrated by symbols," helps me to awaken my consciousness to see these beautiful truths. As a manga artist, Freemasonry has enabled me to draw aside the shadowy curtains to allow my spirit to be absorbed in the quantum energy of the universal flow of life. I look at life through art, and from art I perceive life. From the moment the sun rises until darkness blankets the earth, I lay down ink upon white slim pieces of trees to express my thoughts and truths to the world. What a lovely feeling when I capture the beauty of things concealed to most. Beauty is in the eyes of the beholder, and Freemasonry and art are strands of that same DNA in that they both allow the mind to be free by submerging it down to the bottom depths of the golden ocean of wisdom. Here is where I can become engulfed in the calm and soothing currents of Love.

Living life is living love. Some love to write, sing, work, or teach, others draw, heal, design, or create. These million different propensities are the purposes that makes us linked as one bicycle chain that forms a strong and balanced society. If one link is out of alignment while pulling, stress will occur until a link becomes broken. So in order to maximize the chain's strength to empower the world, we must learn and understand life's balance. Not everyone else's balance, but the balancing strength and weaknesses of our own life links. This automatically creates equanimity for the whole in the chain's work of propulsion.

Do what you love, and love what you do in the harmoniousness of life. Then you will find yourself among the eternal realms of heaven's passions and desires, your consciousness being universally synced with every single tick tock moment of time. When we are not loving, we are unconsciously being a chain link of resistance that does not operate in the circling rotation of life. When this happens, that tick tock clock of the soul's experience becomes the moment of a created hell.

All purposes possess both the spectrums of black and white, a gift and curse. I experience this after having submerged myself so long within the depths of the abstract while drawing that I had became mentally detached and despondent from immediate life around me. When this occurred, I realized I no longer loved what I was doing even though I had been doing what I loved.

Experience has taught me that truly living always require balance. This is hard for the conscious, and even harder for the unconscious. The hoodwink keeps the mortal blissfully dead. They take in the oxygen of creation, but do not breathe the air of life. They digest the food of the earth, but not its spiritual nutrition. They bask in the rays of light, but never feel the glory of it's illumination. In order to fully comprehend the universal purpose of life, we must first balance ourselves in order to feel the balance of all things around us. We are Life and Life is Us. Both are dependent upon each other. So why do we treat the life in our fellow man with irreverence, hate, and imbalance? Is it because we harbor hate, lack reverence, and have no balance within the nature of ourselves?

Are we created in the image and likeness of God? If so, then we are some cruel and abusive lords, the evidence found in the wreckage of our doings. Trash, oil, and plastic are fed into our ocean waters until they are vomited back up upon the laps of our shores. Emission gases, smog, and all sorts of toxins fill the clouds like crack pipes of smoke waiting for mankind to take its hit. We artificially inseminate the womb of mother earth with genetically modified seeds. For what? So we can induce labor to sacrifice her offsprings to our untempered bellies faster. We eat from the troughs of greed while simultaneously lamenting tears over heart diseases, high blood pressure, and other illnesses resulting from obesity. Once momentarily filled, we then politically debate with slander over legislations concerning health care cost and rising medical insurance only to return to the trough like a dog to his vomit. What perfect imbalance! We treat the earth like we treat each other, and we treat each other like we treat the earth. While mother earth applies the healing sage of natural disasters to recalibrate life, we work twice as hard to rub it out with imbalanced living. Things that do not live in balance to itself will not serve as a harmonious balance to another. Therefore, it must be removed from the operations of life as feces is removed from the bowels. Death is nature's natural laxative, and even this has a purpose. To live life with this understanding is understanding life to be lived.

Anchors up for the man who embarks upon the voyage of life, who sets forth to sail the turbulent and yet glorious seas of Eternal Beauty. For all is not amiss. The horizons of Heaven are ever beyond the bow. I have stood upon the decks and beheld the sceneries of life's unfolding canvas and have drawn, projecting myself to share in the same essence of the Creator's joy when He Himself first began to paint upon the trestle-board of existence. It is here, in these suspended moments in time, that with every inhalation of breath, I exhale the manifestation of art. I am one with the creative Spirit, and like the Big Bang of creation, I begin to form galaxies and universes.

All men are creators who have became conscious of their own living purposes, who has discovered the balance between the power of their minds and the true art of living that power in purpose. The seed of a mind's idea is that spark of light that sets life into motion. The moment that spark ignites up the infinite space of our celestial minds, the intense and bright combustion of thought follows, and then the spiritualization of light, and then consciousness, and then manifestation. Scientists report that the Big Bang was caused by two God particles of life having came together. Is this the same workings of the left and right side of our brains interacting with each other to create a thought? What fantastic and immense power! From a spark to whole universes, to galaxies and supernovas, to stars and planets, to the existence of me. Indeed I AM. What an amazing Grand Architect of the Universe to allow man to become Universal Craftsmen of the Temple.

Life is an art that's beautifully illustrated above, below, around, and most of all, within. It has been painted not for external pursuit, but for internal discovery. The road that leads to this discovery is called Truth. The vehicle is Life. The chain of propulsion is Love. Enjoy the sceneries of Life's travels. It's not so much about getting to the destination that you should persue. This is inevitable, But it is the understanding of all the points that gets you to that destination that you should focus on. That way you will never become lost again. Allow the soul to Be, to draw from Life all around it in its experiences. In doing so, you will discover the real truths of life and the understanding of why I say Life Is An Art...But Living Life Is An Artist.

Universal Craftsmen

Universal Craftsmen

GLOSSARY

AARON---The 1st Levitical High Priest of the Hebrews, as recorded in the book of Genesis. The brother of Moses and Miriam who served as Moses's interpreter and voice in discussions with Pharaoh concerning the Hebrew's release from Egypt, it being written that Moses was slow in speech (Exodus 4:10-16).

ABLUTION---Another name for lustration.

ADYTUM---The most sacred part of a shrine or temple, usually reserved for the highest ranking priest in ancient times. It is synonymous with the Sanctum Sanctorum and equivalent to the Holy of Holies of the Jewish Tabernacle and Temple.

ALCHEMY---A philosophical practice, and at one point in the Renaissance period, a practiced chemistry where a universal solvent and its method for transmuting various base metals into gold along with experimental researches for an elixir to life was pursued.

ANTHROPOMORPHIC---The attributings of humanistic characteristics or bodily features to a deity. An example is when one say "..the mighty hand of God."

ANUNIAN---Pertaining to the ancient city of Anu and their religious belief system of gods. The name of this city was called Heliopolis by the Greeks.

BAPTISM---A ritualistic ceremony notably performed among Christian faith practices, where water immersion of a new convert is conducted to symbolically convey both their purification and birth into a new life under the dictates and principles of Jesus Christ.

BEARERS OF BURDENS---A term found in 2nd Chronicles 2:2, which came to be regarded as 70,000 Entered Apprentices in some of the older Masonic monitors. In Hebrew it is translated as ish sabal.

BRUTE---A descriptive condition of a stone in its initial and rough state before the works of hewing has began. A term synonymous with rough ashlar.

CABLE TOW---A chain, rope, or cable used for hoisting and moving heavy objects from one point to another.

CAPSTONE---It is the last stone set in place upon the highest point in the construction of a dome or a cathedral-like temple or building which usually marks the completion of its development. The setting of the Capstone in King Solomon's Temple was accompanied with a solemn and most extravagant dedication offering followed by a two week long celebration.

CASTE WORKERS---An employed system of workers who are socially grouped and then divided by either their economical, religious, or occupational skill sets and statuses. In most instances, especially in remote times, such caste distinctions, along with their certain privileges, were determined by blood lines (the Levitical priesthood being an example of such).

CATECHISM---Instructions or lessons administered in the form of questions and answers which are used in some cases to determine proficiency in the lectures.

CHARGES---The instructions read to the candidate that outlines some of the specific duties and rules of his conduct as a Freemason of that particular degree.

CIRCUMAMBULATION---To travel in a circuit or circular manner.

CIRCUMSPECTION---Careful and prudent observation. It is the watchful consideration, assessment, and wise analysis of conditions, places, circumstances, or things which assists one in the course of action they seek to proceed or perhaps not proceed in.

COEVAL---To occur alongside of in the same time period in history.

CORNERSTONE---In an operative sense of stonemasonry, it is the stone that is placed at the corner of the building structure, the first usually laid in the Northeast corner. It is hollow and deposited with items of honor and sentimental value dedicated by either the builders or owner. It may also possess writings and commemorative signatures on it publicizing its purpose, date of dedication and erecting cause, and is often accompanied with ceremonial honors upon laying.

CORNUCOPIA---A symbol of abundance.

COSMOLOGICAL---Pertaining to the studies of astronomy, its evolution and laws of structure and the various hypothesis of space's first developing formation.

DARKNESS---A symbolization of ignorance and falsehood. It also represents that which is hidden and obscure from consciousness or sight.

DRUID---A high priesthood order believed by some to have been the early habitants of the British Isle and Gaul. Many conjectural ideas and suppositions have been attributed to them out of a lack of written records. It is held that the cairns of Stonehenge may have been one of the sites of their religious worship.

DIVINE SPARK---The soul essence of man that constitutes the core of his Being.

DIURNAL MOTION---The earth's rotation upon its own axis around the Sun that gives the appearance that the Sun is moving in a circular orbit around the earth. Because of such viewpoint from earth, the beginning and ending appearances of the Sun looks as if it's rising and setting.

DIVINE LAW---It is the acting and all pervading force that regulates all seen and unseen life. It is so interwoven in the fabric of creation that if it was somehow able to withdraw itself from life, all aspects of creation would cease to exist. Some say it was instituted by God with the decree of Light in the Book of Genesis, 1st Chapter 3rd Verse, while others contend that it always was, and that it constitutes the self existing nature of God Himself.

DROSS---Needless and excessive matter. Accumulated rubbish that covers or hides the beauty and worth of an object.

E.A.---An acronym for Entered Apprentice. A Mason of this degree.

EPHOD---A beautiful vestment worn by the High Priest of the Jews that had the names of the twelve tribes of Israel engraved upon its breastplate with a particular gem stone assigned to each. It was commanded to be worn by Aaron when entering into the Tabernacle, it being his responsibility as the High Priest to "...bear the judgement of the children of Israel upon his heart before the Lord continually."

ESOTERIC---The inner or concealed nature of a thing. The knowledge or understanding of something which is privy to those who've undergone initiation or proper explanation, compared to that which perhaps is commonly known or openly available to the public at large, which is then regarded as exoteric.

EVOLUTION---Pertaining to both the post and ongoing process of development that leads to formation by means of progressive adaption of its conditions.

F.C.---An acronym for Fellow Craft. A Mason of this degree.

FOUNDATION STONE---A stone mentioned in the writings of the Talmud whose lore found its incorporation in the Select Master's Degree which gives an account of its deposit.

FREEBORN/FREE MAN---One of the requisite qualifications for petitioners seeking candidacy that stems from the Ancient Charges.

T.G.A.O.T.U.---An acronym for The Grand Architect Of The Universe. A descriptive appellation for God among Masons.

GRAND EAST---It symbolically represents the Grand Lodge, which serves as a provisional source of Masonic Light and instructions for all subordinate Lodges under that particular obedience (jurisdiction). In a macrocosmic aspect, it represents the Divine Creator from which the provisional source of all Life and Light emanates.

GREAT WORK---A term of the Rosicrucian Society that expresses the overall regenerative work of establishing the various levels of consciousness. It entails the labor of transmuting the lower base passions of Self in order to bring about that illumination that constitutes the harmonious Oneness between the Soul of man and God's Universal Spirit.

GROUND FLOOR---A term used in Freemasonry to symbolically express the ground floor of King Solomon's Temple on Mt. Moriah where the temple was built (it formerly being a threshing floor owned by Ornan the Jebusite).

HOODWINK---In its most simplistic explanation, it is a blindfold that's used to prohibit sight. To be hoodwinked, but not literally blindfolded, is being incapable of recognizing what is evident or what is transpiring before you.

HERMETIC/HERMETIC RITES---Pertaining to the practices taught by various societies and orders ascribing to the beliefs and teachings of Hermes Trismegistus who is identified by some as being the Egyptian god Thoth.

HIEROPHANT---A term used in ancient Greece to describe the instructors who were directly responsible for the teaching and explanations of the initiatory rites of their particular wisdom school.

HEWN/HEWING---A process of shaping a stone by cutting, chopping, or sanding away all excess and irregularities in order to achieve a desired state of size, shape, or condition for its intended use in structural placement.

INTROSPECTION---To internally examine and consider one's own mental, emotional and moral states of being.

INVESTITURE---The presentation of the Mason's apron, or any other honorary clothing or regalia that comes to be given to a newly made initiate, convert, or graduate of a school, society, or officiating position of some sort.

JORDAN---A 200 mile long river extending from South Lebanon through the Sea of Galilee and further along through Israel and West Jordan which then empties into the Dead Sea. It is biblically noted for such events as the Israelite's crossing prior to their siege of Canaan, the events concerning Jephthah and the Ephraimites, and also the many baptisms that occurred there, especially those pertaining to John the Baptist, Jesus Christ and his disciples.

KABBALAH---A school in which students are instructed in the mystical, philosophical, and metaphysical interpretations of the Hebrew scriptures. It is said to be extremely enigmatic, even having their own particular system of interpreting scriptures.

LANDMARK---A time immemorial custom, practice, or belief that has came to be regarded as an immovable bulwark, standard, or sign post for perpetual observance or adherence. Something, someone, or the occurrence of an event that serves to mark and thenceforth establish an ongoing precedent of action.

LIGHT---A symbolization of knowledge, truth and wisdom. In one aspect, it represents the nature of God. From a moral and philosophical aspect, it represents good. From a metaphysical aspect, it represents the conscious awakening of life materially and spiritually.

LEVEL---A working tool of Speculative Freemasonry derived from the Operative stonemason's trade used to establish a flat surface or foundation that's of equal grade. It speculatively teaches equality towards mankind, irrespective of power, money or social status. It teaches that mankind is of one common species who are all subject to the same conditions of life.

LUX---The Latin word for light. It is found in various mottoes such as Lux e Tenebris, which means Light out of Darkness, and Fiat Lux, which means Let there Be Light.

M.M.---An acronym for Master Mason. A Mason of this degree.

MACROCOSM---The grand totality of the world and its operations. It is the fullest and greatest embodiment of the entire Universe, all that's seen and unseen.

METAPHYSICAL---Pertaining to such studies of science involving abstract thought that's not necessarily based on concrete evidence, but rather upon those theoretical and scientific hypothesis involving ontology, causality and existence, and the philosophical principles of truth and being.

MICROCOSM---Anything that depicts the operations and likenesses of the world or universe, but in a small or miniature embodiment.

MITHRAISM---One of the practices in which some have referred to as the Ancient Mysteries, and others, Ancient Religions. It was regarded as one of the practices of both the Hindu and Persians of earlier times (prior to Zoroastrianism and Brahmanism). Mithra, the god of light, was regarded as their deity of worship. Some of the doctrines pertaining to this particular god can be found in the writings of the Zend, Avesta, and Vedas.

MONITOR---Manuals issued by the Grand Lodges of each state jurisdiction where the moral precepts, lessons, and instructions in the degrees are afforded to their subordinate Lodges, versus the various esoteric aspects that are not committed to writing.

MYSTIC TIE---A term used in former times as a designation of the Craft (Brethren of the Mystic Tie), which was descriptive of the Divine indissoluble bond of Friendship and Love that exists among the brothers of the fraternity.

NEOPHYTE---A candidate who has became an initiate or convert of a religion where he begins to learn the given instructions and lessons pertaining to its beliefs.

OBEISANCE---An act of homage which denotes respect and submission of oneself over to another as in the example of bowing, or kneeling before a king.

OBLIGATIONS---The sacred oath administered and taken by the candidate of his respective degree which outlines his moral duties and responsibilities as a practitioner.

ORACLE---In one sense, it represents the sacred placing where divine instructions or revelations are given by either a priest or priestess, who serves as a medium between a particular deity and the people, the Oracle of Apollo at the city of Delphi being a notable example. It is believed that sorcery and divinations were involved in the invocations of such deities in these oracles. In another sense, this word (as used in the biblical text of 1st Kings, 6th Chapter, 9th -23rd verse) represents the Holy of Holies within King Solomon's Temple, the same location as the Sanctum Sanctorum.

OPERATIVE MASONRY---A term used to designate the workings of the actual stonemason's trade in contradistinction to Freemasonry which is regarded as a speculative practice.

ORDER OF THE EASTERN STAR---An adoptive order that's widely comprised of the wives, daughters, mother's, and sisters of Freemasons. It was formerly known as Adoptive Masonry and also Female Masonry. It was termed Adoptive as it was recognized by the Grand Bodies of Freemasonry. Although not Masonic in the same nature, it no less inculcates the same principles of Truth and Morality found in keeping with those taught to the men of Freemasonry in which its own ritualistic designs, rites, and allegorical expressions beautifully expresses.

ORIENTATION---Masonically, it is the particular manner in which a Lodge is situated.

OMNIPOTENT---All Powerful. An attribute most often used to describe the range or amount of God's power.

OMNIPRESENT---All Existing. An attribute depictive of the nature of God being everywhere simultaneously.

OMNISCIENT---All Knowing. An attribute pertaining to God's possession of all knowledge.

PLUMB---A working tool of Speculative Freemasonry derived from the Operative stonemason's trade which is said to establish the true perpendicularity in the erecting of walls. Achieving a straight up and down state without any deviations to the right or left is what is termed plumb. Speculatively, it teaches the craftsmen the rectitude of life.

PRIMORDIAL---The earliest developing origins of existences and creation.

PROPITIOUS---Actions intended to incur favor or appeasement.

PURIFICATION RITES---A ceremonial practice that involves the cleansing of candidates, priests, temple workers and their ceremonial tools, either by water or oil. When performed as part of an initiation rite, it symbolically conveys the death and rebirth of one's mind. It is performed both as reverence and as a symbolization of the pure and undefiled state of character or condition in which one is to approach God in worship and fellowship.

PYTHAGORAS---A Greek philosopher who founded a wisdom school in Samos Greece. He is most notable for his use of numbers and mathematical formulas in conveying his esoteric lessons.

RELIEF---One of the tenets of Freemasonry that entails not only the aspects of financial assistance and philanthropic donations to various organizations in need, but also the dispensing of aid in its various intangible form that can never be monetarily valued or assessed.

RITE---A ceremony often conducted in a ritualistic manner whose meaning and purposes are intended to leave a significant impression upon the person undergoing such.

S.D.---An acronym for Senior Deacon. A Masonic officer.

SANCTUM SANCTORUM---A place within the Tabernacle and Temple called the Holy of Holies which was regarded as the most sacred area of worship and communion with God. The High Priest was usually the only one permitted entry, and even then, only once a year on Yom Kippur, the Day of Atonement.

SEPHIROTHS---Eleven Emanations of Life shown depicted as spheres (10 seen and 1 unseen), which are taught within the Kabbalah system to symbolize the Tree of Life. Their taught explanations are said to consist of the spiritual and esoteric understanding of creation, life and some say the temple of man.

SHEKINAH GLORY---Among Jewish believers, it was considered to be a representation and sign of the manifesting presence of the glory of God made visible on earth.

SOUL REGENERATION---It is the redemptive process of the Life essence of man by moral and spiritual rebirth that brings about a change in thoughts, feelings and behavior. Such words as reconstruction and re-creation are all synonymous terms (to some degree another), that convey this same understanding of reestablishing something to a whole or better state of condition.

SPECULATIVE---The works of mental and spiritual contemplation for purposes of obtaining insight into abstract Truths and Wisdoms. It is one's consciousness of not only the aspects of Self, but also of the governing laws of creation and one's interrelationship with it.

SQUARE---A working tool of Speculative Freemasonry derived from the Operative stonemason's trade. Operatively its used to achieve 90 degree right angles upon the corners of a stone. Speculatively it teaches one to square their actions with the square of morality, approaching the angles of one's thinking and actions with righteousness and exactitude in all their executions.

THEOLOGICAL The virtues of Faith, Hope, and Charity. Although they are found within the designs of Freemasonry, they derive from 1st Corinthians, Chapter 13.

TILER---A Masonic officer responsible for the prevention of unlawful entry or intrusion into the Lodge.

TRANSFIGURATION---The supernatural change of appearance and form into that of an exalted or glorified nature.

TRANSLITERATION---To assign the alphabet letters of a word from one language to its corresponding alphabet sound of another language.

TRANSMUTATION---The process of changing a base substance into a different and better one altogether. Its practice is notably mentioned in the teachings of the Rosicrucian Society which instructs its students in how to change the lower based passions of their lower natured selves to one of higher refinement in spirituality. Doing so under the taught principles of Alchemy and the Divine Law is what is symbolically understood to be changing lead into gold (an expression in former times that came to be misunderstood by the uninstructed as being literal).

TRANSUBSTANTIATION---A practice in which the significance of a thing is believed to have been transferred upon or onto another thing or person by the rites of ceremonial consecrations and invocations of deity, an example being the bread of the Eucharist.

URIM AND THUMMIN---Two stones (some say metals) found upon the High Priest's breastplate whose uses are not quite definitively certain, but are believed to have been employed for oracular purposes by the High Priest in receiving various instructions and decisions pertaining to the nation of Israel and God. The words Urim and Thummin in Hebrew means Lights.

V.I.T.R.I.O.L.---An acronym whose Latin meaning is Vista Interiora Terrace Rectificando Invenies Ocultum Lapidem, which roughly translates to mean, Visit the Interior of the Earth and by Purification Discover the Occult Stone.

VOLUME OF THE SACRED LAW---Commonly written as the V.S.L. It constitutes the sacred writings of religion in which the candidate becomes to be obligated upon. The particular use of a V.S.L. varies with each candidate's own particular faith practice.

REFERENCES AND BIBLIOGRAPHY

The following is a list of various publications that were used as study aids in drafting these essays. Some are quite old, but are still excellent reads for obtaining insight into the Masonic knowledge and understanding that was once considered in those times. In reading these, I have presented some of the views found in keeping with my own research and personal understandings arrived at. However, it should be kept in mind the era in which some of these authors were writing in, and how, with the ever Eastward travels towards the Light, greater clarity and revelatory understanding in Truth has since came to be offered.

Contemplative Masonry, Basic Applications of Mindfulness, Meditation, and Imagery For The Craft---C.R. Dunning Jr.
The Mysticism of Masonry---R. Swinburne Clymer, M.D.
The Royal Arch, Its Hidden Meaning---George H. Steinmetz
Lectures On Masonic Symbolism And A Second Lecture on Symbolism of the Omkara And Other Ineffable Words---Albert Pike
Coil's Masonic Encyclopedia---Henry Wilson Coil
African Religion Vol. 1 Anunian Theology---Dr. Muata Ashby
African Dionysus, From Egypt To Greece---Dr. Muata Ashby
The Symbolism of Freemasonry---Albert G. Mackey
After Death, The Immortality of Man---Paschal Beverly Randolph
The New Strong's Concise Dictionary of The Words in The Hebrew Bible---James Strong L.L.D., S.T.D.
A Comparison of English Symbols With The Hebrew Bible---Friedrich Portal
Lessons In Capital Masonry---Charles P. Hunt
The Theocratic Philosophy of Freemasonry---Rev. George Oliver
Stellar Theology and Masonic Astronomy---Robert Hewitt Brown
Lexicon of Freemasonry---Albert G. Mackey
Holy Bible, Authorized Version
From Babylon To Timbuktu---Rudolph Windsor
Valley of The Dry Bones---Rudolph Windsor
Dictionary of Symbols---Jean Chevalier And Alain Gheerbrant
Restorations of Masonic Geometry and Symbolry---Henry Bromwell
The Builder---Joseph Fort Newton
Stolen Legacy---George G.M. Jones

Morals and Dogma---Albert Pike

Secret Teachings of All Ages---Manly P. Hall

Historical Landmarks, Volumes I and II---Rev. George Oliver

All monitorial quotes in this work are derivative of Malcolm C. Duncan- which doesn't necessarily reflect the monitorial standard of all Grand Lodges and their jurisdictional subordinates (each having their own).

Pages from the author's upcoming work, titled:

AND THE MORAL OF THE STORY IS...

Why can't he see? This was a question that came to mind the other day when I saw this fellow inmate going to the storebox for ten dollars worth of hygiene items. Sadly it was not even an hour after he had just gotten paid and had left from going to the commissary himself. He does this every week like clock work. He has a real bad gambling habit, so even when he wins, he looses, because he still has to pay out his winnings to those he borrowed the money from. For him the house is everybody, and the house is always winning. And by the way, if you're wondering what a storebox is, it's a penitentiary word for someone who personally lends another commissary items at an interest rate until they are able to pay it back. Actually, it's not a bad service. It's quite convenient for a person who may have just dropped their toothbrush in the toilet and stands in need of a replacement, or for a person whose pen has just ran out of ink in the middle of writing their letter. But for a person enslaved by an addiction, it's the beginning down a slippery road of perpetual debt that often results in conflict. Well sure enough, not even two weeks after that particular loan, this poor fellow caught a serious beat down from trying to dodge one of the guys he owed. Now, you would think that this would have been enough to awaken him to some needed lifestyle changes. Well, it wasn't. Because not even after three days of this whole ordeal, he was right back at it again, which unbelievably led once again to another fight. I don't think the swelling had even gone down in his left eye, before the right one was made shut. I was totally blown away! What's the matter with this guy? Why does he keep doing this to himself? Can't he see the signs? But before I could even finish my thought, a voice came to me and said "Why couldn't you see yours? Maybe if you had, you wouldn't be here criticizing what he's doing." The silence in my ear was deafening.

Why is it we're easily able to see another person's flaws, vices or circumstances, but not clearly our own until it's too late. After choking down some humble pie, I really contemplated this question. I finally came to its answer by remembrance of a story that had been told to me a while back by an older fellow named Soldier. Exactly where he heard it from, or whether it was true, I'm not quite sure, but it serves now to remind me of my own deep seated passions that I allow to unconsciously influence my decisions. Therefore, I share this story as Soldier shared it with me.

There was a breed of wolves in Alaska that was terrorizing the local villages and killing off a great number of their livestock. These wolves were most allusively sneaky and cunning, and despite the best efforts of the locals, they just couldn't seem to capture them. One day, after all seemed hopeless, they were given some information about a famed trapper who they were told could possibly help them. Having been contacted and told about the situation, he sure enough agreed to meet with them. He explained to them that he was quite familiar with this type of wolf and that if left unchecked, they would eventually overpopulate and kill the entire village. Out of concern he agreed to show them how they could get rid of them all by showing them first how to kill the pack leader. He started first by retrieving a long butcher's knife and began sharpening it until its edges on both sides were super thin as razors. He then went out and slit the throats of several chickens and drained their blood into a small pale. He then proceeded to dip the blade into the pale and placed it in ice until it had frozen. Afterwards, he removed it from the ice and immediately placed it back into the pale of blood once again. He kept doing this until the blade developed into a small like glacier. He then went out into the woods and pushed the knife hilt down into the snowy ground and then waited. Later that night the wolf caught wind of the fresh chicken blood in the air and was instinctively drawn to it. After cautiously approaching, he looked around and began to slowly lick it. As he was licking it, the warmth of his tongue began to melt the ice and he could taste the rich saltiness of the iron which drove him mad with pleasure. His eyes rolled in the back of his head as he slowly closed them in sheer delight. He couldn't help but lap faster, all the while not even conscious of the glinting edges of the blade that had started to protrude through. The more he licked, the more blood filled his belly and the more he became ecstatically satisfied with what he thought to be chicken's blood. As he kept on lapping, he never realized that it was not only his own blood that he was drinking, but that it was the ice numbing his would be pain that made him unaware of the blade's cuts. Inevitably, it was not long before the wolf became weak and slowly prostrated before the icicle and died. And The Moral of this Story Is...Don't Allow Your Own Passions To Be What Kill You.

I revert back to that question that I was asking myself that day. Why is it that we are able to see other people's signs of pending danger, vices, or problems, but not so easily our own? What blinds us from seeing ourselves?. It is the effects of our own personal passions that dulls our senses (which in return decreases our awarenesses), and much like the wolf, our over indulgences suspends us in a state of gratification to the point that it makes us unconsciously complacent and lethargic to all of the existing signs around us. It does so until it traps and then destroys us. The same way the wolf was no longer able to differentiate between his own blood and that of the chicken's, is the same way that we become no longer able to differentiate between what's good and what's bad for ourselves. We can't see that it is our own unrestrained passions that is actually serving as our poison. Our faculties becomes so distortedly conditioned to perceive only that which culminates in achieving self gratification, that it blocks anything that poses a threat in preventing its obtainment. It's a defense mechanism, and if not deliberately brought under subjection by a reconstructed mind, it will operate for its own self interest, even unto its own demise. This is why the reconstructing of one's thinking is so critical to our redevelopment. It disrupts the brain's path of energy pattern, and by redirecting it, it challenges the faculties to formulate new and different perceptions. This is the key to changing any and every undesirable habit, whether food, cigarettes, alcohol, drugs, sex, video games, T.V...any passion that has became a stronghold in one's life. It matters not the vice.

So how many times must a person bump his head before they consider their choices and begin to change? The answer is, as many times as it takes for them to get it (hoping all along they do so before they destroy themselves or possibly others). In the case of the compulsive gambler, it may be many more black eyes and swollen lips, or possibly something worse. I hope this isn't the case, but the truth is that life serves some costly lessons in which many have paid high prices in learning. In this aspect, I believe the Divine Law spares no expenses when instructing her students. Some of the greatest truths of man's self discovery has came by way of some of the most greatest tragedies. Furthermore, once we do learn our lesson, this doesn't necessarily mean the black eye will just up and disappear. The matter of correcting the previous mistakes are still there. Even when the swelling goes down, you'll find that the unsightly coloring tends to still stay around for ten to twenty, and often fifty years or more (even life for some)...just ask many of my fellow incarcerees. However, even with my own unsightly appearances, I am thankful to be able to still see. For those who may feel otherwise, just consider the wolf's circumstances.

    Watching the incidents unfold with this guy caused me to step down from my self exalted throne of self righteousness and cultivate more of the virtues of forbearance, humility, and compassion in my own life. It has taught me that not all passions are of a tangible nature, that those, such as egotism and pride, are as detrimental to the soul of man as the bloody knife was to the tongue of the wolf. But what it more so reminded me of was of that great lesson of Circumspection; that when signs can be found to lay around you, they still only point to what's inside of you, and when you think that the lesson is not about you, it's probably more than ever all about you.

www.ingramcontent.com/pod-product-compliance
Lightning Source LLC
Chambersburg PA
CBHW051534020426

42333CB00016B/1921